# CASE MANAGEMENT IN CR

Since the first edition of this book – the first on the new system of case management in Crown Courts – much has happened, and the controversial and often misunderstood elements of case management have gradually evolved into a system which now appears to be having its intended effect. This book is designed to provide all those who work in the Crown Courts – judges, administrators, barristers and solicitors – with a one-stop guide to the day-to-day practical problems that arise both before and during trial. In particular it deals with all the problems that pre-trial case management can pose as well as those management type problems that can arise during the course of a trial such as problems with jurors, witnesses and absent defendants. It deals with all the main applications such as bad character disclosure and abuse of process. This is a unique and invaluable work of reference for all lawyers whose work brings them into contact with the Crown Court, as well as students studying for their Bar Finals.

Criminal Law Library

# Case Management in Criminal Trials

## Second Edition

HH JUDGE RODERICK DENYER QC

·HART·
PUBLISHING

OXFORD AND PORTLAND, OREGON
2012

Published in the United Kingdom by Hart Publishing Ltd
16C Worcester Place, Oxford, OX1 2JW
Telephone: +44 (0)1865 517530
Fax: +44 (0)1865 510710
E-mail: mail@hartpub.co.uk
Website: http://www.hartpub.co.uk

Published in North America (US and Canada) by
Hart Publishing
c/o International Specialized Book Services
920 NE 58th Avenue, Suite 300
Portland, OR 97213-3786
USA
Tel: +1 503 287 3093 or toll-free: (1) 800 944 6190
Fax: +1 503 280 8832
E-mail: orders@isbs.com
Website: http://www.isbs.com

British Library Cataloguing in Publication Data
Data Available

ISBN: 978-1-84946-304-1

Typeset by Hope Services, Abingdon
Printed and bound in Great Britain by
Page Bros (Norwich) Ltd, Norwich

# CONTENTS

# Abbreviations

| | |
|---|---|
| ABE | achieving best evidence |
| CJA 2003 | Criminal Justice Act 2003 |
| CP(AW)A 1965 | Criminal Procedure (Attendance of Witnesses) Act 1965 |
| CPIA 1996 | Criminal Procedure and Investigations Act 1996 |
| ECHR | European Convention on Human Rights |
| PACE 1984 | Police and Criminal Evidence Act 1984 |
| PCMH | plea and case management hearing |
| PII | public interest immunity |
| POA 1985 | Prosecution of Offences Act 1985 |
| YJCEA 1999 | Youth Justice and Criminal Evidence Act 1999 |

# Table of Cases

# Table of Legal Instruments

# 1

# Case Management and the Criminal Procedure Rules

## The Overriding Objective

1.1   Rule 1.1 of the Criminal Procedure Rules 2011 (SI 2011/1709) ('the Rules') sets out the overriding objective of the Rules. It provides as follows:

> 1.1(1) The overriding objective of this new code is that criminal cases be dealt with justly.
>
> (2) Dealing with a criminal case justly includes:
>
> (a) acquitting the innocent and convicting the guilty;
> (b) dealing with the prosecution and the defence fairly;
> (c) recognising the rights of a defendant, particularly those under Article 6 of the European Convention on Human Rights;
> (d) respecting the interests of witnesses, victims and jurors and keeping them informed of the progress of the case;
> (e) dealing with the case efficiently and expeditiously;
> (f) ensuring that appropriate information is available to the court when bail and sentence are considered; and
> (g) dealing with the case in ways that take into account:
>
> (i)   the gravity of the offence alleged;
> (ii)  the complexity of what is in issue;
> (iii) the severity of the consequences for the defendant and others affected; and
> (iv)  the needs of other cases.

Every participant in a criminal case has a duty to conduct the case in accordance with the overriding objective and in compliance with the Rules. This derives from Rule 1.2:

> 1.2(1) Each participant, in the conduct of each case must:
>
> (a) prepare and conduct the case in accordance with the overriding objective;
> (b) comply with the Rules, Practice Directions and directions made by the court; and
> (c) at once inform the court and all parties of any significant failure (whether or not that participant is responsible for that failure) to take any procedural step

required by these Rules, any Practice Direction or any direction of the court. A failure is significant if it might hinder the court in furthering the overriding objective.

(2) Anyone involved in any way with a criminal case is a participant in its conduct for the purposes of this Rule.

The court itself (to the extent that it is not a participant) has a duty to further the overriding objective:

1.3 The court must further the overriding objective in particular when:

    (a)  exercising any power given to it by legislation (including these Rules);
    (b)  applying any Practice Direction; or
    (c)  interpreting any Rule or Practice Direction.

# Active Case Management by the Court: General

1.2   Before looking in detail at particular aspects of case management, it is important to bear in mind that, extensive though the powers of the court are, they are limited. Rule 3.5(1) makes it clear that in fulfilling its duty of active case management, 'the court may give any direction and take any step actively to manage a case unless that direction or step would be inconsistent with legislation, including these Rules'. In *Hubner v Czech Republic*,[1] an attempt was made to argue that to extradite the applicant in respect of £20-worth of stolen petrol was inconsistent with the overriding objective, particularly Rule 1.1(1)(g). In rejecting the submission, Elias LJ said:

7. The purpose of the Criminal Procedure Rules is to deal with what the title suggests, namely matters of procedure. The court must, in the exercise of all its procedural powers, including those given by legislation, have in mind the overriding obligation to deal with cases justly. But this principle cannot affect the way in which the substantive law is interpreted. Firstly, it is plainly not for rules made by the Statutory Rules Committee to modify or change an Act of Parliament. That is what in effect Counsel is suggesting here. He says that there should be an additional exception under the Act for cases where extradition will not be required, namely where the offence is considered by the court to be too trivial. Second, the Rules are only intended to be procedural. They are not seeking to regulate the manner in which principles of law must be interpreted or construed.

8. Counsel accepted that the consequence of his submission is rather startling. It would mean in any criminal trial the court can conclude, in particular circumstances, that it would be unjust to give full effect to what Parliament has enacted and therefore an abuse of process and it could exercise powers given by Rule 1 of the Criminal Procedure Rules to do what it considered was just in the particular case. The judges may indeed like to have that power but, however august the individuals who make up the Criminal

---

[1] [2009] EWHC 2929 (Admin).

Procedure Committee, I am afraid they do not have the power to override what Parliament has enacted.

It is also useful to remember that the idea of case management by the judiciary did not simply come into existence as a consequence of the Rules. The concept was not new. This is clearly apparent from the judgment of Judge LJ in *Chaadan*:[2]

35. The trial judge has always been responsible for managing the trial. This is one of his most important functions. To perform it, he has to be alert to the needs of everyone involved in the case. That obviously includes, but is not limited to, the interests of the defendant. It extends to the prosecution, the complainant, to every witness (whichever side is to call the witness), to the jury or, if the jury has not been sworn, to jurors in waiting. Finally the judge should not overlook the community's interest that justice should be done without unnecessary delay. A fair balance has to be struck between all these interests. . . .

37. We must also consider whether the case was somehow rushed, a submission which gives this court the opportunity to highlight a significant recent change, perhaps less heralded than it might have been, but nowadays, as part of his responsibility for managing the trial, the judge is expected to control the timetable and to manage the available time. Time is not unlimited. No one should assume that trials can continue to take as long or use up as much time as either or both sides may wish, or think, or assert, they need. The entitlement to a fair trial is not inconsistent with proper judicial control over the use of time. At the risk of stating the obvious, every trial which takes longer than it reasonably should is wasteful of limited resources. It also results in delays to justice in cases still waiting to be tried, adding to the tension and distress of victims, defendants, particularly those in custody awaiting trial, and witnesses. Most important of all, it does nothing to assist the jury to reach a true verdict on the evidence.

38. In principle, the trial judge should exercise firm control over the timetable, where necessary, making it clear in advance and throughout the trial that the timetable will be subject to appropriate constraints. With such necessary even-handedness and flexibility as the interests of justice require as the case unfolds, the judge is entitled to direct that the trial is expected to conclude by a specific date and to exercise his powers to see that it does. We find that nothing in the criticisms of the way in which the judge dealt with the timetable, and nothing in the remaining complaints about his management of the case which would justify us interfering with the decisions made whilst exercising his discretion as the trial judge.

This was a theme that Judge LJ returned to in *Jisl*,[3] when he said:

114. The starting point is simple. Justice must be done. The defendant is entitled to a fair trial: and, which is sometimes overlooked, the prosecution is equally entitled to a reasonable opportunity to present the evidence against the defendant. It is not however a concomitant of the entitlement to a fair trial that either or both sides are further entitled to take as much time as they like, or for that matter, as long as Counsel and solicitors for the defendants themselves think appropriate. Resources are limited. The funding for courts and judges and for prosecuting and the vast majority of defence

lawyers, is dependent on public money, for which there are many competing demands. Time itself is a resource. Every day unnecessarily used, while the trial meanders sluggishly to its eventual conclusion, represents another day's stressful waiting for the remaining witnesses and the jurors in that particular trial and no less important, continuing and increasing tension and worry for another defendant or defendants, some of whom are remanded in custody, and the witnesses in trials which are waiting their turn to be listed. It follows that the sensible use of time requires judicial management and control. . . .

116. The principle therefore is not in doubt. This appeal enables us to re-emphasise that its practical application depends on the determination of trial judges and the cooperation of the legal profession. Active hands-on case management, both pre-trial and throughout the trial itself, is now regarded as an essential part of the judge's duty. The profession must understand that this has become and will remain part of the normal trial process and that cases must be prepared and conducted accordingly. . . .

118. Once the issue has been identified, in a case of any substance at all . . . the judge should consider whether to direct the timetable to cover pre-trial steps, and eventually the conduct of the trial itself, not rigid nor immutable and fully recognising that during the trial at any rate the unexpected must be treated as normal and making due allowance for it in the interests of justice. To enable the trial judge to manage the case in a way which is fair to every participant, pre-trial, the potential problems as well as the possible areas for time-saving should be canvassed . . . When trial judges act in accordance with these principles, the directions they give and, where appropriate, the timetables they prescribe in the exercise of their case management responsibilities, will be supported in this court. Criticism is more likely to be addressed to those who ignore them.

# Active Case Management by the Court and the Rules

1.3   Part 3 of the Rules specifically deals with case management. Rule 3.2 imposes a duty on the court to further the overriding objective by actively managing the case. It identifies some of the matters involved:

3.2(1) The court must further the overriding objective by actively managing the case.
(2) Active case management includes:

  (a)   the early identification of the real issues;
  (b)   the early identification of the needs of witnesses;
  (c)   achieving certainty as to what must be done, and by whom, and when, in particular by the early setting of a timetable for the progress of the case;
  (d)   monitoring the progress of the case in compliance with directions;
  (e)   ensuring that evidence, whether disputed or not, is presented in the shortest and clearest way;
  (f)   discouraging delay, dealing with as many aspects of the case as possible on the same occasion, and avoiding unnecessary hearings;
  (g)   encouraging the participants to cooperate in the progression of the case; and
  (h)   making use of technology.

(3) The court must actively manage the case by giving any direction appropriate to the needs of that case as early as possible.

The parties have a duty to assist the court in carrying out its duties of active case management:

3.3 Each party must:

    (a) actively assist the court in fulfilling its duty under Rule 3.2 without, or if necessary with, a direction; and

    (b) apply for a direction if needed to further the overriding objective.

This obligation is further amplified in Rule 3.9:

3.9(1) This Rule applies to a party's preparation for trial or appeal, and in this Rule and Rule 3.10 trial includes any hearing at which evidence will be introduced.

(2) In fulfilling his duty under Rule 3.3, each party must:

    (a) comply with directions given by the court;

    (b) take every reasonable step to make sure his witnesses will attend when they are needed;

    (c) make appropriate arrangements to present any written or other material; and

    (d) promptly inform the court and the other parties of anything that may:

        (i) affect the date or duration of the trial, or

        (ii) significantly affect the progress of the case in any way.

(3) The court may require a party to give a certificate of readiness.

An important link between the court and the parties in and about active case management is the Case Progression Officer:

3.4(1) At the beginning of the case each party must, unless the court otherwise directs:

    (a) nominate an individual responsible for progressing that case; and

    (b) tell other parties and the court who he is and how to contact him.

(2) In fulfilling its duty under Rule 3.2, the court must, where appropriate:

    (a) nominate a court officer responsible for progressing the case; and

    (b) make sure the parties know who he is and how to contact him.

(3) In this part a person nominated under this Rule is called a Case Progression Officer.

(4) A Case Progression Officer must:

    (a) monitor compliance with directions;

    (b) make sure that the court is kept informed of events that may affect the progress of that case;

    (c) make sure that he can be contacted promptly about the case during ordinary business hours;

    (d) act promptly and reasonably in response to communications about the case; and

    (e) if he will be unavailable, appoint a substitute to fulfil his duties and inform the other Case Progression Officers.

1.4    Rules 3.5, 3.8 and 3.10 are at the heart of judicial case management:

3.5(1) In fulfilling its duty under Rule 3.2, the court may give any direction and take any
step actively to manage a case unless that direction or step would be inconsistent
with legislation including these Rules.

(2) In particular, the court may:

   (a)  nominate a judge to manage the case;
   (b)  give a direction on its own initiative or on application by a party;
   (c)  ask or allow a party to propose a direction;
   (d)  for the purpose of giving directions, receive applications and representations
        by letter, by telephone or by any other means of electronic communication,
        and conduct a hearing by such means;
   (e)  give a direction without a hearing;
   (f)  fix, postpone, bring forward, extend or cancel a hearing;
   (g)  shorten or extend (even after it has expired) a time limit fixed by a direction;
   (h)  require that issues in the case should be determined separately, and decide in
        what order they will be determined; and
   (i)  specify the consequences of failing to comply with a direction.

(3) A Magistrates' Court may give a direction that will apply in the Crown Court if the
case is to continue there.

(4) The Crown Court may give a direction that will apply in a Magistrates' Court if the
case is to continue there.

(5) Any power to give a direction under this part includes a power to vary or revoke
that direction.

(6) If a party fails to comply with a Rule or a direction, the court may:

   (a)  fix, postpone, bring forward, extend, cancel or adjourn the hearing;
   (b)  exercise its powers to make a costs order; and
   (c)  impose such other sanctions as may be appropriate.

3.8(1) At every hearing, if a case cannot be concluded there and then the court must
give directions so that it can be concluded at the next hearing or as soon as possible
after that.

(2) At every hearing the court must, where relevant:

   (a)  if the defendant is absent, decide whether to proceed nonetheless;
   (b)  take the defendant's plea (unless already done) or if no plea can be taken then,
        find out whether the defendant is likely to plead guilty or not guilty;
   (c)  set, follow or revise a timetable for the progress of the case, which may include
        a timetable for any hearing including the trial;
   (d)  in giving directions, ensure continuity in relation to the court and to the par-
        ties' representatives where that is appropriate and practicable; and
   (e)  where a direction has not been complied with, find out why, identify who was
        responsible and take appropriate action.

(3) In order to prepare for a trial in the Crown Court, the court must conduct a plea
and case management hearing unless the circumstances make that unnecessary.

(4) In order to prepare for the trial, the court must take every reasonable step to
encourage and to facilitate the attendance of witnesses when they are needed.

3.10  In order to manage a trial the court:

(a)  must establish, with the active assistance of the parties, what are the disputed issues;

(b)  must consider setting a timetable that:

  (i)   takes account of those issues and of any timetable proposed by a party; and

  (ii)  may limit the duration of any stage of the hearing;

(c)  may require a party to identify:

  (i)    which witnesses that party wants to give evidence in person;

  (ii)   the order in which that party wants those witnesses to give their evidence;

  (iii)  whether that party requires an order compelling the attendance of a witness;

  (iv)   what arrangements are desirable to facilitate the giving of evidence by a witness;

  (v)    what arrangements are desirable to facilitate the participation of any other person, including the defendant;

  (vi)   what written evidence the party intends to introduce;

  (vii)  what other material, if any, that person intends to make available to the court in the presentation of the case; and

  (viii) whether that party intends to raise any point of law that could affect the conduct of the trial; and

(d)  may limit:

  (i)   the examination, cross-examination or re-examination of a witness; and

  (ii)  the duration of any stage of the hearing.

1.5   A number of areas broadly pertinent to the case management provisions above have been the subject of rulings by the Court of Appeal or the Divisional Court.

## Time Saving

The importance of controlling the timetable has been stressed in a number of cases. In *D and others*,[4] the estimate for the length of the trial was four months; it lasted 235 days but the court only sat on 132 of those days. Moses LJ said:

> 31. Thus, to deal with a case justly requires efficiency and expedition. The right to a fair trial enshrined in Article 6 of the Convention requires not only that the trial start within a reasonable time but also that a charge is determined at a hearing within a reasonable time . . . That is not to say that the mere length of the trial in itself is a sufficient ground for characterising a conviction as unsafe; the important question is whether the length of the trial rendered a fair trial impossible.

---

[4]  [2007] EWCA Crim 2485.

32. . . . The fact that Criminal Procedure Rules were broken and the Protocol[5] disregarded are only factors which should be taken into account in assessing the fairness of the trial. Such breaches are not themselves dispositive. . . .

37. We are not in a position to reach any fair conclusion as to whether any part of the serious disruption and delay of the trial should be laid at the door of Counsel who defended . . . The essential point is that the main cause of the delay lay in the failure of the Judge to ensure that a sufficient number of hours were sat during the day in order to hear and read the evidence. . . .

41. . . . But we record with some dismay that when Counsel was asked how long the cross-examination of certain witnesses would take, he declined to tell the Judge. Whilst precision is not possible, the Judge is entitled and should require Counsel to give some estimate and, absent unforeseeable events, require him to keep to that estimate. Case management cannot be impeded by the mere bland assertion of Defence Counsel that he will take no longer than is necessary.

To like effect is the decision in *Kyham*[6] (a case dealt with at first instance before the Terrorism Protocol came into force[7]) where Judge P said:

152. Much closer judicial case management and the exercise of the powers now available under the Criminal Procedure Rules, have produced a significant reduction in the number of pre-trial hearings as well as the length of most terrorist cases. The parties focus proper attention on case preparation. Each new case is subject to judicial control of the timetable . . . Many matters which might otherwise have required an oral hearing are now dealt with administratively or, by consent, electronically. The subsequent trial is now conducted in accordance with the now familiar Criminal Procedure Rules and with the cooperation and assistance of the profession, the administration of justice has improved. Adherence to, and if necessary, judicial enforcement of the rules is and remains a high priority, and judges and practitioners who fulfil their own responsibilities within the trial process on the basis that time is a limited resource can anticipate wholehearted support in this court if and when they are criticised for doing so. None of these measures interferes with the due administration of justice, rather they enhance it.

In *Kay*,[8] the Court of Appeal stressed the important time-saving properties of written submissions:

6. The Judge was rightly concerned to save as much time as possible. One way for him to do so was to invite Counsel who wished to make submissions to reduce them into writing with a consequent curtailment of oral argument . . . We should therefore emphasise that when dealing with matters preliminary to the trial, if the Judge thought it right to do so, his new case management powers permitted him to deal with these

---

[5] This is a reference to the Protocol on the Control and Management of Heavy Fraud and other complex criminal cases, issued by the Lord Chief Justice on 22 March 2005. It is generally included in the standard practitioners' books. It is required reading for anyone likely to be involved in a lengthy case.

[6] [2008] EWCA Crim 1612.

[7] Protocol on the Management of Terrorism Cases, issued on 30 January 2007. It is generally included in the standard practitioners' books.

[8] [2006] EWCA Crim 835.

issues exclusively by reference to written submissions, and again if he saw fit, submissions limited to a length specified by him. He is not bound to allow oral submissions and he is certainly entitled to put a time limit on them. A necessary public element of any hearing is sufficiently achieved if the defendants themselves are supplied with copies of written submissions . . . and the representatives of the media present in court for any hearing are similarly so supplied.

In *Lee*,[9] the appellant had been charged with a series of serious sexual assaults including the rape of his nieces. The grounds of appeal centred very much around allegations that the trial judge had been unduly interventionist and had unfairly curtailed cross-examination and prevented the defence from calling certain witnesses. In rejecting these submissions, Thomas LJ said:

> 28. It is clear that the Judge's interventions during cross-examination were either for the purpose of suggesting to Counsel he moves on where a point has been gone over sufficiently, or to keep the trial focused on the issues, or to clarify questions: the interventions were quite proper . . . all of that was good case management . . . Secondly, as to raising with Counsel the need to call witnesses, so far from this founding a ground of criticism of a judge, it is our view that this is what a judge ordinarily ought to do in the course of a case as part of good trial management.

## Controlling Cross-examination

Rule 3.10 now makes explicit what had always been the position, namely the right of a judge to control prolix and unnecessary cross-examination.

In *Kalia*,[10] Roskill LJ said:

> What we are saying, though of course in immediate relation to the present case, applies at all times. The trial judge can and should do his utmost to restrain unnecessary, prolonged cross-examination, and this court will unhesitatingly support him when he does.

*Butt*[11] is a more recent example. The trial judge had imposed a time limit on cross-examination. This ruling was the main ground of appeal. Supporting the trial judge and upholding the conviction, Dyson LJ said:

> 10. Counsel would emphasise the duty to present the defence fearlessly. That is obviously very important. But so too is the obligation to avoid wasted time, repetition and prolixity. It is no part of the duty of Counsel to put every point of the defendant's case (however peripheral) to a witness or to embark on lengthy cross-examination on matters which are not really in issue. It is the duty of Counsel to discriminate between important and relevant features of a defence case which must be put to a witness and minor and/or unnecessary matters which do not need to be put.

---

[9]   [2007] EWCA Crim 764.
[10]   (1974) 60 Crim App R 200, 211.
[11]   [2005] EWCA Crim 805.

11. We are in no doubt that the cross-examination was repetitious and prolix and that it did involve a good deal of wasted time . . . Counsel spent far too much time getting to the real issue. In our judgement, the Judge showed remarkable patience in forbearing to intervene until page 33 of the transcript . . . In our judgement the Judge was quite right to intervene at page 65 and seek to bring the cross-examination to an end . . . We are not saying that it should become a routine feature of trial management that judges should impose time limits for evidence in chief and cross-examination of witnesses. If Counsel performed their duty properly, this should rarely be necessary. But where . . . Counsel indulge in prolix and repetitious questioning, judges are fully entitled, and indeed we would say obliged, to impose reasonable time limits.

## Overstepping the Line

In respect of the foregoing matters, there are limits beyond which a judge must not go: gross rudeness and bullying is still not permissible.

In *Cordingley*,[12] one of the grounds of appeal was that 'the Judge behaved oppressively towards Defence Counsel and the appellant and that in consequence the appellant did not receive a fair trial'. Allowing the appeal, Laws LJ said:

13. We have been greatly troubled by the Judge's conduct in this case. We are bound to say we consider that the exchanges between Judge and Counsel betray a rudeness and discourtesy of which the Judge should be ashamed. His treatment of the issue about the appellant's change of clothes brutal, his withdrawal of bail was at least questionable. . . .

15. . . . It is to be remembered that every defendant is entitled to be tried fairly – that is courteously and with due regard to the presumption of innocence. This appellant was not treated fairly. There was a failure of due process by reason of the Judge's conduct.

To similar effect is the decision in *Cole*.[13] One of the grounds of appeal was that 'the Judge's interventions during the course of the trial was such as to show marked hostility to the appellant and to the appellant's case and to the appellant's Counsel as to render the conduct of the trial unfair'. The Judge had made a number of unhelpful interventions. On the second day of the trial, he had sent defence counsel a note. It was headed 'Six Ps' and went on: 'Prior planning prevents piss poor performance'. The conviction was quashed.

Closely allied to judicial bad manners is the problem that can arise from excessive judicial intervention, particularly by asking too many questions, especially when those questions are hostile in nature. In *Copsey*,[14] the Judge asked 60 questions during the first defendant's evidence-in-chief and 50 during his cross-examination. He then asked 57 questions during the examination-in-chief of the co-accused and 36 during the cross-examination. The Court of Appeal concluded that the trial had been unfair.

[12] [2007] EWCA Crim 2174.
[13] [2008] EWCA Crim 3234.
[14] [2008] EWCA Crim 2043.

In *Perren*,[15] there were repeated occasions during the course of the appellant's evidence-in-chief where the Judge intervened with hostile questions. Many of these suggested incredulity on the part of the Judge as to aspects of the appellant's account. Quashing the conviction and ordering a retrial, Toulson LJ said:

> 34. We must evaluate the effect of these interventions in the context of the trial as a whole. We are particularly concerned about the questions put in the course of examination in chief. It is not a sufficient answer to say that because questions were likely to be put in cross-examination, there was no harm in them being put by the Judge in the course of examination in chief . . . there are good reasons why a judge should be particularly careful about refraining from intervening during evidence in chief, except insofar as it is necessary to clarify, to keep the evidence moving on and, if necessary, to avoid prolixity or irrelevance. The first is that it is for the prosecution to cross-examine, not the judge. The second is that the right time for the prosecution to cross-examine is after a witness has given his evidence in chief.

> 35. The appellant's story may have been highly improbable but he was entitled to explain it to the jury without being subjected to sniper fire in the course of doing so. The potential for injustice is that, if the jury, at the very time when they are listening to the witness giving his narrative account of events, do so to the accompaniment of questions from the bench indicating to anybody with common sense that the judge does not believe a word of it, this may affect the mind of the jury as they listen to the account.

Most recently, there was the Privy Council decision in *Michel*.[16] The opening paragraph in the opinion of Lord Brown reads as follows:

> 1. Not often is Defence Counsel, appealing against conviction on the grounds of an unfair hearing, able to turn the appeal court's feeling from initial rueful concern to eventual deep dismay simply by reference to the number and character of the judge's interventions in the course of the trial. Such, alas, is the position in this case and, overwhelming though the evidence against the appellant may appear to have been, the board can see no alternative but to set his conviction aside.

What had happened was that the appellant had spent eight days in the witness box during which time the Judge asked him 273 questions of which 138 were during examination-in-chief. The questions were generally hostile and evinced incredulity as to the defence being advanced. Acknowledging the strength of the prosecution case, nevertheless, said Lord Brown:

> 27. There is, however, a wider principle in play in this case merely than the safety, in terms of its correctness, of the conviction. Put shortly there comes a point when, however obviously guilty an accused person may be, the appeal court reviewing his conviction cannot escape the conclusion that he has simply not been fairly tried: so far from the Judge having umpired the contest, rather he has acted effectively as a second prosecutor.

[15] [2009] EWCA Crim 348.

[16] [2009] UKPC 41. See also *Andrew* [2010] EWCA Crim 789, where Laws LJ said (at para 12): 'In our judgement it is necessary to stand back and look at the Recorder's conduct of this trial as a whole . . . Doing so, we are of the clear view that the Recorder behaved as if he were an advocate for the prosecution. His interventions in the appellant's evidence, which we have enumerated, were deeply prejudicial. His summing up was unbalanced to say the least'.

Having quoted from *Perren* (above), His Lordship then went on to articulate the relevant principle as follows:

> 31. Not merely is the accused in such a case deprived of the opportunity of having his evidence considered by the jury in the way that he was entitled, he is denied too the basic right underlying the adversarial system at trial . . . that of having an impartial judge to see fair play in the conduct of the case against him. Under the common law system, one lawyer makes the case against the accused, another his case in response, and a third holds the balance between them, ensuring that the case against the accused is properly and fairly advanced in accordance with the rules of evidence and procedure.

# Cards on the Table and End of the Ambush

1.6    The proper and early identification of the real issues in the case, coupled with pronounced disapproval of non-disclosure of such issues, has been a significant feature of a number of recent decisions.

In *Gleeson*,[17] the question for the Court of Appeal was whether 'where a defendant with an unanswerable legal challenge to the indictment which, unless amended, would entitle him to an acquittal, leaves it until the end of the prosecution case before raising it, does justice require that, although the defect is remediable by amendment, no amendment should be admitted at that stage'. In rejecting the appeal based upon the fact that the trial judge had allowed the amendment, Auld LJ spelt out very clearly what is now required of the defence in such circumstances. He said:

> 34.  Counsel should have drawn attention to his proposed legal challenge to the indictment . . . at the plea and directions hearing and in the defence statement. If he had done that, he could have had no valid objection to the prosecution correcting their error at that stage, or certainly by the beginning of the trial . . .

> 35.  Just as a defendant should not be penalised for errors of his legal representatives in the conduct of his defence, if he is unfairly prejudiced by this, so also should a prosecution not be frustrated by errors of the prosecutor unless such errors have irremediably rendered a fair trial for the defendant impossible. For defence advocates to seek to take advantage of such errors by deliberately delaying identification of an issue of fact or law in this case until the last possible moment is, in our view, no longer acceptable, given the legislative and procedural changes to our criminal justice process in recent years.

In *DPP v Chorley Justices*,[18] an issue arose as to whether the analyst's certificate in a breathalyser case had been served on the defendant for the purposes of the Road Traffic Offenders Act 1988. Having referred to Parts 1 and 3 of the Rules, Thomas LJ said:

---

[17] [2003] EWCA Crim 3357.
[18] [2006] EWHC 1795 (Admin).

26. The pertinent point relevant to what happened in this case is the early identification of the real issues. It is, it seems to us, clear that what should have happened is that
at the first hearing of a case of this kind, after entry of the plea of not guilty, the defendant should have been asked first what was in issue. At that stage and at the first hearing
he should then have been asked what witnesses did he need . . . He should have been
asked what issues were taken by the defence. In our experience, it is very rare in a court,
when such a question is asked, that parties do not reply. Most people approach the case
on the basis that they want justice done as they wish to be acquitted if innocent: it is our
experience that the cases when a defendant refuses to identify the issue are rare indeed.
If a defendant refuses to identify what the issues are, one thing is clear: he can derive no
advantage from that or seek, as appears to have happened in this case, to attempt an
ambush at trial. The days of ambushing and taking last-minute technical points are
gone. They are not consistent with the overriding objective of deciding cases justly,
acquitting the innocent and convicting the guilty.

27. In this case . . . if when the point on service was taken, the CPS had invited the court
to ask the defendant if the blood alcohol level was in issue and, if it was, was an adjournment needed, then the obvious justice of the case would have been that the case should
have been adjourned because no defendant can, by seeking to take an ambush point of
this kind and failing to cooperate and identify the issues at an early stage, derive any
advantage therefrom. The duty of the court is to see that justice is done. That does not
involve allowing people to escape on technical points or by attempting, as here, an
ambush. It involves the court in looking at the real justice of the case and seeing whether
the rules have been complied with by 'cards being put on the table' at the outset and the
issues being clearly identified.

28. For the future, no solicitor should expect that his client will be able to rely on this
sort of technical point or this type of ambush. The days for that sort of tactic to succeed
are over.

Observations to a similar effect can be found in *Malcolm v DPP*.[19] In that case,
the defence took a point in the closing speech to the effect that the appropriate
breathalyser procedure had not been gone through. The Justices took the view
that the prosecution had failed to produce evidence in respect of this but gave the
prosecution leave to recall a police officer to remedy the defect. The Divisional
Court upheld this approach. Stanley Burnton J said:

31. It is the duty of the Defence to make its defence and the issues it raises clear to the
Prosecution and the court at an early stage. This duty is implicit in Rule 3.3 of the
Criminal Procedure Rules . . . It is the duty of the Defence to make the real issues clear
at the latest before the Prosecution closes its case.

In the same case, Maurice Kay LJ said:

44. In my judgement, the Justices did not fall into error. Indeed they are to be
commended for refusing to succumb to this kind of forensic *legerdemain*. Of course a
defendant is entitled to put the prosecution to strict proof. However, it is then for his
advocate to raise the issues in a timely and appropriate way.

---

[19] [2007] EWHC 363 (Admin). To similar effect are the observations in *JL v DPP* [2009] EWHC 238
(Admin).

In *Writtle v DPP*,[20] at a late stage and after the case had gone part heard, the defence sought to introduce expert evidence which raised some wholly new issues, none of which had been canvassed with prosecution witnesses who had already given evidence. The Justices refused to hear it. Upholding the Justices and noting the failure by the defence to comply with the rules relating to the calling of expert evidence, Simon J said:

> 15. The days when the Defence can assume that they will be able successfully to ambush the Prosecution are over.

In *Penner*,[21] the Court of Appeal again stressed the need for the criminal trial process to be freed from the notion of the ambush. Thomas LJ said:

> 6. The Criminal Procedure Rules have been in force in this country for some time. They have abolished what is known as 'trial by ambush'. Sometimes, it appears that people do not appreciate that and the duties that arise at the PCMH [plea and case management hearing]. . . .

> 18. So this case is an ample demonstration of why it is essential that Counsel at the PCMH stage carefully examine and identify the issues. As Counsel in this case failed to do so, when the point, as he tells us, ocured to him in the course of cross-examination, it was then his duty to have identified it to the Judge, before going any further with his cross-examination. He should not have left the matter for half-time. He should have told the Judge that there was a new issue and asked the Judge how the matter should be dealt with.

> 19. . . . It is no longer possible to have cases conducted in the way in which this case was conducted by Counsel for the appellant, when points occur to someone and then an attempt is made to ambush the prosecution by a submission of no case to answer.

---

[20] [2009] EWHC 236 (Admin).
[21] [2010] EWCA Crim 1155.

# 2

# The Plea and Case Management Hearing

2.1   Rule 2.2 of the Criminal Procedure Rules 2011 (SI 2011/1709) ('the Rules') defines 'Practice Direction' as 'the Lord Chief Justice's consolidated criminal practice direction as amended'.

Rule 3.8(3) of the Rules provides that:

> In order to prepare for a trial in the Crown Court, the court must conduct a plea and case management hearing unless the circumstances make that unnecessary.

Rule 3.11 of the Rules provides that:

> (1) The case management forms set out in the Practice Direction must be used . . .
> (2) The court must make available to the parties a record of directions given.

2.2   Part IV.41 of the Practice Direction contains important guidance in respect of the plea and case management hearing (PCMH) as well as setting out certain time-lines. (It also spells out that a preliminary hearing is not required in respect of every case sent to the Crown Court pursuant to section 51 of the Crime and Disorder Act 1998, a provision which seems frequently to be ignored (see IV.41.3); if there is to be a preliminary hearing it should be held about 14 days after the sending of the case.)

## Cases sent for Trial

IV.41.5 of the Practice Direction is in these terms:

> Where the Magistrates' Court do not order a preliminary hearing, it should order a PCMH to be held within about 14 weeks after sending for trial when a defendant is in custody and within about 17 weeks after sending for trial when a defendant is on bail. These periods accommodate the periods fixed by the relevant Rules for the service of the prosecution case papers and for making all potential preparatory applications. When the parties realistically expect to have completed their preparations for the PCMH in less time than that, then the Magistrates' Court should order it to be held earlier. But it will not normally be appropriate to order that the PCMH be held on a date before the expiry of at least four weeks from the date on which the prosecutor expects to serve the prosecution case papers to allow the defence a proper opportunity to consider them. To order that a PCMH be held before the parties have had a reasonable opportunity to complete

their preparations in accordance with the Criminal Procedure Rules risks compromising the effectiveness of this most important pre-trial hearing and risks wasting their time and that of the court.

# Cases Committed for Trial

IV.41.6 of the Practice Direction is in these terms:

> For cases committed to the Crown Court for trial under section 6 of the Magistrates' Courts Act 1980 . . . a PCMH should be ordered by the Magistrates' Court in every case, to be held within about 7 weeks after committal. That period accommodates the periods fixed by the relevant Rules for making all potential preparatory applications. Where the parties realistically expect to have completed their preparations for the PCMH in less time than that, then the Magistrates' Court should order it to be held earlier. However, to order that a PCMH be held before the parties have had a reasonable opportunity to complete their preparations in accordance with the Criminal Procedure Rules risks compromising the effectiveness of this most important pre-trial hearing and risks wasting their time and that of the court.

2.3    Both the Practice Direction and the Rules recognise the importance of the PCMH and the need for it to be properly conducted. It is apparent from the matters set out at 2.2 above that the parties should have adequate time to prepare for the hearing. IV.41.8 of the Practice Direction provides:

> Active case management at the PCMH is essential to reduce the number of ineffective and cracked trials and delays during the trial to resolve legal issues. The effectiveness of a PCMH in a contested case depends in large measure upon preparation by all concerned and upon the presence of the trial advocate or an advocate who is able to make decisions and give the court the assistance which the trial advocate could be expected to give. Resident judges in settling the listing policy should ensure that list officers fix cases as far as possible to enable the trial advocate to conduct the PCMH and the trial.

With this in mind, it is instructive to look at the current PCMH form, particularly with regard to time limits. The references in square brackets below are to the numbered paragraphs in the current form.

## Case Progression Officers [3.2]

The names and email addresses of the parties' case progression officer must be set out as well as the name of the court's case progression officer. This is not an optional requirement. Rule 3.4 of the Rules provides as follows:

> (1) At the beginning of the case each party must, unless the court otherwise directs:
>     (a) nominate an individual responsible for progressing that case; and
>     (b) tell other parties and the court who he is and how to contact him.

(2) In fulfilling its duty under Rule 3.2 the court must where appropriate:

    (a) nominate a Court Officer responsible for progressing the case; and

    (b) make sure the parties know who he is and how to contact him.

(3) In this part a person nominated under this Rule is called a case progression officer.

(4) A case progression officer must:

    (a) monitor compliance with directions;

    (b) make sure that the court is kept informed of events that may affect the progress of that case;

    (c) make sure that he can be contacted promptly about the case during ordinary business hours;

    (d) act promptly and reasonably in response to communications about the case; and

    (e) if he will be unavailable, appoint a substitute to fulfil his duties and inform the other case progression officers.

## Credit for Guilty Plea

It is almost inconceivable that advice about credit for a guilty plea will not have been given; see section 144 of the Criminal Justice Act 2003 and the Sentencing Council guidelines.

## Trial in Absence

This is important. The defendant should be warned that the trial may proceed in his absence. The proven giving of the warning may well be relevant to the subsequent exercise of the discretion to try him in his absence, see *Jones*.[1]

## Prosecution Disclosure [10.1]

This should already have taken place. By virtue of section 3(8) and 13 of the Criminal Procedure and Investigations Act (CPIA) 1996, the prosecution must act 'as soon as is reasonably practicable' after committal or service of the papers in a 'sent' case.

## Defence Statement [10.2, 10.3]

Assuming that the prosecution have complied with their initial disclosure obligations, the defence statement should have been filed within 28 days thereafter unless application had been made within that period for an extension of time within which to file the same, see CPIA 1996, sections 5 and 12 and regulations 2

---

[1] [2001] EWCA Crim 168 (reported as *Hayward*) and [2002] UKHL 5.

and 3 of the Criminal Procedure and Investigations Act 1996 (Defence Disclosure Time Limits) Regulations 2011 (SI 2011/209). Further, the court should ensure that any defence statement filed complies with section 6A. There is or may be a duty to warn the accused as to the potential consequences of non-compliance with these obligations, see CPIA 1996, section 6E(2).

## What are the Real Issues [10.4]

In the 'ambush' cases,[2] both the Court of Appeal and the Divisional Court have stressed the importance of ascertaining at the PCMH what the real issues in the case are regardless of the adequacy or otherwise of any defence statement filed.

## Any Defence Application Pursuant to CPIA 1996, Section 8[10.5]

Such an application by a defendant seeking further disclosure pursuant to this section can only be made when a defence statement has been filed. The appropriate procedure is set out in Rule 22.5.

## Details of Expert Evidence [12]

A party who wants to introduce expert evidence must serve it 'as soon as practicable' (Rule 33.4). The court's power to direct that in a multi-handed case evidence should be given by one expert only should be noted, see Rule 33.7.

## Measures to Assist Witnesses and Defendants in Giving Evidence [17]

Parties seeking special measures directions, a defendant's evidence direction, directions about the use of an intermediary, or a witness anonymity order, should apply in writing 'as soon as is reasonably practicable' and in any event 'not more than 14 days after the defendant pleads not guilty', see Rule 29.3.

## Reporting Restrictions [19]

Possible orders include those to be made pursuant to section 39(1) of the Children and Young Persons Act 1933, the Sexual Offences Amendment Act 1992, section 46 of the Youth Justice and Criminal Evidence Act (YJCEA) 1999, and section 4 of the Contempt of Court Act 1981; see also Rule 16.

---

[2] *DPP v Chorley Justices* [2006] EWHC 1795 (Admin) and *Penner* [2010] EWCA Crim 1155.

## Third Party Material [20]

Any application for a witness summons by a party pursuant to section 2 of the Criminal Procedure (Attendance of Witnesses) Act 1965 must be made 'as soon as practicable after becoming aware of the grounds for doing so', see Rule 28.3.

## Video Evidence [22]

YJCEA 1999, section 27 deals with the use in evidence of a video-recording of an interview with a vulnerable witness. The section includes the possibility of excluding part of the recording on prejudice grounds. The section is amplified by Part IV.40 of the Practice Direction.

## Cross-examination on Sexual History [26]

An application pursuant to YJCEA 1999, section 41 should be made in writing and not more than 28 days after the prosecution has complied or purported to comply with its initial disclosure obligations pursuant to CPIA 1996, section 3, see Rule 36.2.

## Bad Character [27]

Any prosecution application to adduce the bad character of a defendant must be served within 14 days of the defendant having pleaded not guilty; the defendant must make any objection within 14 days thereafter, see Rule 35.4. In respect of any application relating to the bad character of a person other than the defendant, it must be served as soon as is reasonably practicable and in any event 'not more than 14 days after the prosecution disclosed material upon which it is based', see Rule 35.3.

## Hearsay [28]

Any prosecution application to introduce hearsay evidence pursuant to the following provisions of the Criminal Justice Act 2003, namely sections 114, 116 and 121, must be made within 14 days of the defendant having pleaded not guilty. Any such application by a defendant must be made 'as soon as reasonably practicable', see Rule 34.2.

## Admissibility and Legal Issues [29]

Arguably, many of the matters to be dealt with under this heading should have featured in the defence statement or in the discussion of 'the real issues'. However, Part IV.36 of the Consolidated Criminal Practice Direction suggests that a defendant gives notice of any abuse of process application 'not later than 14 days before the date fixed for the trial'. But in any event, where the defence are contemplating the making of such an application, they should raise it with the judge at the PCMH, see IV.36.5.

## Timetable [30]

The question is asked whether a provisional timetable can be fixed at this stage for the conduct of the trial and, if not, why not? Although in reality it may not be possible to set a firm timetable until the start of the trial, nevertheless, by virtue of Rule 3.10 and the court's duty to manage the trial, many of the matters set out in that Rule may have to be or should be canvassed at the PCMH.

## Public Interest Immunity [31]

The question specifically relates to 'on notice' PII applications. Such applications are governed by Rule 22.3. No specific timetable is laid down.

2.4 Although not strictly related to the PCMH form itself, there are certain other time limits that may have some relevance so far as the pre-trial management of a case is concerned:

(1) Any notice of an intention to make an application to dismiss the charges in a 'sent' case pursuant to section 51 of the Crime and Disorder Act 1998 should be made not later than 14 days after service of the documents, though the time may be extended, see Rule 13.2.
(2) A draft indictment must be served not more than 28 days after service of the documents on a defendant in a 'sent' case or within 28 days of committal, see Rule 14.1.

# 3

# Non-compliance with Case Management and Other Procedural Orders and the Sanctions Available to the Court

3.1  Sometimes, statute provides a sanction for a failure to comply with a procedural rule. However, in the absence of statutory authority the nature of the sanctions that can be imposed for non-compliance with case management orders, or indeed other procedural breaches, are somewhat limited. Sir Robin Auld noted that:

> I have anxiously searched here and abroad for just and efficient sanctions and incentives to encourage better preparation for trial. A study of a number of recent and current reviews in other commonwealth countries and in the USA shows that we are not alone in this search and that, as to sanctions at any rate, it is largely in vain.[1]

3.2  As set out in chapter one, Rule 3.5 of the Criminal Procedure Rules 2011 (SI 2011/1709) ('the Rules') specifies the case management powers of the Crown Court. The relevant parts of Rule 3.5 are as follows:

> 3.5(1) In fulfilling its duty under Rule 3.2 the Court may give any direction and take any step actively to manage a case unless that direction or step would be inconsistent with legislation including these Rules.
> (2) In particular the Court may:
>   (a)  nominate a judge . . . to manage the case;
>   (b)  give a direction on its own initiative or an application by a party;
>   (c)  ask or allow a party to propose a direction;
>   (d)  for the purposes of giving directions, receive applications and representations by letter, by telephone or by any other means of electronic communication, and conduct a hearing by such means;
>   (e)  give a direction without a hearing;
>   (f)  fix, postpone, bring forward, extend or cancel a hearing;
>   (g)  shorten or extend (even after it has expired) a time limit fixed by a direction;
>   (h)  require that issues in the case should be determined separately and decide in what order they will be determined; and
>   (i)  specify the consequences of failing to comply with a direction.
> . . .

---

[1]  Sir Robin Auld, *Review of the Criminal Courts of England and Wales* (2001) para 231.

(5) Any power to give a direction under this part includes a power to vary or revoke that direction.

(6) If a party fails to comply with a rule or a direction, the court may:

    (a) fix, postpone, bring forward, extend, cancel or adjourn a hearing;

    (b) exercise its powers to make a costs order; and

    (c) impose such other sanction as may be appropriate.

# Costs

3.3 In this connection, it is worth bearing in mind what was said by Auld at paragraphs 229 and 230 of his report:

> 229. I have mentioned the lack of reflective sanctions and the need for better incentives to encourage all concerned in the preparation of criminal cases for trial, to cooperate when they reasonably can and to get on with it. Orders of costs, wasted costs orders, the drawing of adverse inferences or depriving one or other side of the opportunity of advancing all or part of its case at trial, are not, in the main, apt means of encouraging and enforcing compliance with criminal pre-trial procedures. In these respects criminal courts have much less control than civil courts.

> 230. In criminal cases an order for costs against a defendant personally is rarely an option because of his lack of means and because it may be hard to apportion fault as between him and his legal representative. And there are problems about the fairness of a trial if a defendant is under threat of a sanction of that sort . . . an order for costs against the prosecution for procedural default is possible and sometimes imposed. But, where it serves as a mark of the court's disfavour and dents a departmental budget, judges are disinclined in publicly funded defence cases to order what amounts to a transfer of funds from one public body to another. The third possible financial sanction is to make a wasted costs order against the legal representative on one side or the other. But again there are often practical limitations on the court in identifying who is at fault – on the prosecution side, counsel, those instructing him or the police – and on the defence side, counsel, his solicitors or the defendant.

So far as costs are concerned, the regime derives from the Prosecution of Offences Act (POA) 1985 and Part 76 of the Criminal Procedure Rules.

## Costs Against a Defendant

POA 1985, section 18 provides as follows:

18. – (1) Where:

. . .

    (c) any person is convicted of an offence before the Crown Court, the Court may make such order as to costs to be paid by the accused to the prosecution as it considers just and reasonable . . .

(3)  The amount to be paid by the accused in pursuance of an order under this section shall be specified in the order.

The relevant provisions of Part 76 of the Rules are set out below.

The obvious point that arises is that such an order can only be made on conviction.

## Costs Against a Party

This is provided for by POA 1985, section 19 and the Costs in Criminal Cases (General) Regulations 1986 (SI 1986/1335) made thereunder:

19. – (1) The Lord Chancellor may by regulations make provisions empowering . . . the Crown Court . . . in any case where the court is satisfied that one party to criminal proceedings has incurred costs as a result of an unnecessary or improper[2] act or omission by or on behalf of another party to the proceedings, to make an order as to the payment of those costs.

(2)  Regulations made under sub-section (1) above may in particular:

(a)   allow the making of such an order at any time during the proceedings.[3]

Regulation 3 of the 1986 Regulations provides:

3.(1)  Subject to the provisions of this Regulation, where at any time during criminal proceedings:

. . .

(b)   the Crown Court is satisfied that costs have been incurred in respect of the proceedings by one of the parties as a result of an unnecessary or improper act or omission by or on behalf of another party to the proceedings, the court may, after hearing the parties, order that all or part of the costs so incurred by that party shall be paid to him by the other party. . . .

(3)  An order made under paragraph (1) shall specify the amount of costs to be paid in pursuance of the order.

Rule 76.8 of the Criminal Procedure Rules is set out below.

## Wasted Costs

POA 1985, section 19A and the 1986 Regulations provide for the making of wasted costs orders against legal or other representatives. Section 19A reads as follows:

---

[2]  *DPP v Denning* (1992) 94 Crim App R 274, where Nolan LJ said (at 280): 'The word improper in this context does not necessarily connote some grave impropriety. Used as it is in conjunction with the word unnecessary, it is in my judgement intended to cover an act or omission which would not have occurred if the party concerned had conducted his case properly'.

[3]  In *Denning* (above), Nolan LJ said (at 279): 'The purpose and effect of section 19(2) and Regulation 3(1) seems to me to have been not to vary the normal procedure by which a final order for costs is made at the end of the proceedings – that is to say, after they have been ended by a verdict or a notice of discontinuance – but to give the court power to make an interim order of costs whilst the proceedings are still in progress'.

19A. – (1) In any criminal proceedings:

. . .

    (b)   the Crown Court may . . . order the legal or other representative concerned to meet the whole of any wasted costs or such part of them as may be determined in accordance with the Regulation.

. . .

(3)  In this section:

'Legal or other representative' in relation to any proceedings, means a person who is exercising a right of audience or a right to conduct litigation on behalf of any party to the proceedings;

'Wasted costs' means any costs incurred by a party:

    (a)   as a result of any improper, unreasonable or negligent act or omission on the part of any representative or any employee of a representative; or

    (b)   which, in the light of any such act or omission occurring after they were incurred, the court considers it unreasonable to expect that party to pay.

## Regulation 3B of the 1986 Regulations provides as follows:

3B.(1)  A wasted costs order may provide for the whole or any part of the wasted costs . . . ordered to be paid and the court shall specify the amount of such costs.

(2)  Before making a wasted costs order the court shall allow the legal or other representative and any party to the proceedings to make representations.

Guidance as to the approach to be adopted by the court when considering a wasted costs order is set out in Part VIII of the Practice Direction (Costs): Criminal Proceedings[4], paragraph 1.4 of which reads as follows:

Judges contemplating making a wasted costs order should bear in mind the guidance given by the Court of Appeal in *Re a Barrister* . . . The guidance which is set out below, is to be considered together with all the statutory and other rules and recommendations set out by Parliament and in this Practice Direction:

    (i)   There is a clear need for any judge or court intending to exercise the wasted costs jurisdiction to formulate carefully and concisely the complaint and grounds upon which such an order may be sought. These measures are draconian and, as in contempt proceedings, the grounds must be clear and particular.

    (ii)  Where necessary a transcript of the relevant part of the proceedings under discussion should be available and in accordance with the rules a transcript of any wasted costs hearing must be made.

    (iii)  A defendant involved in a case where such proceedings are contemplated should be present if, after discussion with Counsel, it is thought that his interests may be affected and he should certainly be present and represented if the matter might affect the course of his trial. Regulation 3B(2) of the Costs in Criminal Cases (General) (Amendment) Regulations 1991 furthermore requires that before a wasted costs order is made 'the court shall allow the legal or other representative and any party to the proceedings to make representations'. There may be cases where it may be appropriate for counsel for the Crown to be present.

---

[4]  [2004] 2 Crim App R 26.

(iv)  A three-stage test or approach is recommended when a wasted costs order is contemplated:

    (a)  Has there been an improper, unreasonable or negligent act or omission?

    (b)  As a result, have any costs been incurred by a party?

    (c)  If the answers to (a) and (b) are yes, should the court exercise its discretion to disallow or order the representative to meet the whole or any part of the relevant costs and if so what sum is involved?

(v)  It is inappropriate to propose any settlement that the representative might forego fees. The complaint should be formally stated by the judge and the representative invited to make his own comments. After any other party has been heard, the judge should give his formal ruling.

(vi)  The judge must specify the sum to be allowed or ordered. Alternatively, the relevant available procedure should be substituted should it be impossible to fix the sum.

Furthermore, reference has also to be made to paragraph 1.5 of Part VIII which reads as follows:

The Court of Appeal has given further guidance in *Re P* . . . as follows:

(i)  The primary object is not to punish but to compensate, albeit as the order is sought against a non-party, it can from that perspective be regarded as penal.

(ii)  The jurisdiction is a summary jurisdiction to be exercised by the court which has tried the case in the course of which the misconduct was committed.

(iii)  Fairness is assured if the lawyer alleged to be at fault has sufficient notice of the complaint made against him and a proper opportunity to respond to it.

(iv)  Because of the penal element, a mere mistake is not sufficient to justify an order – there must be a more serious error.

(v)  Although the trial judge can decline to consider an application in respect of costs, for example on the ground that he or she is personally embarrassed by the appearance of bias, it will only be in exceptional circumstances that it will be appropriate to pass the matter to another judge, and the fact that, in the proper exercise of his judicial function, a judge has expressed views in relation to the conduct of a lawyer against whom an order is sought, does not of itself normally constitute bias or the appearance of bias so as to necessitate a transfer.

Rule 76.9 of the Criminal Procedure Rules is set out below.

## Costs Against Third Parties

Section 93 of the Courts Act 2003 added a new section 19B to the POA1985, the relevant parts of which are as follows:

19B. – (1) The Lord Chancellor may by regulation make provision empowering . . . the Crown Court . . . to make a third party costs order if the conditions in sub-section (3) are satisfied.

(2)  A third party costs order is an order as to the payment of costs incurred by a party to criminal proceedings by a person who is not a party to those proceedings ('the third party').

(3) The condition is that:

    (a)  there has been serious misconduct (whether or not constituting a contempt of court) by the third party; and

    (b)  the court considers it appropriate, having regard to that misconduct, to make a third party costs order against him.

As to procedure, the relevant parts of regulation 3F of the 1986 Regulations are as follows:

(2) The court may make a third party costs order:

    (a)  subject to paragraph (3) at any time during or after criminal proceedings; and

    (b)  on the application of any party or of its own initiative.

(3) The court shall make a third party costs order during the proceedings only if it decides that there are good reasons to do so, rather than making the order after the proceedings, and it shall notify the parties and the third party of those reasons and allow any of them to make representation.

(4) Before making a third party costs order the court shall allow the third party and any party to make representations and may hear evidence . . .

(6) A third party costs order shall specify the amount of costs to be paid in pursuance of the order.

The procedure is further refined in regulation 3G:

3G. . . . (2) An application for a third party costs order shall be in writing and shall contain:

    (a)  the name and address of the applicant;

    (b)  the name and addresses of the other parties;

    (c)  the name and address of the third party against whom the order is sought;

    (d)  the date of the commencement of the criminal proceedings;

    (e)  a summary of the facts upon which the applicant intends to rely in making the application including details of the alleged misconduct of the third party.

(3) The application shall be sent to the appropriate officer and upon receiving it the appropriate officer shall serve copies of it on the third party and the other parties.

(4) Where the court decides that it might make a third party costs order of its own initiative, the appropriate officer shall serve notice in writing accordingly on the third party and the parties.

(5) At the same time as serving notice under paragraph (4) the appropriate officer shall serve a summary of the reasons why the court might make a third party costs order, including details of the alleged misconduct of the third party.

(6) Where the appropriate officer serves copies of an application under paragraph (3) or serves notice under paragraph (4) he shall at the same time serve notice on the parties and the third party of the time and place fixed for the hearing.

# Relevant Provisions of the Criminal Procedure Rules in Relation to Costs

The matter is governed by Part 76 of the Rules, which applies to all costs orders made under the foregoing provisions, see Rule 76.1.

Rule 76.2 sets out certain general rules applicable to costs applications and hearings. It provides as follows:

76.2(1) The court must not make an order about costs unless each party and any other person directly affected:

    (a)  is present; or

    (b)  has had an opportunity:

        (i)   to attend; or

        (ii)  to make representations.

(2)  The court may make an order about costs:

    (a)  at a hearing in public or in private; or

    (b)  without a hearing.

(3)  In deciding what order, if any, to make about costs, the court must have regard to all the circumstances including:

    (a)  the conduct of all the parties; and

    (b)  any costs order already made.

(4)  If the court makes an order about costs it must:

    (a)  specify who must, or must not, pay what, to whom; and

    (b)  identify the legislation under which the order is made, where there is a choice of powers.

(5)  The court must give reasons if it:

    (a)  refuses an application for a costs order; or

    (b)  rejects representations opposing a costs order.

(6)  If the court makes an order for the payment of costs:

    (a)  the general rule is that it will be for an amount that is sufficient reasonably to compensate the recipient for costs:

        (i)   actually reasonably and properly incurred; and

        (ii)  reasonable in amount; but

    (b)  the court may order the payment of:

        (i)   a proportion of that amount;

        (ii)  a stated amount less than that amount;

        (iii) costs from or until a certain date only;

        (iv) costs relating only to particular steps taken; or

        (v)  costs relating only to a distinct part of the case.

(7) On an assessment of the amount of costs, relevant factors include:

    (a)   the conduct of all the parties;

    (b)   the particular complexity of the matter or the difficulty or novelty of the questions raised;

    (c)   the skill, effort, specialised knowledge and responsibility involved;

    (d)   the time spent on the case;

    (e)   the case where, and the circumstances in which work or any part of it was done; and

    (f)   any direction or observations by the court.

As to costs against a defendant (section 18), this is dealt with by Rule 76.5. Costs against a party (section 19) are dealt with by Rule 76.8, and wasted costs (section 19A) by Rule 76.9. As to costs against third parties (section 19B), this is governed by Rule 76.10.

# Sanctions Directly Provided for by Statute and/or Regulation and/or Rule

## Expert Evidence

3.4   Pursuant to section 81 of the Police and Criminal Evidence Act 1984 and section 20(3) of the Criminal Procedure and Investigations Act 1996 (both as amended), rules may require the disclosure of expert evidence before it can be introduced as part of the party's case and, if not disclosed, may prohibit its introduction without the permission of the court. Rule 33.4 of the Criminal Procedure Rules 2011 now governs:

33.4(1) A party who wants to introduce expert evidence must:

    (a)   serve it on:

        (i)   the court officer; and

        (ii)  each other party;

    (b)   serve it:

        (i)   as soon as practicable; and in any event

        (ii)  with any application in support of which that party relies on that evidence; and

    (c)   if another party so requires, give that party a copy of, or a reasonable opportunity to inspect:

        (i)   a record of any examination, measurement, test or experiment on which the expert's findings and opinion are based or that were carried out in the course of reaching those findings and opinion; and

        (ii)  anything on which any such examination, measurement, test or experiment was carried out.

(2) A party may not introduce expert evidence if that party has not complied with this rule unless:

    (a)   every other party agrees; or

    (b)   the court gives permission.

In *Ensor*,[5] at the end of the prosecution case the defence produced a psychiatric report whose existence had not previously been disclosed, intending to rely upon it for the purpose of justifying the decision of the defendant not to give evidence. The trial judge refused leave to introduce the report or call the psychiatrist, pointing out the breach of the rules and taking the view that the late disclosure was 'a tactical ploy' by the defence. In upholding that decision, Aikens LJ in the Court of Appeal (after referring to Parts 1 and 3 of the Rules and the parties' obligations thereunder) said:

> 30. In our view the effect of the CPR Parts 1.2 and 3.3 together is that it is incumbent upon both prosecution and defence parties to criminal trials to alert the court and the other side at the earliest practical moment if it is intending or may be intending to adduce expert evidence. That should be done if possible at a PCMH. If it cannot be done then, it must be done as soon as the possibility becomes live . . .

> 32. We entirely agree with the Judge" view that the defence was in grave breach of the Criminal Procedure Rules . . . it was nothing less than an attempt to ambush the prosecution.

## Hearsay

The law governing the nature of and the admissibility of hearsay evidence is set out in Chapter 2 of the Criminal Justice Act 2003, sections 114–136. The relevant parts of section 132 of the Act are as follows:

> 132. – (1) Rules of court may make such provision as appears to the appropriate authority to be necessary or expedient for the purposes of this chapter: and the appropriate authority is the authority entitled to make the rules. . . .
>
> (3) The rules may require a party proposing to tender the evidence to serve on each other party to the proceedings such notice, and such particulars of or relating to the evidence, as may be prescribed. . . .
>
> (5) If a party proposing to tender evidence fails to comply with a prescribed requirement applicable to it:
>
>     (a)   the evidence is not admissible except with the court's leave;
>
>     (b)   where leave is given, the court or jury may draw such inferences from the failure as appear proper;
>
>     (c)   the failure may be taken into account by the court in considering the exercise of its powers with respect to costs.
>
> (6) In considering whether or how to exercise any of its powers under sub-section (5), the court shall have regard to whether there is any justification for the failure to comply with the requirement.

---

[5] [2009] EWCA Crim 2519; see also *Rittle v DPP* [2009] EWHC 236 (Admin).

(7) A person shall not be convicted of an offence solely on an inference drawn under sub-section 5(b).[6]

The rules governing the introduction of hearsay evidence are set out in Part 34 of the Criminal Procedure Rules 2010 (dealt with in chapter seventeen on hearsay). It is worth noting that pursuant to Rule 34.5, the court has a dispensing power in respect of the requirements to give notice and may shorten or extend time limits.

In *Musone*,[7] application was made at a late stage by the defendant to introduce hearsay evidence affecting a co-defendant: no attempt had been made to comply with Part 34 of the Rules. Moses LJ said:

> 37. The Act thus gives power to the Judge to prevent that which, in the Judge's assessment, might cause incurable unfairness either to the prosecution or to a fellow defendant. Plainly, the procedural rule should not be used to discipline one who has failed to comply with them in circumstances where unfairness to others may be cured and where the interests of justice would otherwise require the evidence to be admitted. But there will be cases in which the Judge can properly deploy section 132(5)(a) not merely as a matter of discipline, but to prevent substantive unfairness which cannot be cured by an adjournment.

## Defence Statements

Section 5(5) of the Criminal Procedure and Investigations Act (CPIA) 1996 requires an accused to give a defence statement. Section 6A sets out what has to be in the defence statement. This includes giving particulars of any alibi. Where there has been a failure to provide a defence statement or where it is inadequate in various respects, or where no or no proper particulars of alibi have been given in an alibi case, then by virtue of section 11(5), the court or any other party may make such comment as appears appropriate and the court or jury may draw such inferences as appear proper in deciding whether the accused is guilty of the offence charged.

# Sanctions Not Expressly Provided for by Statute, Regulation or Rule

## Abuse of Process

3.5 This, of course, can only apply to the prosecution. In *CPS v LR*,[8] the defence needed access to allegedly indecent images of children, partly so that the lawyers

---

[6] For that at least, we should be grateful!
[7] [2007] EWCA Crim 1237.
[8] [2010] EWCA Crim 924.

could properly advise the defendant. The Judge ordered the Crown to make copies of the images, which were then to be made available to the defence. The Crown refused to comply. The Judge stayed the proceedings. The Court of Appeal dismissed the prosecution appeal. Lord Judge CJ said:

> 16. The starting point is simple. Orders made by Crown Court judges must be obeyed. The normal consequence of disobedience by the prosecution to an order made by the Judge in the interests of a fair trial is either the exclusion of any evidence to which the order relates, or as in this case, where the entire case depended on the 240 images which were covered by the order, the stay ordered by the Judge.

## Miscellaneous

Chapter 1 of the Criminal Justice Act 2003, comprising sections 98–113, contains no provision for a sanction for non-compliance with procedural rules governing bad character applications (unlike the hearsay provisions set out above). In particular, section 111, which provides for the making of rules, only refers to a costs sanction for non-compliance. In *Musone*,[9] at a late stage in a murder trial and without any prior notice to the co-accused as required by the Rules, the appellant indicated an intention to give bad character evidence relating to the co-accused to the effect that he had admitted committing a murder on a previous occasion. It might be thought that this was evidence that had 'substantial probative value in relation to an important matter in issue between the defendant and the co-defendant' for the purposes of section 101(1)(e). The trial Judge (for wholly understandable reasons) refused to allow the evidence to be given. His decision was upheld by the Court of Appeal. Moses LJ said:

> 55.–60. For reasons that are not apparent to us, section 132(5) appears to envisage a more stringent sanction for a failure to comply with a requirement by prohibiting the admission of evidence except with the court's leave, in relation to hearsay evidence. Notwithstanding the absence of any such specific provision within section 111, we take the view that the rules made under section 111 in relation to bad character evidence, do confer power on a court to exclude such evidence in circumstances where there has been a breach of a prescribed requirement . . . In our judgement, the Judge was entitled to exclude that evidence in circumstances where he concluded that the appellant had deliberately manipulated the trial process so as to give his co-defendant no opportunity of dealing properly with the allegation . . . In our judgement, it is not possible to see how the overriding objective can be achieved if a court has no power to prevent a deliberate manipulation of the rules by refusing to admit evidence which it is sought to adduce in deliberate breach of those rules. We emphasise that cases in which a breach of the procedural rules will entitle a court to exclude evidence of substantial probative value will be rare.

The jurisprudential basis for this ruling is slightly difficult to ascertain.

---

[9] [2007] EWCA Crim 1237.

3.6   Very often, failures to comply with time limits, other pre-trial orders or the Rules themselves, go unpunished. To some extent this is inevitable. The state has an interest in ensuring that those who commit serious crime are tried and convicted and do not escape simply because of procedural mistakes by the prosecution. Equally, procedural mistakes or non-compliance with orders by or on behalf of a defendant cannot be allowed to affect the defendant's right to a fair trial. Some examples are set out below.

## Prosecution Failures

In *Phillips*,[10] the Crown had completely failed to comply with various orders made by different judges as to the disclosure of certain documents. Giving the judgment of the Court of Appeal, Clark J said:

> 36. Not only must judges be robust in their case management decisions . . . but the parties who are ordered to take steps must take them. Case progression staff, both on the prosecution and the defence side, must ensure compliance with case management orders. The responsibilities of prosecution and defence, particularly in accordance now with the Criminal Procedure Rules, are well known.

In spite of describing the Crown's failure as lamentable, this non-compliance was not the ground upon which the conviction of the appellant was quashed.

In *Owens*,[11] the Crown had regularly been supplying notices of additional evidence. The defence legitimately complained of this 'drip feeding'. Eventually, the Judge made an order in these terms: 'Anything served following 21 days from today will not be admitted. I will stand by that one . . . whatever is served after that will definitely not be admitted'. Approximately two weeks before the trial, the prosecution served 18 pages of witness statements and 100 pages of exhibits which subsequently led to the further disclosure of thousands of pages of unused material. Not surprisingly, the defence objected and wanted the evidence excluded. The Judge refused. This refusal was not a successful ground of appeal. Rix LJ said:

> 52. The Judge was entitled, having satisfied himself that there was ultimately no unfairness and no undue prejudice in the service of this material, to conclude that, his own order notwithstanding, it would be in the interests of justice to permit the material encompassed by the NAE to go forward for consideration as to its admissibility or exclusion on its own merits.

In *Sutton Coldfield Magistrates*,[12] a bad character application was made by the prosecution. There had been a complete failure to comply with the time limit set out in Part 35 of the Rules. The Magistrates allowed the evidence to be given. In refusing to quash the conviction a number of observations were made by the Divisional Court:

---

[10]   [2007] EWCA Crim 1042.
[11]   [2006] EWCA Crim 2206.
[12]   *R (Robinson) v Sutton Coldfield Magistrates' Court* [2006] EWHC 307 (Admin).

14. The first point to make is that time limits must be observed. The objective of the Criminal Procedure Rules . . . depends upon adherence to the timetable set out in the Rules. Secondly, Parliament has given the court a discretionary power to shorten a time limit or extend it even after it has expired. In the exercise of that discretion, the court will take account of all the relevant considerations, including the furtherance of the overriding objective. I am not persuaded that the discretion should be fettered in the manner for which the claimant contends, namely that time should only be extended in exceptional circumstances.

15. In this case there were two principal material considerations: first the reason for the failure to comply with the Rules. As to that, a party seeking an extension must plainly explain the reasons for its failure. Secondly, there was the question of whether the claimant's position was prejudiced by the failure.

16. . . . Any application for an extension will be closely scrutinised by the court. A party seeking an extension cannot expect the indulgence of the court unless he clearly sets out the reasons why it is seeking the indulgence.

In *Malone*,[13] for reasons which are understandable in the context of that case, the prosecution introduced bad character evidence (a forged report) without having given any notice pursuant to Part 35 of the Rules. In the Court of Appeal, Gage LJ said:

53. Finally, the Criminal Procedure Rules provide for notice to be given orally and time limits to be abridged. Whilst we would not wish to say anything which might encourage prosecuting authorities not to comply with those rules, we do not see the fact that in this case no notice had been served under Rule 35 as an insuperable obstacle to the document being admitted under section 101(1)(d).

In *Culhane*,[14] on the first day of the trial the prosecution sought to introduce the previous convictions of both defendants. No notice had been given pursuant to Rule 35.4. Refusing leave to appeal on this ground, Rix LJ said:

25. . . . Ultimately the question for the court is whether there could be any conceivable prejudice involved . . . The court has specific power under Rule 35.8 . . . to waive the time limit or the giving of notice.

In *Chapman*,[15] having written a letter to the defence indicating that they were not going to make a bad character application, the Crown had a change of heart shortly before trial. The Judge admitted the evidence and the defendant was convicted. In the Court of Appeal, Hooper LJ said:

20. Counsel was not able to point out to the trial judge or to us any particular prejudice which was suffered by this appellant as a result of the late application.

It thus seems fairly clear that so far as prosecution failures to comply with time limits and notice periods are concerned, the only test that matters is whether the

[13] [2006] EWCA Crim 1860.
[14] [2006] EWCA Crim 1053.
[15] [2006] EWCA Crim 2545.

defendant can point to some specific prejudice to him occasioned by the failure which has adversely affected his right to a fair trial. It is to be assumed that the fact that he might not have been convicted if the evidence had been excluded does not amount to prejudice for these purposes.

## Defence Failures

The Criminal Procedure Rules are of course binding on defendants, as is the obligation to give a defence statement pursuant to the CPIA 1996. However, procedural mistakes or non-compliance with orders by or on behalf of a defendant cannot be allowed to affect his right to a fair trial. Accordingly, although the failure to serve a defence statement and an associated failure to give notice of an alibi might occasion strong comment, might give rise to the possibility of the drawing of an adverse influence or might occasion an adjournment to give the Crown time to investigate it, it is inconceivable that the defendant could be prevented from giving that evidence or calling his witnesses in support.

In *Tinnion*[16] (a case where in fact the defendant was probably under no obligation to give a defence statement disclosing an alibi), the trial Judge had refused to allow the defendant to call two alibi witnesses. Quashing the conviction, Clarke J said:

> 8. . . . None of the reasons given amounts to any proper basis for ruling the evidence inadmissible so that it could not be called or heard at all. Even if the Recorder had been right to hold that the claimant was under a requirement to provide a defence statement, either in the Youth Court or in the Crown Court on appeal, with details of his alibi witnesses, it does not follow that the failure to comply with this requirement rendered the evidence inadmissible. The sanction against a defendant who fails to give such notice is not that a witness cannot be called, but that adverse comment can be made and cross-examination can be conducted, and that the court or jury may draw such inference as is proper from the failure to give such notice (see section 11 of the Criminal Procedure and Investigations Act 1996 as now in force). It may be that the Recorder was thinking back to the time when leave of the court was required before a defendant in the Crown Court could call an alibi witness when no notice had been served.

Problems arise when two defendants are running a 'cut-throat' defence. The case of *Musone* has already been dealt with. In *Chapman*,[17] one of the grounds upon which leave to appeal was sought was on the basis that the trial Judge had given leave to a co-defendant to serve a bad character application out of time. Refusing leave, Hooper LJ said:

> 21. Counsel was unable and remains unable to point to any prejudice suffered by the appellant as a result of the lateness of the application.

---

[16] [2009] EWHC 2930 (Admin).
[17] [2006] EWCA Crim 2545.

In *Lawson*,[18] counsel for the co-accused put a previous conviction of the appellant to him during the course of his cross-examination. No notice had been given, either formally pursuant to Part 35 of the Rules or informally to his counsel, and nor had leave been sought from the judge. Giving judgment, Hughes LJ said:

14. We are quite unable to understand how that came to happen. It was directly contrary to the Rules . . . we are wholly unsurprised by the Judge's description of the conduct of counsel as reprehensible.

15. It is contended that in the absence of notice the Judge should not have allowed the question to be asked or the evidence to stand . . . we entirely agree with the way the Judge dealt with it. He had a discretion under Rule 35.8 to allow evidence of bad character to be adduced, notwithstanding that the required notice had not been given, by permitting notice to be given orally or in a different form from that prescribed and he had power to shorten time for it. It must be implicit in the power to shorten time that it can be shortened to any degree and thus dispensed with.

16. Whenever a co-accused proposes to adduce bad character evidence . . . he should always, without exception, alert counsel for the other defendant of his intention. That is so that the latter can take objection . . . and that the Judge can rule, after proper argument on both sides, whether the evidence is admissible or not. The requirement that counsel be alerted is not a substitute for the notice called for by the Criminal Procedure Rules, where the possibility of such an application can be anticipated.

However, if there has been a complete non-compliance with the Rules in and about the giving of notice and the making of an application and if there is serious prejudice to the co-accused caused thereby, it is worth bearing in mind what Richards LJ said in *Ramirez*.[19] Having referred to both *Musone* and *Jarvis*,[20] he said:

44. . . . It is right to say, however, that we remain very concerned at the potential implication in other cases of what happened here. We make clear that in another case, the giving of bad character evidence by one defendant in relation to a co-defendant without prior notice or application could well lead to the discharge of the jury and to a retrial, with the possibility of severe sanctions in the form at least of wasted costs order against any legal representative found to have been involved in the deliberate manipulation of the Rules leading to such a consequence.

---

[18] [2006] EWCA Crim 2572.
[19] [2009] EWCA Crim 1721.
[20] [2008] EWCA Crim 488.

# 4

---

# Defence Statement and Disclosure

---

## The Defence Statement

4.1   Part 1 of the Criminal Procedure and Investigations Act (CPIA) 1996 (as amended by the Criminal Justice Act 2003) governs the requirement to give (and the contents of) a defence statement. Section 1 of the CPIA 1996 provides that:

1. ... (2) This part applies when:

   (a)   a person is charged with an indictable offence and he is committed for trial for the offence concerned

   ...

   (cc)   a person is charged with an offence for which he is sent for trial.

By CPIA 1996, section 5:

5. – (1) ... this section applies when:

   (a)   this part applies by virtue of section 1(2); and
   (b)   the prosecutor complies with section 3 or purports to comply with it.[1]

   ...

   (5)   Where this section applies, the accused must give a defence statement to the court and the prosecutor.

In *Essa*,[2] the appellant had, on legal advice, not filed a defence statement. Hughes LJ said:

> 18. We should, we think, briefly say that we are at a loss to understand how any lawyer can properly give that advice to any defendant in the face of section 5(5) of the Act. Whatever may be the primary purpose of the statute, its requirement is that the accused give a defence statement to the court and the prosecution. It is not open to those who advise defendants to pick and choose which statutory rules applicable to the conduct of criminal proceedings they obey and which they do not.

4.2   This paragraph is concerned with time limits. By CPIA 1996, section 5(5C):

> A defence statement that has to be given to the court and the prosecutor ... must be given during the period which by virtue of section 12 is the relevant period for this section.

---

[1]   Compliance or purported compliance by the prosecution with its duties of initial disclosure.
[2]   [2009] EWCA Crim 43.

Section 12 provides as follows:

> 12. ... (2) ... the relevant period is a period beginning and ending with such days as the Secretary of State prescribes by regulations for the purposes of the section concerned.[3]

The relevant regulations were the Criminal Procedure and Investigations Act 1996 (Defence Disclosure Time Limits) Regulations 1997 (SI 1997/2680), which came into force on 1 April 1997. From 28 February 2011, they have been replaced by the Criminal Procedure and Investigations Act 1996 (Defence Disclosure Time Limits) Regulations 2011 (SI 2011/209). The relevant parts are as follows:

> 2.(1) The relevant notification period for Section 5 (compulsory disclosure) ... begins with the day on which the prosecutor complies or purports to comply with Section 3 (initial duty of the prosecutor to disclose).
>
> (2) ...
>
> (3) ... the relevant period for Section 5 ... expires at the end of 28 days beginning with the first day of the relevant period.
>
> 3.(1) The court may by order extend (or further extend) the relevant period by so many days as it specifies.
>
> (2) The court may only make such an order:
>
> > (a) on an application by the accused; and
> > (b) if it is satisfied that it would be unreasonable to require the accused to give a defence statement under section 5 ... within the relevant period.
>
> (3) Such an application must:
>
> > (a) be made within the relevant period;
> > (b) specify the grounds on which it is made; and
> > (c) state the number of days by which the accused wishes the relevant period to be extended.
>
> (4) There is no limit on the number of applications that may be made under paragraph 2(a).

The current Regulation is a considerable improvement upon its predecessor both in terms of clarity and by providing a more sensible 28-day period for service of the defence statement rather than the previous 14 days. It should be noted, though, that any application to extend the period for filing the same has to be made within the initial 28-day period and that the court has to be satisfied that it would be 'unreasonable' to expect compliance by the defendant within that 28-day period. There is no power to extend the time limit if no application is made within the 28-day period. Accordingly, a late defence statement will still invite the sanctions (such as they are) set out in CPIA 1996, section 11, discussed below.

---

[3] The regulations therefore are to be made (and are made) by the Secretary of State at the Ministry of Justice. They are not made by the Criminal Procedure Rules Committee.

4.3   The contents of a defence statement are prescribed by CPIA 1996, section 6A:

6A. – (1) . . . a defence statement is a written statement:

(a)   setting out the nature of the accused's defence, including any particular defences on which he intends to rely;

(b)   indicating the matters of fact on which he takes issue with the prosecution;

(c)   setting out, in the case of each such matter, why he takes issue with the prosecution;

(ca)  setting out particulars of the matters of fact on which he intends to rely for the purposes of his defence; and

(d)   indicating any point of law (including any point as to the admissibility of evidence or an abuse of process) which he wishes to take and any authority on which he intends to rely for that purpose.

(2)   A defence statement that discloses an alibi must give particulars of it including:

(a)   the name, address and date of birth of any witness the accused believes is able to give evidence in support of the alibi, or as many of those details as are known to the accused when the statement is given;

(b)   any information in the accused's possession which might be of material assistance in identifying or finding any such witness in whose case any of the details mentioned in paragraph (a) are not known to the accused when the statement is given.

(3)   For the purposes of this section evidence in support of an alibi is evidence tending to show that by reason of the presence of the accused at a particular place or in a particular area at a particular time, he was not, or was unlikely to have been, at the place where the offence is alleged to have been committed at the time of its alleged commission.

In *Bryant*,[4] Judge LJ (as he then was) said:

12. In passing, we note that the defence case statement was woefully inadequate. It consisted of a general denial of the counts in the indictment, accompanied by the sentence 'the defendant takes issue with any witness purporting to give evidence contrary to his denials'. This sort of observation is not worth the paper it is written on. It is not the purpose of a defence case statement.

In *K*,[5] the Court of Appeal stressed the importance of practitioners being familiar with the Protocol on Disclosure which has a number of trenchant things to say about defence statements. In particular:

34. In the past, the prosecution and the court have too often been faced with a defence case statement that is little more than an assertion that the defendant is not guilty. As was stated by the Court of Appeal in *Bryant* . . . such a reiteration of the defendant's plea is not the purpose of a defence statement. Defence statements must comply with the requisite formalities set out in the CPIA . . .

---

[4]   4 [2005] EWCA Crim 2079.
[5]   [2006] EWCA Crim 385.

35. Where the enhanced requirements for defence disclosure apply under section 6A of the CPIA, namely when the case involves a criminal investigation commencing on or after 4 April 2005, the defence statement must spell out in detail the nature of the defence and particular defences relied upon: it must identify the matters of fact upon which the accused takes issue with the prosecutor and the reasons why, in relation to each disputed matter of fact. It must further identify any point of law . . . which the accused proposes to take and identify authorities relied on in relation to each point of law . . . Judges will expect to see defence case statements that contain a clear and detailed exposition of the issues of fact and law in the case. . . .

37. There must be a complete change in the culture. The defence must file the defence case statement by the due date. Judges should then examine the defence case statement with care, to ensure that it complies with the formalities required by the CPIA.

38. If no defence case statement – or no sufficient case statement – has been served by the PCMH the Judge should make a full investigation of the reasons for this failure to comply with the mandatory obligation of the accused.

39. If there is no or no sufficient defence statement by the date of the PCMH or any pre-trial hearing where the matter falls to be considered, the Judge must consider whether the defence should be warned . . . that an adverse inference may be drawn at the trial. In the usual case, where section 6E(2) applies and there is no justification for the deficiency, such a warning should be given.

In *Rochford*,[6] the defendant was charged with dangerous driving. His defence statement read: 'The defendant was not the driver of the vehicle in question at the material time. He accepts he may have been the person shown on the CCTV at the garage'. The trial Judge was underwhelmed by this defence statement (as will be seen later). The Court of Appeal made the following relevant comments, applicable to all cases:

1.16. The first question which we think we ought to address is whether there was in this case a failure to comply with section 6A. The answer is that we do not know and neither did the Judge. If the defendant was going to say that he was somewhere else rather than in the driving seat then there had been a failure to comply with section 6A. If he was going to call evidence from some source other than himself that he was somewhere else other than in the driving seat then there had been a failure to comply with section 6A. If the possibility that he had been somewhere else was going to be raised distinctly before the jury by way of submission or argument, that too would entail a failure to comply with section 6A. Once the issue is going to be raised in any of those manners (and there may be other ways in which it could be) section 6A(1)(ca) and (c) would apply and would require the defendant to set out why he took issue with the Crown on his location and to give particulars of the matters of fact on which he intended to rely for that purpose. However, if the defendant was going to make no positive case at all and not raise the issue of his possible location elsewhere and if he was simply going to sit tight and ensure that the Crown proved its case then, as it seems to us, there would have been no failure to comply with section 6A. . . .

---

[6] [2010] EWCA Crim 1928.

1.21. . . . do legal professional privilege and the defendant's privilege against self-incrimination survive section 6A? The answer to that is 'yes'. What the defendant is required to disclose by section 6A is what is going to happen at the trial. He is not required to disclose his confidential discussions with his advocate although of course they may bear on what is going to happen at the trial. Nor is he obliged to incriminate himself if he does not want to. Those are fundamental rights and they have certainly not been taken away by section 6A.

1.22. . . . can the lawyer properly advise a defendant not to file a defence statement? The answer to that is 'no'. The obligation to file a defence statement is a statutory obligation on the defendant. It is not open to a lawyer to advise his client to disobey the client's statutory obligation. It is as simple as that. . . .

1.24. The remaining question is this. What is the duty of the lawyer if the defendant has no positive case to advance at trial but declines to plead guilty? . . . A less extreme but equally possible example is the defendant who refuses to give instructions either at all or on specific points. In neither of those situations can it possibly be the obligation of the defendant to put into his defence statement an admission of guilt or a refusal to give instructions. What are the lawyers to do? . . . But in general terms our answer is this. The defence statement must say that the defendant does not admit the offence or the relevant part of it as the case may be and calls for the Crown to prove it. But it must also say that he advances no positive case because if he is going to advance a positive case that must appear in the defence statement and notice of it must be given. Unless the requirement is that the statement is made but no positive case is advanced, it would be open to defendants simply to ignore sections 5(5) and 6A.

4.4    CPIA 1996, section 6C came into force on 1 May 2010. It provides as follows:

6C. – (1) The accused must give to the court and the prosecutor a notice indicating whether he intends to call any person (other than himself) as witnesses at his trial and if so:
   (a) giving the name, address and date of birth of each such proposed witness or as many of those details as are known to the accused when the notice is given;
   (b) providing any information in the accused's possession which might be of material assistance in identifying or finding any such proposed witness in whose case any of the details mentioned in paragraph (a) are not known to the accused when the notice is given.
(2) Details do not have to be given under this section to the extent that they have already been given under section 6A(2).
(3) The accused must give a notice under this section during the period which, by virtue of section 12, is the relevant period for this section.
(4) If, following the giving of a notice under this section, the accused:
   (a) decides to call a person (other than himself) who is not included in the notice as a proposed witness or decides not to call a person who is so included; or
   (b) discovers any information which under sub-section (1) he would have had to include in the notice if he had been aware of it when giving the notice,

   he must give an appropriately amended notice to the court and the prosecutor.

The same time limits as apply to defence statements apply to the defence witness notice. They are now set out in SI 2011/209, see 4.2 above. To the extent that section 6C and the Regulations apply, they must be taken to have overruled the decision in *Warley Magistrates*.[7]

With the coming into force of section 6C, a new Code of Practice has been issued pursuant to CPIA 1996, section 21A in respect of the police or prosecuting authorities interviewing witnesses who have been named by the defence in the defence witness notice, entitled Code of Practice for Arranging and Conducting Interviews of Witnesses Notified by the Accused. It is not proposed to set it out here.

4.5 CPIA 1996, section 6E sets out certain other matters in respect of defence statements.

Authority

6E. – (1) Where an accused's solicitor purports to give on behalf of the accused:

    (a)   a defence statement under section 5 . . . the statement shall, unless the contrary is proved, be deemed to be given with the authority of the accused. . . .

Pre-trial warning

    (2)  If it appears to the Judge at a pre-trial hearing that an accused has failed to comply fully with section 5 or 6C so that there is a possibility of comment being made or inferences drawn under section 11(5) he shall warn the accused accordingly.

. . .

Jury having copy of defence statement

    (4)  The Judge in a trial before a Judge and jury:

        (a)   may direct that the jury be given a copy of any defence statement; and
        (b)  if he does so, may direct that it be edited so as not to include references to matters evidence of which would be inadmissible.

    (5)  A direction under sub-section (4):

        (a)   may be made either of the Judge's own motion or on the application of any party;
        (b)  may be made only if the Judge is of the opinion that seeing a copy of the defence statement would help the jury to understand the case or to resolve any issues in the case.

4.6   In this paragraph I deal with the sanctions which may be applied in the event of non-compliance with the foregoing rules about defence statements. In *Rochford* (see 4.3 above) the trial Judge was of the view that the defence statement which had been filed failed to comply with CPIA 1996, sections 5 and 6A. He said that any refusal by the defendant to amend the document would be regarded by him as

---

[7]  [2007] EWHC 1836 (Admin).

a contempt of court (and possibly a contempt of court by his counsel!). The defendant persisted in his refusal and the Judge sentenced him to 28 days in prison for contempt of court for disobedience of the order to amend the defence statement. The Court of Appeal held that he had no power to do so:

> 1.18. The second question which we need to address is, if it is plain that there is a breach of section 6A, either because there is no defence statement or because it has not got in it what it ought to have, can the court by ordering compliance then vest itself with the power to punish as a contempt of court disobedience to the order. The answer to that is 'no'. Any order such as a Judge might make would be no more than an emphatic articulation of the statutory obligation created by sections 5(5) and 6A. The sanction for non-compliance is explicit in the statute in section 11. It is not open to the court to add an additional extra-statutory sanction of punishment for contempt of court.

Before looking at section 11, it is also worth remembering that, unlike the 'old' law in respect of alibi notices applies, there is no power to prevent the calling, for example, of an alibi witness simply because the witness has not been named in the defence statement. In *Tinnion*[8] (where the defendant was in fact probably under no obligation to give a defence statement, it being a Youth Court matter), the trial Judge on an appeal in the Crown Court had refused to allow the defendant to call two alibi witnesses. Quashing the conviction, Clark J said:

> 8. . . . none of the reasons given amounts to any proper basis for ruling the evidence inadmissible so that it could not be called or heard at all. Even if the Recorder had been right to hold that the applicant was under a requirement to provide a defence statement . . . with details of his alibi witnesses, it does not follow that the failure to comply with the requirement rendered the evidence inadmissible. The sanction against a defendant who fails to give such a notice is not that a witness cannot be called, but that adverse comment can be made and cross-examination can be conducted and that the court or jury may draw such inference as is proper from the failure to give such notice (see section 11 of the CPIA). It may be that the Recorder was thinking back to the time when leave of the court was required before a defendant in the Crown Court could call an alibi witness when no notice had been served.

I turn now to CPIA 1996, section 11. It provides as follows:

11. – (1) This section applies in the three cases set out in sub-sections (2), (3) and (4).
(2) The first case is where section 5 applies and the accused:

   (a)  fails to give an initial defence statement;
   (b)  gives an initial defence statement but does so after the end of the period which, by virtue of section 12, is the relevant period for the purposes of section 5;
   . . .
   (e)  sets out inconsistent defences in his defence statement; or
   (f)  at his trial:

      (i)   puts forward a defence which was not mentioned in his defence statement or is different from any defence set out in that statement;

[8] [2009] EWHC 2930 (Admin).

       (ii)   relies on a matter (or any particular of any matter of fact) which, in breach of the requirements imposed by or under section 6A was not mentioned in his defence statement;

      (iii)  adduces evidence in support of an alibi without having given particulars of the alibi in his defence statement; or

      (iv)  calls a witness to give evidence in support of an alibi without having complied with section 6A(2)(a) or (b) as regards the witness in his defence statement.

(3) ...

(4) The third case is when the accused:

    (a)  gives a witness notice but does so after the end of the period which, by virtue of section 12, is the relevant period for the purpose of section 6C; or

    (b)  at his trial calls a witness (other than himself) not included or not adequately identified in a witness notice.

(5) Where this section applies:

    (a)  the court or any other party may make such comment as appears appropriate;

    (b)  the court or jury may draw such inferences as appear proper in deciding whether the accused is guilty of the offence concerned.

(6) Where:

    (a)  this section applies by virtue of sub-section (2)(f)(ii); and

    (b)  the matter which was not mentioned is a point of law (including any point as to the admissibility of evidence or an abuse of process or an authority),

comment by another party under sub-section (5) may be made only with the leave of the court.

(7) Where this section applies by virtue of sub-section (4), comment by another party under sub-section (5)(a) may be made only with the leave of the court.

(8) Where the accused puts forward a defence which is different from any defence set out in his defence statement, in doing anything under sub-section (5) or in deciding whether to do anything under it, the court shall have regard:

    (a)  to the extent of the difference in the defence; and

    (b)  to whether there is any justification for it.

(9) Where the accused calls a witness whom he has failed to include or to identify adequately in a witness notice, in doing anything under sub-section (5) or in deciding whether to do anything under it, the court shall have regard to whether there is any justification for the failure.

(10) A person shall not be convicted of an offence solely on an inference drawn under sub-section (5).

The position would therefore seem to be as follows. By virtue of section 11(2), where there is no defence statement; the defence statement is out of time; the defence statement sets out inconsistent defences; the defence statement does not mention the defence which is run at trial; matters are run at trial which are not mentioned in the defence statement; no particulars of alibi have been given; or no notice of alibi witnesses has been given; or, by virtue of section 11(4), there is a late witness notice or the defence call a witness whose name is not included in the witness notice, then by virtue of section 11(5) the court or another party may comment on that failure and the jury may draw such inferences as may be proper by virtue of that failure. But where the matter not mentioned is a point of law, then comment can only be made with leave. Likewise, where the failure consists of the serving of a witness notice late or where a witness is not mentioned in that notice, comment can only be made by another party with leave of the court. Where the defence at trial is different from the defence set out in the defence statement, the court is to have regard to the extent of the difference and any justification put forward for it in deciding whether to allow the making of comment or the drawing of inferences. Likewise, in deciding whether to allow comment to be made or inferences to be drawn where a witness is called who is not mentioned in the witness notice or not adequately identified, the court has to have regard as to whether there is any justification for the failure in deciding whether to allow comment and/or the drawing of inferences.

# Disclosure

4.7 CPIA 1996, section 3 (as amended by Criminal Justice Act 2003, section 32) sets out the duties of a prosecutor in respect of initial disclosure and the time for compliance with that obligation. The relevant provisions of section 3 are as follows:

> 3. – (1) The prosecutor must:
>
> > (a) disclose to the accused any prosecution material which has not previously been disclosed to the accused and which might reasonably be considered capable of undermining the case for the prosecution against the accused or of assisting the case for the accused; or
> >
> > (b) give to the accused a written statement that there is no material of a description mentioned in paragraph (a). . . .
>
> (8) The prosecutor must act under this section during the period which by virtue of section 12 is the relevant period for this section.

CPIA 1996, section 12 enabled the Secretary of State to make regulations defining 'the relevant period'. No such regulations have been made so far as prosecution disclosure is concerned. Accordingly, section 13 of the Act applies. That provides that where no regulation has been made, section 3(8) above should be read as follows:

> (8) The prosecutor must act under this section as soon as is reasonably practicable after: . . .
>
> > (b) the accused is committed for trial;
> >
> > (c)(a) copies of the documents containing the evidence on which the charge or charges are based are served on the accused.

When considering its duty pursuant to section 3(1), it is important that the prosecution bear in mind what was said by Lord Bingham in *H*:[9]

> 17. Section 3 does not require disclosure of material which is either neutral in its effect or which is adverse to the defendant, whether because it strengthens the prosecution or weakens the defence. . . .
>
> 35. If material does not weaken the prosecution case or strengthen that of the defendant, there is no requirement to disclose it. For this purpose, the parties' respective cases should not be restrictively analysed. But they must be carefully analysed, to ascertain the specific facts the prosecution seek to establish and the specific grounds on which the charges are resisted. The trial process is not well served if the defence are permitted to make general and unspecified allegations and then seek far-reaching disclosure in the hope that material may turn up to make them good. Neutral material, or material damaging to the defendant need not be disclosed and should not be brought to the attention of the court. Only in truly borderline cases should the prosecution seek a judicial ruling on the disclosability of material in its hands. If the material contains information which the prosecution would prefer that the defendant did not have on forensic as opposed to public interest grounds, that will suggest that the material is disclosable. If the disclosure test is faithfully applied, the occasions on which a Judge will be obliged to recuse himself because he has been privately shown material damning to the defendant will . . . be very exceptional indeed.

Likewise, the Protocol for the Control and Management of Unused Material in the Crown Court is relevant.[10] This tells prosecutors that:

> (4) The overarching principle is therefore that unused prosecution material will fall to be disclosed if, and only if, it satisfies the test for disclosure applicable to the proceedings in question, subject to any overriding public consideration. . . .
>
> (18) Where the single test for disclosure applies under the amended CPIA disclosure regime, the prosecution is under a duty to consider, at an early stage of proceedings, whether there is any unused prosecution material which is reasonably capable of assisting the case for the accused. What a defendant has said by way of defence or explanation either in interview or by way of a prepared statement, can be a useful guide to making an objective assessment of the material which would satisfy the test.

Reference should also be made to the revised guidelines issued by the Attorney General in 2005, full details of which are set out in the standard practitioners' textbooks.

The duty is to disclose 'prosecution material'. This is defined in CPIA 1966, section 3(2) as follows:

> 3. . . . (2) For the purposes of this section prosecution material is material:
>
> > (a)  which is in the prosecutor's possession and came into his possession in connection with the case for the prosecution against the accused; or

---

[9]  [2004] UKHL 3.
[10]  Issued in 2006.

(b)   which, in pursuance of a code . . . he has inspected in connection with the case
for the prosecution against the accused.

So far as a code is concerned, this was issued by the Secretary of State pursuant
to CPIA 1996, sections 23 to 25 and applies to investigations begun after 4 April
2005.[11] In respect of certain basic obligations, we can précis the code requirements
as follows:

(1)   In respect of any criminal investigation there should be a 'disclosure officer'.
He is the person responsible for examining material retained by the police
during the investigation and revealing that information to the prosecutor
and certifying that he has done so.
(2)   The 'disclosure officer' is a different entity than 'the officer in charge of the
investigation' whose job, inter alia, includes the responsibility to see that all
material relevant to the investigation is kept and made available to the disclosure officer.
(3)   Any police officer acting as an investigator must retain information obtained
in a criminal investigation which may be relevant to the investigation. That
duty applies in particular to material which may satisfy the test for prosecution disclosure.
(4)   Material which has been obtained in accordance with the code which the
disclosure officer does not believe will form part of the prosecution case must
be listed in a schedule. Material which he regards as not being sensitive will
be listed in a schedule of 'non-sensitive material' whilst that which he believes
to be sensitive will be listed in a schedule of 'sensitive material'. Material is to
be regarded as 'sensitive' where the disclosure officer believes that its disclosure 'would give rise to a real risk of serious prejudice to an important public
interest'.

At 4.12 below, possible prosecution obligations in respect of material not held
by them or the police are examined. It should be remembered, as Ousley J said in
*Wood*:[12]

55. The disclosure duties are created in respect of material which, put shortly, the CPS
or the police have and which the CPS has inspected or must be allowed to inspect. The
code reflects that position.

4.8   The duties of the prosecution in connection with disclosure are continuing
duties. Section 37 of the Criminal Justice Act 2003 inserted a new section 7A into
the CPIA 1996. The section is headed 'Continuing duty of prosecutor to disclose'
and reads as follows:

---

[11] Criminal Procedure and Investigations Act 1996 (Code of Practice) Order 2005 (SI 2005/985).
[12] [2006] EWHC 32 (Admin).

7A. – (1) This section applies at all times:

    (a)   after the prosecutor has complied with section 3 or purported to comply with it. . . .

(2)  The prosecutor must keep under review the question whether at any given time (and in particular following the giving of a defence statement) there is prosecution material which:

    (a)   might reasonably be considered capable of undermining the case for the prosecution against the accused, or of assisting the case for the accused; and

    (b)   has not been disclosed to the accused.

(3)  If at any time there is any such material as is mentioned in sub-section (2), the prosecutor must disclose it to the accused as soon as is reasonably practicable.

The duty of the prosecutor to keep things under review applies regardless of whether or not a defence statement has been served. When a defence statement has been served, then CPIA 1996, sections 7A(5) and 8 apply:[13]

(5)  Where the accused gives a defence statement under section 5:

    (a)   if as a result of that statement the prosecutor is required by this section to make any disclosure or further disclosure he must do so during the period which, by virtue of section 12, is the relevant period for this section.

Given that no regulations have been made under section 12, the default provisions of section 13(2) apply so that the time for compliance is 'as soon as reasonably practicable after the accused gives the statement in question':

    (b)   if the prosecutor considers that he is not so required, he must during that period give the accused a statement to that effect.

If a defendant who has given a defence statement and who has received (or not received) a section 7A(5) notice remains dissatisfied, he can utilise the provisions of section 8:

8. – (1) This section applies where the accused has given a defence statement under section 5 . . . and the prosecutor has complied with section 7A(5) or has purported to comply with it or has failed to comply with it.

(2)  If the accused has at any time reasonable cause to believe that there is prosecution material which is required by section 7A to be disclosed to him and has not been, he may apply to the court for an order requiring the prosecutor to disclose it to him.

A question arises as to what constitutes a 'defence statement' for the purpose of activating section 7A(5) and which gives rise to the right of a defendant to make an application pursuant to section 8. In particular, what is to happen if the statement is late or somewhat deficient in terms of its content? This was dealt with by Ousley J in *Wood*.[14]

---

[13]  Inserted by Criminal Justice Act 2003, s 38.
[14]  See n 12 above.

24. and 25. I reject the submission . . . that the defence statement was not a defence statement given under section 5 because it was late . . . The concept of a statement given under section 5 must be the same for the purposes of applying section 8. I also find it difficult to see that the late provision of such a statement could deprive a Judge of jurisdiction to hear a section 8 application . . . The next argument . . . was that the defendant could not make a section 8 application because the defence statement was not in substance a defence statement because it did not comply with the requirements of section 5(6). Of course, there may be so-called defence statements which are so deficient in their fulfilment of the requirements . . . that they cannot properly be termed defence statements at all . . . But there are real dangers of injustice in treating deficient written defence statements as so wholly ineffective as to be non-existent in reality and thus remove the Judge's jurisdiction to make a section 8 order.

As to the procedure to be adopted by a defendant in making a section 8 application, this is set out in Rule 22.5 of the Criminal Procedure Rules 2011 (SI 2011/1709) ('the Rules'). It reads as follows:

22.5(1) This rule applies where the defendant:

    (a)  has served a defence statement . . .; and
    (b)  wants the court to require the prosecutor to disclose material.

(2)  The defendant must serve an application on:

    (a)  the Court Officer; and
    (b)  the prosecutor.

(3)  The application must:

    (a)  describe the material that the defendant wants the prosecutor to disclose;
    (b)  explain why the defendant thinks there is reasonable cause to believe that:

        (i)   the prosecutor has that material; and
        (ii)  it is material that the CPIA requires the prosecutor to disclose; and

    (c)  ask for a hearing, if the defence wants one and explain why it is needed.

(4)  The court may determine an application under this rule:

    (a)  at a hearing in public or in private; or
    (b)  without a hearing.

(5)  The court does not require the prosecutor to disclose material unless the prosecutor:

    (a)  is present; or
    (b)  has had at least 14 days in which to make representations.

This leaves one question unresolved. If the prosecution are resisting the application on grounds other than public interest immunity, it must mean that in their view the material is not disclosable: it does not undermine the case for the prosecution or assist the case for the accused. If the defence, who by definition are claiming that they have not seen the material, are asserting that it is disclosable, it must follow that the judge will have to look at it and make the decision. It would not be a proper exercise of the judicial function simply to accept the assertion of the prosecution and dismiss the application out of hand. In any event, this is implicit in the speech of Lord Bingham in *H*,[15] when he said:

> 35. Only in truly borderline cases should the prosecution seek a judicial ruling on the disclosability of material in its hands.

This clearly assumes the existence of a set of circumstances when the decision has to be taken by the judge.

4.9 Under CPIA 1996, section 3(6), 'material must not be disclosed under this section to the extent that the court, on an application by the prosecutor, concludes that it is not in the public interest to disclose it and orders accordingly'; see also section 7A(8). We are here dealing with public interest immunity (PII). Any application by the prosecution for a ruling from a judge should be made in accordance with Part 22 of the Rules. The relevant rules are as follows:

22.3(1) This rule applies where:

  (a) without a court order, the prosecutor would have to disclose material; and
  (b) the prosecutor wants the court to decide whether it would be in the public interest to disclose it.

(2) The prosecutor must:

  (a) apply in writing for such a decision; and
  (b) serve the application on:
  
    (i) the Court Officer;
    (ii) any person who the prosecutor thinks would be directly affected by the disclosure of the material; and
    (iii) the defendant, but only to the extent that serving it on the defendant would not disclose what the prosecutor thinks ought not to be disclosed.

(3) The application must:

  (a) describe the material and explain why the prosecutor thinks that:
  
    (i) it is material that the prosecutor would have to disclose;
    (ii) it would not be in the public interest to disclose that material; and
    (iii) no measure such as the prosecutor's admission of any fact, or disclosure by summary, extract or edited copy, adequately would protect both the public interest and the defendant's right to a fair trial;
  
  (b) omit from any part of the application that is served on the defendant anything that would disclose what the prosecutor thinks ought not to be disclosed (in which case paragraph (4) of this rule applies); and
  (c) explain why, if no part of the application is served on the defendant.

(4) Where the prosecutor serves only part of the application on the defendant, the prosecutor must:

  (a) mark the other part to show that it is only for the court; and
  (b) in that other part, explain why the prosecutor has withheld it from the defendant.

---

[15] See n 9 above.

(5) Unless already done, the court may direct the prosecutor to serve an application on:

   (a)  the defendant;

   (b)  any other person who the court considers would be directly affected by the disclosure of the material.

(6) The court must determine the application at a hearing which:

   (a)  will be in private unless the court otherwise directs; and

   (b)  if the court so directs, may take place, wholly or in part, in the defendant's absence.

(7) At a hearing at which the defendant is present:

   (a)  the general rule is that the court will receive in the following sequence:

      (i)  representations first by the prosecutor and any other person served with the application and then by the defendant in the presence of them all; and then

      (ii)  further representations by the prosecutor and any such other person in the defendant's absence; but

   (b)  the court may direct other arrangements for the hearing.

(8) The court may only determine the application if satisfied that it has been able to take adequate account of:

   (a)  such rights of confidentiality as apply to the material; and

   (b)  the defendant's right to a fair trial.

(9) Unless the court otherwise directs, the Court Officer:

   (a)  must not give notice to anyone other than the prosecutor:

      (i)  of the hearing of an application under this rule, unless the prosecutor served the application on that person; or

      (ii)  of the court's decision on the application;

   (b)  may:

      (i)  keep a written application or representation; or

      (ii)  arrange for the whole or any part to be kept by some other appropriate person subject to any conditions that the court may impose.

It is open to a defendant to apply to the court to review a decision that material is not disclosable on PII grounds. The appropriate procedure is set out in Rule 22.6 of the Rules.

As to the proper approach of both the Crown and the court when considering PII matters, reference should again be made to the speech of Lord Bingham in *H*.[16] He said:

35. If material does not weaken the prosecution case or strengthen that of the defendant, there is no requirement to disclose it . . . When any issue of derogation from the golden rule of full disclosure comes before it, the court must address a series of problems:

---

[16]  See n 9 above.

(1) What is the material which the prosecution seek to withhold? This must be considered by the court in detail.

(2) Is the material such as may weaken the prosecution case or strengthen that of the defendant? If no, disclosure should not be ordered. If yes, full disclosure should be ordered (subject to (3), (4) and (5) below).

(3) Is there a real risk of serious prejudice to an important public interest (and if so what) if full disclosure of the material is ordered? If no, full disclosure should be ordered.

(4) If the answer to (2) and (3) is yes, can the defendant's interests be protected without disclosure or disclosure be ordered to an extent or in a way which will give adequate protection to the public interest in question and also afford adequate protection to the interests of the defence? This question requires the court to consider, with specific reference to the material which the prosecution seeks to withhold and the facts of the case and the defence as disclosed, whether the prosecution should formally admit what the defence seek to establish or whether disclosure, short of full disclosure, may be ordered. This may be done in appropriate cases by the preparation of summaries or extracts of evidence or the provision of documents in an edited or anonymised form provided the documents supplied are in each case approved by the Judge.

(5) Do the measures proposed in answer to (4) represent the minimum derogation necessary to protect the public interest in question? If no, the court should order such greater disclosure as will represent the minimum derogation from the golden rule of full disclosure.

(6) If limited disclosure is ordered pursuant to (4) or (5), may the effect be to render the trial process, viewed as a whole, unfair to the defendant? If yes, then fuller disclosure should be ordered even if this leads or may lead the prosecution to discontinue the proceedings so as to avoid having to make disclosure.

(7) If the answer to (6) when first given is no, does that remain the correct answer as the trial unfolds, evidence is adduced and the defence advanced? It is important that the answer to (6) should not be treated as a final once-and-for-all answer but as a provisional answer which the court must keep under review.

Normally, the judge who has examined undisclosed material should continue to act as trial judge – he is after all the one who has to keep the position under review as the trial proceeds. The judge has a discretion to recuse himself if in his opinion the interests of justice require it, but it is difficult to think of any circumstances in which a judge might reach that conclusion.[17]

# Third Party Material

4.10    This paragraph is concerned with obtaining the production of documents and things not in the hands of the parties: third party material. The distinction between production and disclosure should be noted. In many cases the court will

---

[17] *Dawson* [2007] EWCA Crim 822 at paras 58, 59 and 60.

still have to decide whether the material produced by the third party to the court should be disclosed to the parties. The starting point is section 2 of the Criminal Procedure (Attendance of Witnesses) Act (CP(AW)A) 1965 (as amended):

2. – (1) This section applies when the Crown Court is satisfied that:

    (a)  a person is likely to be able to . . . produce any document or thing likely to be material evidence for the purpose of any criminal proceedings before the Crown Court; and

    (b)  it is in the interests of justice to issue a summons under this section to secure the attendance of that person to . . . produce the document or thing.

(2)  In such a case the Crown Court shall, subject to the following provisions of this section, issue a summons (a witness summons) directed to the person concerned and requiring him to:

    (a)  attend before the Crown Court at the time and place stated in the summons; and

    (b)  . . . produce the document or thing.

(3)  A witness summons may only be issued under this section on an application: and the Crown Court may refuse to issue the summons if any requirement relating to the application is not fulfilled.

. . .

(7)  An application must be made in accordance with criminal procedure rules.

The requirement that the documents or thing must be 'material evidence' has generated (and continues to generate) much confusion. The strict position was set out by the House of Lords in *R v Derby Magistrates*.[18] Lord Taylor said:

Section 97 contemplates the production by a witness of documents which are immediately admissible per se and without more . . . section 97 cannot be used to obtain discovery . . . It was not open to the defence to obtain a witness summons . . . to secure discovery of documents for use in cross-examination.

The scope of documents which might now be regarded as 'immediately admissible per se' has probably been widened by the provisions governing admissible hearsay in sections 114, 116, 117, 119 and 121 of the Criminal Justice Act 2003, though to what extent is not entirely clear. Be that as it may, the test in respect of ordering the production and disclosure of third party material is clearly different from the test that has to be applied in respect of the disclosure of prosecution material. Some assistance in reconciling the two approaches can be found in the decision of the Court of Appeal (sadly still unreported) in *Bruschett*.[19] This was a case involving historic allegations of violence and buggery against a former headmaster of a special school and where there were voluminous social services files. Otton LJ said:

---

[18] [1996] 1 Crim App R 385, 393 (the case actually dealt with the directly analogous provisions of Magistrates' Courts Act 1980, s 97).

[19] Court of Appeal, 21 December 2000 (the decision is available on Casetrack at www.casetrack. com).

In our judgement the learned Judge approached his task in a most conscientious and praiseworthy manner. He remained loyal to the stringent restrictions on disclosure imposed by the *Reading* test but he decided to adopt a more flexible approach. He first identified two categories of documents which the *Reading* test suggested might not be disclosed. The first concerned false allegations in the past, the second where if there was anything which suggested that some other adult had indulged in similar activity with the child. In either case it would be disclosed. We consider this an eminently sensible and pragmatic approach.

The procedure to be followed in respect of applications regarding material held by third parties is set out in Part 28 of the Rules:

28.3(1) A party who wants the court to issue a witness summons . . . must apply as soon as practicable after becoming aware of the grounds for doing so.

(2) The party applying must:

   (a)   identify the proposed witness;
   (b)   explain:

      (i)    what evidence the proposed witness can give or produce;
      (ii)   why it is likely to be material evidence; and
      (iii)  why it would be in the interests of justice to issue a summons.

(3) The application may be made orally unless:

   (a)   Rule 28.5 applies; or
   (b)   the court otherwise directs.

28.4(1) An application in writing under Rule 28.3 must be in the form set out in the Practice Direction containing the same declaration of truth as a witness statement.

(2) The party applying must serve the application:

   (a)   in every case on the Court Officer and as directed by the court; and
   (b)   as required by Rule 28.5 if that rule applies.

28.5(1) This rule applies to an application under Rule 28.3 for a witness summons requiring the proposed witness:

   (a)   to produce in evidence a document or thing; or
   (b)   to give evidence about information apparently held in confidence, that relates to another person.

(2) That application must be in writing in the form required by Rule 28.4.

(3) The party applying must serve the application:

   (a)   on the proposed witness, unless the court otherwise directs; and
   (b)   on one or more of the following if the court so directs:

      (i)    a person to whom the proposed evidence relates;
      (ii)   another party.

(4) The court must not issue a witness summons when this rule applies unless:

   (a)   everyone served with the application has had at least 14 days in which to make representations, including representations about whether there should be a hearing of the application before the summons is issued; and

(b) the court is satisfied that it has been able to take adequate account of the duties and rights, including rights of confidentiality, of the proposed witness and of any person to whom the proposed evidence relates.

It cannot be stressed strongly enough that the foregoing provisions relate to an application for the issue of a witness summons; in other words, it is only the first part of the process which may or may not lead the court to actually issue the summons. This is important because the rights of the third party in respect of the privacy/confidential information of the third party or of the person to whom the documents held by the third party relate, have to be considered. Indeed, the current form of Rule 28.5 is an attempt to meet the criticism of the previous rule made by the Divisional Court in *R v Crown Court at Stafford*,[20] where an attempt was made at short notice to obtain the medical records of a 14-year-old complainant. May LJ said:

> 25. In my judgement, procedural fairness in the light of Article 8 undoubtedly required in the present case that B should have been given notice of the application for the witness summons and given the opportunity to make representations before the order was made . . . I would firmly reject the suggestion that it would have been sufficient for the interests of B to be represented only by the NHS Trust. The confidence is hers not theirs.

That this is so is clear from Rule 28.6, which provides as follows:

28.6(1) This rule applies where a person served with an application for a witness summons requiring the proposed witness to produce in evidence a document or thing objects to its production on the ground that:

(a) it is not likely to be material evidence; or
(b) even if it is likely to be material evidence, the duties or rights, including rights of confidentiality, of the proposed witness or of any person to whom the document or thing relates, outweigh the reasons for issuing a summons.

(2) The court may require the proposed witness to make the document or thing available for the objection to be assessed.
(3) The court may invite:

(a) the proposed witness or any representative of the proposed witness; or
(b) a person to whom the document or thing relates or any representative of such a person,

to help the court assess the objection.

It follows from the foregoing that prior to the issue of a summons, if the proposed witness has signalled an objection to producing the documents on one of the grounds specified, the court can require the witness to produce the documents to the court for the validity of the objection to be assessed. When the third party is a local authority or a hospital or education authority, they may well take the point that, regardless of materiality, production of the document should not be ordered

---

[20] [2006] EWHC 1645 (Admin).

on grounds of the confidentiality of the information or indeed PII grounds.[21] The court can request (though not order) the assistance of the third party in assessing the validity of the objection. Clearly, the final decision as to both the issue of a summons and indeed the ordering of the subsequent disclosure of the material rests with the judge. In *K*,[22] Lord Taylor said:

> When public interest immunity is claimed for a document, it is for the court to rule whether the claim should be upheld or not. To do that involves a balancing exercise. The exercise can only be performed by the Judge himself examining or viewing the evidence so as to have the facts of what it contains in mind. Only then can he be in a position to balance the competing interests of public interest immunity and fairness to the party claiming disclosure.

However, frequently a local authority and the like will instruct counsel or an in-house lawyer to go through the files and flag up what might be regarded as 'material evidence' and in respect of which a ruling on disclosure or otherwise on PII grounds is sought. This is a permissible approach. In *W*,[23] Staughton LJ said:

> The court by issuing a summons cannot make a person disclose all the documents in his possession if they are all or any of them irrelevant. The court can only require people to disclose relevant documents. In the first instance, it is for the possessor of the documents to decide whether they are relevant or not. He is entitled to claim that some or all are irrelevant and give his reasons for saying so. The next stage is with the Judge. He may either accept the assertion of the possessor of the document or he may look at the documents himself. That is a decision to be taken in his discretion but of course the discretion must be exercised judicially . . . He may regard an assurance from an independent and competent member of the bar as sufficient reason for treating the documents as irrelevant . . . At the end of the day, the Judge in his discretion may either accept an assurance by or on behalf of the possessor of the document that they are irrelevant, or else look at them and decide for himself.

In reality therefore, decisions both about the issuing of a summons and the disclosure of material will be dealt with pursuant to Rules 28.5 and 28.6 without the necessity of a subsequent hearing following the issue of a summons. Nevertheless, the possibility remains that a summons is issued and that subsequent thereto the witness wants to object either to the issuing of the summons or to producing the documents. In those circumstances, CPIA 1996, section 2C and Rule 28.7 of the Rules apply.

Section 2C provides as follows:

2C. – (1) If a witness summons issued under section 2 above is directed to a person who:

    (a) applies to the Crown Court;

    (b) satisfies the court that he was not served with notice of the application to issue the summons and that he was neither present nor represented at the hearing of the application; and

---

[21] *D v NSPCC* [1978] 1 AC 171.
[22] (1993) 97 Crim App R 342.
[23] [1997] 1 Crim App R 166, 170.

(c)  satisfies the court that he cannot give any evidence likely to be material evidence or as the case may be produce any document or thing likely to be material evidence,

the court may direct that the summons shall be of no effect. . . .
(8)  Where the direction is made under this section that a witness summons shall be of no effect, the person on whose application the summons was issued may be ordered to pay the whole or any part of the costs of the application under this section.

Rule 28.7 provides as follows:

28.7(1) The court may withdraw a witness summons . . . if one of the following applies for it to be withdrawn:

(a)  the party who applied for it on the ground that it is no longer needed;
(b)  the witness on the grounds that:

(i)  he was not aware of any application for it; and
(ii)  he cannot give or produce evidence likely to be material evidence; or
(iii)  even if he can, his duties or rights including rights of confidentiality or those of any person to whom the evidence relate, outweigh the reasons for the issue of the summons; or

(c)  any person to whom the proposed evidence relates on the grounds that:

(i)  he was not aware of any application for it; and
(ii)  that evidence is not likely to be material evidence; or
(iii)  even if it is, his duties or rights including rights of confidentiality or those of the witness outweigh the reasons for the issue of the summons.

(2)  A person applying under this rule must:

(a)  apply in writing as soon as practicable after becoming aware of the grounds for doing so, explaining why he wants the summons . . . to be withdrawn; and
(b)  serve the application on the Court Officer and as appropriate on:

(i)  the witness;
(ii)  the party who applied for the summons; and
(iii)  any other person who he knows was served with the application for the summons.

(3)  Rule 28.6 applies to an application under this rule that concerns a document or thing to be produced in evidence.

The 'dispensing power' in Rule 28.8 should be noted:

28.8(1) The court may:

(a)  shorten or extend (even after it has expired) a time limit under this part; and
(b)  where a rule or direction requires an application under this part to be in writing, allow the application to be made orally instead.

(2)  Someone who wants the court to allow an application to be made orally under paragraph (1)(b) of this rule must:

(a)  give as much notice as the urgency of his application permits to those on whom he would otherwise have served an application in writing; and

(b) in doing so explain the reasons for the application and for wanting the court to consider it orally.

Lastly, it should be noted that if a witness summons is granted pursuant to CPIA 1996, section 2, then by virtue of section 2A there is a power to require production of the documents and inspection thereof prior to the main hearing of the case.

4.11 The foregoing paragraph dealt with applications by a party. However, the court itself has power to act of its own motion. This derives from CPIA 1996, section 2D:

> 2D. For the purpose of any criminal proceedings before it, the Crown Court may of its own motion issue a summons (a witness summons) directed to a person and requiring him to:
>
> (a) attend before the court at the time and place stated in the summons; and
> (b) ... produce any document or thing specified in the summons.

The recipient of such a summons may still apply to set it aside. This derives from section 2E:

> 2E. – (1) If a witness summons issued under section 2D above is directed to a person who:
>
> (a) applies to the Crown Court; and
> (b) satisfies the court that he cannot ... produce any document or thing likely to be material evidence,
>
> the court may direct that the summons shall be of no effect.

## Prosecution Duties in Respect of Third Party Material

4.12 Applications in respect of material held by third parties are most often made by the defence. However, it should be remembered that the prosecution have duties in this area. At 4.7 above, there was a discussion as to what constituted 'prosecution material' and reference was made to the code. The current code, issued pursuant to CPIA 1996, sections 23–25, is the Criminal Procedure and Investigations Act 1996 (Code of Practice) Order 2005.[24] Paragraph 3.6 of the Code provides as follows:

> If the officer in charge of an investigation believes that other persons may be in possession of material that may be relevant to the investigation . . . he should ask the disclosure officer to inform them of the existence of the investigation and invite them to retain the material in case they receive a request for its disclosure. The disclosure officer should inform the prosecutor that they may have such material. However, the officer in charge of an investigation is not required to make speculative enquiries of other persons.

[24] SI 2005/985.

Perhaps of greater significance are the Revised Guidelines issued by the Attorney General in 2005. Relevant provisions include:

51. There may be cases where the investigation disclosure officer or prosecutor believes that a third party . . . has material or information which might be relevant to the prosecution case. In such cases, if the material or information might reasonably be considered capable of undermining the prosecution case or of assisting the case for the accused, prosecutors should take such steps they regard as appropriate in the particular case to obtain it.

52. If the investigator, disclosure officer or prosecutor seeks access to the material or information but the third party declines or refuses to allow access to it, the matter should not be left. If despite any reasons offered by the third party it is still believed that it is reasonable to seek production of the material or information and the requirements of section 2 of the Criminal Procedure (Attendance of Witnesses) Act 1965 . . . are satisfied, then the prosecutor or investigator should apply for a witness summons causing a representative of the third party to produce the material to the court.

53. Relevant information which comes to the knowledge of investigators or prosecutors as a result of liaison with third parties should be recorded by the investigator or prosecutor in a durable or retrievable form (for example, potentially relevant information revealed in discussions at a child protection conference attended by police officers).

54. Where information comes into the possession of the prosecution in the circumstances set out in paragraphs 51 to 53 above, consultation with the other agency should take place before disclosure is made: there may be public interest reasons which justify withholding the disclosure and which would require the issue of disclosure of the information to be placed before the court.

The nature of the prosecution's obligations in respect of third party material has been considered by the courts, though quite how far those obligations extend is not entirely clear. Both the relevant Court of Appeal cases have concerned material held abroad.

In *Alibhai*,[25] Longmore LJ said:

32. Nevertheless the Crown does have obligations in respect of material in the hands of third parties and a conviction would, in any event, be unsafe if the absence of disclosure of material in the possession of a third party meant that the accused could not have a fair trial. . . .

63 [after referring to the guidelines] Secondly, even if there is a suspicion that triggers these provisions, the prosecutor is not under an absolute obligation to secure the disclosure of the material or information. He enjoys what might be described as a 'margin of appreciation' as to what steps he regards as appropriate in the particular case. If criticism is to be made of a failure to secure third party disclosure, it would have to be shown that the prosecutor did not act within the permissible limits afforded by the Guidelines.

---

[25] [2004] EWCA Crim 681.

64  In saying this, we are not ruling out the possibility that in an extreme case it might be so unfair for a prosecution to proceed in the absence of material which a third party declines to produce that it would appear proper to stay it, regardless of whether the prosecutor is in breach of the Guidelines.

Commenting on *Alibhai*, Ousley J said in *Wood*:[26]

61.  The circumstances in which a failure to pursue a witness summons could found an abuse are considered in *Alibhai* which I would summarise as follows: the material has to be of significance in relation to a real issue, damaging to the prosecution case or helpful to the defence – the fact that material could not be obtained by the prosecutor from a third party did not show dishonourable conduct or abuse of power by the prosecutor as it was not under an absolute obligation to secure disclosure of the material – it would have to be shown that it had not acted in accordance within the permissible limits of the Attorney General's guidelines.

The most recent Court of Appeal decision is *Flook*.[27] Here the argument related to material in South Africa which was in the possession of the South African police and prosecution authorities and with whom the British police had had close liaison. Much material had been obtained but there were certain matters that the British police had not been allowed to copy. In his judgment, Thomas LJ referred both to the Code and the Attorney General's guidelines. He said:

35.  In our view the provisions of the Code and the 2005 Guidelines, although expressed in a domestic context, make clear the obligation of the Crown . . . is to pursue reasonable lines of enquiry in relation to material that may be held overseas in states outside the European Union.

36.  However, it is self-evident that where there may be material . . . outside the European Union, the power of the Crown and the courts of England and Wales to obtain material is limited . . . There may be cases where a foreign entity will simply not make the material available . . .

37.  There cannot for these reasons be any absolute obligation on the Crown to disclose relevant material held overseas outside the European Union . . . The obligation is one to take reasonable steps. Whether the Crown has complied with that obligation is for the court to judge in each case on the provision of full information. It is not necessary for us to decide whether the Crown any longer has the margin of consideration referred to in *Alibhai*.

In the area of foreign material, the Crown has powers which are not available to the defence; see section 7 of the Crime (International Cooperation) Act 2003.

---

[26] [2006] EWHC 32 (Admin).
[27] [2009] EWCA Crim 682.

# 5

# Reporting Restrictions

5.1 Section 39(1) of the Children and Young Persons Act 1933[1] provides as follows:

> 39. – (1) In relation to any proceedings in any court . . . the court may direct that:
>
> (a) no newspaper report of the proceedings shall reveal the name, address or school, or include any particulars calculated to lead to the identification of any child or young person[2] concerned in the proceedings, either as being the person by or against or in respect of whom the proceedings are taken, or as being a witness therein, except insofar (if at all) as may be permitted by the court.

Unless the child or young person is either a victim, a witness or a defendant, the section does not bite.

In *Ex parte Crook*,[3] Glidewell LJ said (at 217):

> The Judge has a complete discretion to allow representatives of those parties whom he considers have a legitimate interest in the making of, or in opposing the making of, an order under section 39 to make representations to him about the order before he makes it. In a case such as this, where the children concerned are in the care of a local authority, the Judge is clearly empowered . . . to allow or invite the representative of the local authority to make representations to him.

He went on to say (at 220):

> If the Judge decides in his discretion to make an order, he should make clear what the terms of the order are. Normally there is no problem about this. It will suffice to use the words of section 39(1) of the Act of 1933 or a suitable adaption and to relate the order to the child or children named in the indictment. But, if there is possible doubt as to which child or children the order relates, the Judge should identify the relevant child or children with clarity. Secondly, a written copy of the order should be drawn as soon as possible after the Judge has made the order orally.

Although section 39 does not empower a court to order in terms that the names of defendants who are not young persons should not be published, an order may

---

[1] Section 39 is to be replaced at some time by Youth Justice and Criminal Evidence Act 1999, ss 44 and 45. We have waited 10 years for this, so it is not dealt with here!

[2] A 'child' is a person under the age of 14 years and a 'young person' is someone aged between 14 and 17 years (ie under 18), see Children and Young Persons Act 1933, s 107.

[3] [1995] 2 Crim App R 212.

have that effect.[4] An order under section 39 can be made at any time, even after the proceedings have ended.[5]

5.2   Recent authority has shown a willingness on the part of the senior judiciary to prevent illegitimate extensions of the ambit of section 39. In *Ex Parte Trinity Mirror*,[6] the children of the defendant were not witnesses in the case, nor victims of his crimes. The Crown Court made an order preventing the media from identifying the defendant on the basis that his children would suffer serious harm. The case obviously did not fall within the ambit of section 39. The Judge had purported to use section 45(4) of the Senior Courts Act 1981 as giving him jurisdiction.[7] Giving the judgment of the Court of Appeal, the President said:

> 30. In our judgement, for the purposes of section 45(4) . . . matters are 'incidental to' the jurisdiction of the Crown Court only when the power to be exercised relates to the proper despatch of the business before it . . . The Crown Court has no general power to grant injunctions. There is no inherent jurisdiction to do so on the basis that it is seeking to achieve 'a desirable' or indeed 'a just and convenient' objective. Unless the proposed injunction is directly linked to the exercise of the Crown Court's jurisdiction and the exercise of its statutory functions, the appropriate jurisdiction is lacking.

He went on to say:

> 32. In our judgement it is impossible to over-emphasise the importance to be attached to the ability of the media to report criminal trials.

This decision is entirely consistent with the approach taken by the House of Lords in *Re S (a Child)*.[8] A mother was indicted for the murder of her son. Her other son had been taken into care and placed with his father. The guardian of the child sought an injunction restraining any publication of photos of the mother or her name or any photo of the dead child. Evidence was provided by a psychiatrist who said that any publicity would have a very adverse effect on the living child. Upholding the Judge at first instance in his refusal to grant an injunction, Lord Steyn said:

> 18. and 20. . . . the ordinary rule is that the press, as the watchdog of the public, may record everything that takes place in a criminal court. I would add that in European jurisprudence and in domestic practice, this is a strong rule. It can only be displaced by unusual or exceptional circumstances . . . Given the number of statutory exceptions, it

---

[4]   *Ex Parte Godwin* [1992] QB 190, 196: 'If the inevitable effect of making an order is that it is apparent that some details, including for instance names of defendants, may not be published because publication would breach the order, that is the practical application of the order: it is not part of the terms of the order itself'.

[5]   See *R v Harrow Crown Court ex parte Perkins* (1998) 162 JP 527, where Sullivan J said: 'I can see no reason why as a matter of law a direction should not be made in relation to proceedings which have been concluded at an earlier stage'. (The full transcript is available on Casetrack at www.casetrack.com.)

[6]   *R v Croydon Crown Court ex parte Trinity Mirror* [2008] EWCA Crim 50.

[7]   Supreme Court Act 1981, s 45(4) reads as follows: 'the Crown Court shall, in relation to . . . the enforcement of its orders, and all other matters incidental to its jurisdiction, have the like powers, rights, privileges and authority as the High Court'.

[8]   [2004] UKHL 47.

needs to be said clearly and unambiguously that the court has no power to create by a process of analogy, except in the most compelling circumstances, a further exception to the general principle of open justice.

He went on to say:

26. This is an application for an injunction beyond the scope of section 39, the remedy provided by Parliament to protect juveniles directly affected by criminal proceedings. No such injunction has been granted in the past under the inherent jurisdiction or under the provisions of the ECHR.

However, it should be noted that in extreme circumstances the court has power to protect the identity of defendants. In *R v Times Newspapers Ltd*,[9] an order had been made (at a court martial) banning the publication of the names of the defendants. In the Court of Appeal, Latham LJ said:

12. But there is no doubt that a court may, in appropriate circumstances, order that the identity of a defendant can be protected from publicity by withholding his or her name. This is recognised by section 11 of the Contempt of Court Act 1981.[10]

He went on to say:

16. and 17. In common law, there is therefore no authority for the proposition that anonymity can be ordered for any purpose which is not connected to, or does not have effect on, the administration of justice, or is not provided for in any statutory exception . . . In order therefore for us to be entitled to make any order for anonymity for all or any of the soldiers, we must be satisfied either that the administration of justice would be seriously affected were we not to grant anonymity, or that there is 'a real and immediate' risk to the life of any of the soldiers were anonymity not granted.

5.3    Alleged victims of varieties of sexual assault, including rape, enjoy the anonymity provisions of the Sexual Offences Amendment Act 1992.[11] This provides as follows:

1. – (1) Where an allegation has been made that an offence to which this Act applies has been committed against a person, no matter relating to that person shall during that person's lifetime be included in any publication if it is likely to lead members of the public to identify that person as the person against whom the offence is alleged to have been committed.

(2)    Where a person is accused of an offence to which this Act applies, no matter likely to lead members of the public to identify a person as the person against whom the offence is alleged to have been committed (a complainant) shall during the complainant's lifetime be included in any publication. . . .

(3A) The matters relating to a person in relation to which the restrictions imposed by sub-section (1) or (2) apply (if their inclusion is likely to have the result mentioned in that sub-section) include in particular:

---

[9]  [2008] EWCA Crim 2396.

[10]  It should be emphasised that the section does not itself provide the power to make such an order. It provides the mechanism for doing so but only where the power exists in law.

[11]  The full list of offences covered is set out in Sexual Offences Amendment Act 1992, s 2.

(a) the person's name;
(b) the person's address;
(c) the identity of any school or other educational establishment attended by the person;
(d) the identity of any place of work; and
(e) any still or moving picture of the person.

Section 3 of the 1992 Act gives a dispensing power to a judge to waive the non-identification prohibition where it is necessary to persuade witnesses to come forward and the defence may be substantially prejudiced if waiver is not granted, or where the effect of the ban is to impose substantial and unreasonable restrictions on the reporting of the proceedings. The fact that a defendant has been acquitted is not a substantial reason for lifting the ban.

5.4    For many years the common law had permitted a court to ban the naming by the press of the alleged victim of a blackmail attempt. Breach of the prohibition was punishable by way of contempt proceedings.[12] Nowadays, the matter is more generally governed by section 46 of the Youth Justice and Criminal Evidence Act (YJCEA) 1999, in force since October 2004. It applies to all criminal proceedings. The relevant provisions are as follows:

46. – (1) This section applies where:

(a) in any criminal proceedings in any court in England and Wales . . . a party to the proceedings makes an application for the court to give a reporting direction in relation to a witness in the proceedings (other than the accused) who has attained the age of 18.[13] . . .

(2) If the court determines:

(a) that the witness is eligible for protection; and
(b) that giving a reporting direction in relation to the witness is likely to improve:

   (i)   the quality of evidence given by the witness; or
   (ii)  the level of cooperation given by the witness to any party to the proceedings in connection with that party's preparation of its case,

the court may give a reporting direction in relation to the witness.

(3) For the purposes of this section, a witness is eligible for protection if the court is satisfied:

(a) that the quality of evidence given by the witness; or
(b) the level of cooperation given by the witness to any party to the proceedings in connection with that party's preparation of its case,

is likely to be diminished by reason of fear or distress on the part of the witness in connection with being identified by members of the public as a witness in the proceedings.

---

[12]  *R v Socialist Worker* [1975] QB 637.
[13]  A reporting direction is defined by YJCEA 1999, s 46(6) as follows: 'For the purpose of this section, a reporting direction in relation to a witness is a direction that no matter relating to the witness shall during the witness's lifetime be included in any publication if it is likely to lead members of the public to identify him as being a witness in the proceedings'.

(4) In determining whether a witness is eligible for protection, the court must take into account in particular:

  (a) the nature and alleged circumstances of the offence to which the proceedings relate;

  (b) the age of the witness;

  (c) such of the following matters as appear to the court to be relevant, namely:

    (i) the social and cultural background and ethnic origins of the witness;

    (ii) the domestic and employment circumstances of the witness; and

    (iii) any religious beliefs or political opinions of the witness;

  (d) any behaviour towards the witness on the part of:

    (i) the accused;

    (ii) members of the family or associates of the accused; or

    (iii) any other person who is likely to be an accused or a witness in the proceedings.

(5) In determining that question, the court must in addition consider any views expressed by the witness . . .

(8) In determining whether to give a reporting direction the court shall consider:

  (a) whether it would be in the interests of justice to do so; and

  (b) the public interest in avoiding the imposition of a substantial and unreasonable restriction on the reporting of the proceedings.

The procedure governing the making of an application for a reporting direction is set out in Part 16 of the Criminal Procedure Rules 2011 (SI 2011/1709) ('the Rules'):

16.1(1) An application for a reporting direction made by a party to any criminal proceedings, in relation to a witness in those proceedings, must be made in the form set out in the Practice Direction or orally under Rule 16.3.

(2) If an application for a reporting direction is made in writing, the applicant shall send that application to the Court Officer and copies shall be sent at the same time to every other party to those proceedings.

16.2(1) If an application for a reporting direction is made in writing, any party to the proceedings who wishes to oppose that application must notify the applicant and the Court Officer in writing of his opposition and give reasons for it.

(2) . . .

(3) The notification under paragraph (1) must be given within 5 business days of the date the application was served on him unless an extension of time is granted under Rule 16.6.

16.3(1) The court may give a reporting direction under section 46 . . . in relation to a witness in those proceedings, notwithstanding that the 5 business days specified in Rule 16.2(3) have not expired if:

  (a) an application is made to it for the purposes of this Rule; and

  (b) it is satisfied that, due to exceptional circumstances, it is appropriate to do so.

(2) Any party to the proceedings may make the application under paragraph (1) whether or not an application has already been made under Rule 16.1.

(3) An application under paragraph (1) may be made orally or in writing.

(4) If an application is made orally, the court may hear and take into account representations made to it by any person who in the court's view has a legitimate interest in the application before it.

(5) The application must specify the exceptional circumstances on which the applicant relies.

. . .

16.6(1) An application may be made in writing to extend the period of time for notification under Rule 16.2(3) before that period has expired.

(2) An application must be accompanied by a statement setting out the reasons why the applicant is unable to give notification within that period.

(3) An application must be sent to the Court Officer.

16.7(1) The court may:

    (a) determine any application made under Rule 16.1 and Rules 16.3 to 16.6 without a hearing; or

    (b) direct a hearing of any application.

(2) The Court Officer shall notify all the parties of the court's decision as soon as reasonably practicable.

(3) If a hearing of an application is to take place, the Court Officer shall notify each party to the proceedings of the time and place of the hearing.

(4) A court may hear and take into account representations made to it by any person who in the court's view has a legitimate interest in the application before it.

By virtue of YJCEA 1999, section 46(9) and (10), a court has the power to vary (make an 'excepting direction') or revoke a reporting direction. The relevant procedure is set out in Rules 16.4 and 16.5 of the Rules.

5.5    There is a power in the Crown Court to postpone (though not ultimately ban) press reporting of particular proceedings. This derives from section 4 of the Contempt of Court Act 1981, which provides as follows:

4. – (1) Subject to this section, a person is not guilty of contempt of court in respect of the strict liability rule[14] in respect of a fair and accurate report of legal proceedings held in public, published contemporaneously and in good faith.

(2) In any such proceedings the court may, where it appears to be necessary for avoiding a substantial risk of prejudice to the administration of justice in those proceedings, or in any other proceedings pending or imminent, order that the publication of any report of the proceedings, or any part of the proceedings, be postponed for such period as the court thinks necessary for that purpose.

The proper approach to the application of this section is set out in the judgment of the Court of Appeal in *R v Central Criminal Court ex parte The Telegraph*.[15]

---

[14]  By virtue of Contempt of Court Act 1981, s 1, the strict liability rule means the rule of law whereby conduct may be treated as a contempt of court as tending to interfere with the course of justice, in particular legal proceedings, regardless of an intent so to do.

[15]  (1994) 98 Crim App R 91, 95 and following.

In that case, the then Lord Chief Justice said:

> The sub-section contains two requirements for the making of a postponement order, first that the publication would create 'a substantial risk of prejudice to the administration of justice' and, second, that the postponement of publication 'appears to be necessary for avoiding that risk' . . . It seems to us that this discretion indicated by the use of the word 'may' in the provision is catered for by the second requirement that the court may only make an order where it appears to be 'necessary for avoiding' the substantial risk of prejudice to the administration of justice that it perceives. In forming a view whether it is necessary to make an order for avoiding such a risk, a court will inevitably have regard to the competing public considerations of ensuring a fair trial and of open justice.

He went on to say (dealing with the approach of the court below):

> Having satisfied himself that there would be a substantial risk of prejudice to the administration of justice in the respects that he identified, he appears to have assumed the necessity to avoid it and to have searched for a solution by tailoring the order to a form which he considered would eliminate the risk. Having identified the risk there would be . . . he should then have considered whether in the light of the competing public interest . . . it was necessary for avoiding that risk to make the order, whether in his discretion he should make it and, if so, with all or only some of the restrictions sought.

5.6    There is a useful general guide to reporting restrictions in criminal courts in a document on the Judicial Studies Board website, published in October 2009.

# 6

## Abuse of Process Applications

6.1    This is not the place to recite all the case law that has now accumulated around the rules relating to abuse of process. For our purposes, it is sufficient to identify the two strands which have developed, namely cases where it is said that the defendant cannot have a fair trial and those in which it is said that it would be unfair to try the defendant.[1]

6.2    As to delay and the inability to have a fair trial, the law was summarised thus by Rose LJ in S.[2] He said:

> 21. In the light of the authorities, the correct approach for a Judge to whom an application for a stay for abuse of process on the ground of delay is made, is to bear in mind the following principles:
>
> (i)    Even where delay is unjustifiable, a permanent stay should be the exception rather than the rule.
> (ii)    Where there is no fault on the part of the complainant or the prosecution, it will be very rare for a stay to be granted.
> (iii)    No stay should be granted in the absence of serious prejudice to the defence so that no fair trial can be held.
> (iv)    When assessing possible serious prejudice, the Judge should bear in mind his or her power to regulate the admissibility of evidence and that the trial process itself should ensure that all relevant factual issues arising from delay will be placed before the jury for their consideration in accordance with appropriate directions from the Judge.
> (v)    If having considered all these factors, a Judge's assessment is that a fair trial will be possible, a stay should not be granted.

As to cases where evidence has been lost or destroyed, the following passage from the judgment of Mantell LJ in *Medway*[3] is relevant:

> We recognise that in cases where evidence has been tampered with, lost or destroyed, it may well be that a defendant will be disadvantaged. It does not necessarily follow that in such a case the defendant cannot have a fair trial or that it would be unfair for him to be tried. We would think that there would need to be something wholly exceptional about the circumstances of the case to justify a stay on the ground that evidence has been lost

---

[1]    See *Beckford* [1996] 1 Crim App R 94, 100.
[2]    [2006] EWCA Crim 756.
[3]    Case no 98/7579/Y3, unreported. Reference should also be made to *R (Ebrahim) v Feltham Magistrates* [2001] 2 Crim App R 23, and *DPP v Cooper* [2008] EWHC 507 (Admin).

or destroyed. One such circumstance might be if the interference with the evidence was malicious.

6.3   In respect of situations where it is said that it is not fair to try the defendant (a problem which often arises when entrapment is alleged by the defence) the following passage from the speech of Lord Steyn in *Latif*[4] suffices to illustrate the point. He said:

> In this case the issue is whether, despite the fact that a fair trial was possible, the Judge ought to have stayed the criminal proceedings on broader considerations of the integrity of the criminal justice system. The law is settled. Weighing countervailing considerations of policy and justice, it is for the Judge in the exercise of his discretion to decide whether there has been an abuse of process which amounts to an affront to the public conscience and requires the criminal proceedings to be stayed . . . The speeches in *Bennett* conclusively establish that proceedings may be stayed in the exercise of the Judge's discretion not only where a fair trial is impossible but also where it would be contrary to the public interest and the integrity of the criminal justice system that a trial should take place.

6.4   As to the appropriate procedure to be followed in connection with an abuse of process application, the law now seems to be in something of a mess. Part IV.36 of the Consolidated Criminal Practice Direction provides as follows:

> 36.1  In all cases where a defendant in the Crown Court proposes to make an application to stay an indictment on the grounds of abuse of process, written notice of such application must be given to the prosecuting authority and to any co-defendant not later than 14 days before the date fixed or warned for the trial . . . Such notice must:
>
> (a)   give the name of the case and the indictment number;
> (b)   state the fixed date or the warned date as appropriate;
> (c)   specify the nature of the application;
> (d)   set out in numbered paragraphs the grounds upon which the application is to be made;
> (e)   be copied to the Chief Listing Officer at the court centre where the case is to be heard.
>
> 36.2  Any co-defendant who wishes to make a like application must give a like notice not later than 7 days before the relevant date, setting out any additional grounds relied upon.
>
> 36.3  In relation to such applications, the following automatic directions shall apply:
>
> (a)   The advocate for the applicant must lodge with the court and serve on all other parties his skeleton argument in support of the application at least five clear working days before the relevant date. If reference is to be made to any document not in the existing trial documents, a paginated and indexed bundle of such documents is to be provided with the skeleton argument.

---

[4]  [1996] 1 WLR 104, 112.

(b) The advocate for the prosecution must lodge with the court and serve on all other parties a responsive skeleton argument at least two clear working days before the relevant date, together with a supplementary bundle if appropriate.

36.4 All skeleton arguments must specify any propositions of law to be advanced (together with the authorities relied upon in support, with page references to passages relied upon) and, where appropriate, include a chronology of events and a list of *dramatis personae*. In all instances where reference is to be made to a document, the reference in the trial documents or supplementary bundle is to be given.

36.5 The above time limits are minimum time limits. In appropriate cases the court will order longer lead times. To this end, in all cases where defence advocates are, at the time of the plea and directions hearing, considering the possibility of an abuse of process application, this must be raised with the Judge dealing with the matter, who will order a different timetable if appropriate, and may wish, in any event, to give additional directions about the conduct of the application.

It seems abundantly clear that this direction is based on the premise that the application will be made before or at the start of the trial. However, a recent Court of Appeal decision seems to cast some doubt on this approach, at least in cases based upon delay. In *Smolinski*,[5] Lord Woolf said:

8. and 9. The making of applications to have cases stayed where there has been delay on the basis of abuse of process has become prevalent . . . The court questions whether it is helpful to make applications in relation to abuse of process before any evidence has been given by the complainant in a case of this nature. Clearly, having regard to the period of time which has elapsed, the court expects that careful consideration has been given by the prosecution as to whether it is right to bring the prosecution at all. If, having considered the evidence to be called, and the witnesses having been interviewed on behalf of the prosecution, a decision is reached that the case should proceed, then in the normal way we would suggest that it is better not to make an application based on abuse of process. Unless the case is exceptional, the application will be unsuccessful . . . If an application is to be made to a Judge, the best time for doing so is after any evidence has been called. This means that, on the one hand, the court has had an opportunity of seeing the witnesses and, on the other hand, the complainants have had to go through the ordeal of giving evidence. However, despite the latter point . . . it seems to us that on the whole it is preferable for the evidence to be called and for a Judge then to make his decision as to whether the trial should proceed or whether the evidence is such that it would not be safe for a jury to convict.

Quite how this differs from a judge dealing in the ordinary way with a submission of no case at the close of the prosecution is not immediately obvious. In particular, it is not clear whether the judge is simply to apply the conventional *Galbraith* test or whether some enhanced power is envisaged. It is hard to see how, if it is proper in applying conventional *Galbraith* principles for a judge to decide that the case should continue, he should then be able to decide on abuse grounds that the case should be stayed. It is not a logical division. It might involve a judge in making a fairly naked usurpation of the function of the jury.

[5] [2004] EWCA Crim 1270.

Be that as it may, a differently constituted Court of Appeal in *Burke*[6] endorsed the *Smolenski* approach. Giving judgment, Hooper LJ said:

31. The appropriate time for the Judge to consider whether a fair trial is possible is, in most cases, at the conclusion of the evidence. Counsel for the appellant accepted that proposition.

32. Prior to the start of the case it will often be difficult if not impossible to determine whether a defendant can have a fair trial because of the delay coupled with the destruction of documents and the unavailability of witnesses. Issues which might seem very important before the trial may become unimportant or of less importance as a result of developments during the trial, including the evidence of the complainant and of other witnesses, including the defendant should he choose to give evidence. Issues which seemed unimportant before the trial may become very important . . .

33. In the light of these authorities, we take the view that the Judge should not have been asked to stay the case before it started. This was pre-eminently a case in which the fairness of the trial could only properly be determined when all the evidence had been called and any particular difficulties caused by the passage of time and the destruction of documents and unavailability of witnesses could be identified and considered against the background of all the evidence in the case.

It is not without interest that there are subsequent decisions of the Court of Appeal where the application to stay had been made at the start of the trial and no adverse comment was made, see, for example, *Jones*[7] and *Abu Hamza*.[8] In any event, such an approach, namely deferring the decision, surely cannot be correct in the context of an application based on the assertion that it is not fair to try the defendant because of some police/government impropriety.

6.5   Not only is there an inconsistency between the Practice Direction and the *Smolenski* approach, there are other procedural rules which are predicated on the basis that an application will be made before or at the start of the trial. For example, section 6A(1)(d) of the Criminal Procedure and Investigations Act 1996, dealing with the contents of a defence statement, requires that any point to be taken about abuse of process should be indicated in that statement. If in truth we are simply dealing with an 'enhanced' *Galbraith* submission which, by definition, can only be made after the prosecution case has closed, it is hard to see how a defendant could spell that out in advance of the trial in his defence statement.[9]

---

6  [2005] EWCA Crim 29.
7  [2007] EWCA Crim 1118.
8  [2006] EWCA Crim 2918.
9  The contradiction has largely been resolved by the decision of the Court of Appeal in *CPS v F* (2011) EWCA Crim 1844 – 'abuse' and 'Galbraith' remain separate.Delay will rarely found an abuse application. If relevant, it will form part of a Galbraith submission. Abuse applications are to be made at the outset of the trial.

# 7

---

# Fitness to Plead

---

7.1 Section 4 of the Criminal Procedure and Insanity Act 1964 provides as follows:

4. – (1) This section applies where, on the trial of a person, the question arises (at the instance of the defence or otherwise) whether the accused is under a disability, that is to say, under any disability such that apart from this act, it would constitute a bar to his being tried.
(2) If, having regard to the nature of the supposed disability, the court are of opinion that it is expedient to do so and in the interests of the accused, they may postpone consideration of the question of fitness to be tried until any time up to the opening of the case for the defence.
(3) If, before the question of fitness to be tried falls to be determined, the jury return a verdict of acquittal on the count . . . on which the accused is being tried, that question shall not be determined.
(4) Subject to sub-section (2) and (3) above, the question of fitness to be tried shall be determined as soon as it arises.
(5) The question of fitness to be tried shall be determined by the court without a jury.
(6) The court shall not make a determination under sub-section (5) above except on the written or oral evidence of two or more registered medical practitioners at least one of whom is duly approved.

7.2 The old definition as to what constituted a disability of such a nature as to amount to a bar to the defendant being tried derived from the case of *Pritchard*,[1] and the direction of Baron Alderson to the jury. Bringing matters up to date, the essential points are:

(1) Can the defendant understand the evidence?
(2) Can he participate in the trial if he wants to, including giving evidence on his own behalf?
(3) Can he give instructions to his lawyers?

If he cannot do any of the foregoing, then prima facie he is not fit to plead.

7.3 Section 4(1) refers to the question arising 'at the instance of the defence or otherwise'. In *McCarthy*,[2] Lord Parker said:

[1] (1836) 7 C&P 303.
[2] (1966) 50 Crim App R 109: the whole phrasing of the quotation has to be put in the context of the world as it was then, long before the PCMH regime or even the plea and directions hearing regime came in. Now, the question usually surfaces, whoever raises it, at the PCMH when normally a defendant is arraigned.

The issue here depends upon the true construction of section 4(1) . . . in particular on the meaning of the words 'when the question arises (at the instance of the defence or otherwise)' . . . It seems to the court that the question arises in the ordinary case when the prosecution or the defence get up before arraignment and say to the Judge that there is a preliminary issue, namely whether the defendant is fit to plead. There seems no reason why any different interpretation should be given to the section when considering the Judge himself . . . It is not until he, at the trial, and before arraignment decides that he should raise the question, that a question does arise.

7.4    Section 4(2) is important; the court may postpone the issue of fitness to be tried until any time prior to the start of the case for the defence. Given the consequences that may flow from a finding of unfitness, this is an important safeguard of a defendant's rights. In *Burles*,[3] Lord Parker said:

It seems to the court that a Trial Judge must, in applying the sub-section, first consider the apparent strength and weakness of the case for the prosecution as disclosed on the depositions or statements. He should then go on to consider the nature and degree of the suggested disability . . . and having paid attention to these two matters he must ask himself, 'what is expedient and in the prisoner's interests?' Approaching the matter on that basis, one can envisage cases to which there can really only be one answer: the case for the prosecution may appear so strong and the suggested condition of the prisoner so disabling that postponement of the trial of the issue would be wholly inexpedient. Again, the case for the prosecution may be so thin that, whatever the degree of disablement, it clearly would be expedient to postpone the trial. Between these two extremes it falls to the Judge to weigh up the various considerations and as a matter of discretion to order that the issue be either tried forthwith or postponed.

In *Webb*,[4] Sachs LJ said:

It is of course clear that if there are reasonable chances of the case for the prosecution being successfully challenged so that the defence may not be called on, then clearly it is as a rule in the interests of the accused that trial of the issue be postponed until after arraignment.

In *Norman*,[5] Thomas LJ said:

34.(i) Once it is clear that there is an issue, such cases need very careful case management to ensure that full information is provided to the court without the delay so evident in this case.

(ii) When full information is available the court will need carefully to consider whether to postpone the issue of trial of fitness to plead under section 4(2) given the consequences that a finding of unfitness has for the defendant.

7.5    Assuming that the court decides that it would not be expedient nor in the interests of the defendant to postpone the issue then, by virtue of section 4(4), the issue should be determined straightaway. In a major recent change, section 4(5)

---

[3]  (1970) 54 Crim App R 196, 200.
[4]  (1969) 53 Crim App R 360, 364.
[5]  [2008] EWCA Crim 1810.

provides that the issue should be determined by the judge and not a jury. A determination of the question can only be made on the written or oral evidence of at least two registered medical practitioners, at least one of whom is 'duly approved'.[6]

7.6    Assuming that a finding of unfitness has been made by the judge, then the provisions of section 4A become relevant. This provides as follows:

4A. – (1) This section applies where in accordance with section 4(5) above it is determined by a court that the accused is under a disability.

(2)  The trial shall not proceed or further proceed but it shall be determined by a jury:

(a)  on the evidence (if any) already given in the trial; and

(b)  on such evidence as may be adduced or further adduced by the prosecution, or adduced by a person appointed by the court under this section to put the case for the defence

. . . whether they are satisfied, as respects the count or each of the counts on which the accused was to be or was being tried, that he did the act or made the omission charged against him as the offence.

Before considering the section further, the often overlooked words in section 4A(2)(b), namely 'adduced by a person appointed by the court under this section to put the case for the defence' must be considered. In *Norman*, Thomas LJ said:

34(iii).  If the court determines that the appellant is unfit to plead, then it is the court's duty under section 4A(2) of the Criminal Procedure (Insanity) Act 1964 carefully to consider who is the best person to be appointed by the court to put the case for the defence . . . The duty under section 4A(2) is a duty personal to the court, which must consider afresh the person who is to be appointed: it should not necessarily be the same person who has represented the defendant to date, as it is the responsibility of the court to be satisfied that the person appointed is the right person for this difficult task . . . The responsibility placed on the person so appointed is quite different to the responsibility placed on an advocate when he or she can take instructions from the client. The special position of the person so appointed is underlined by the fact that the person is remunerated not through the criminal defence service but out of central funds. Given the responsibility that the act places on the court, it would not be unusual if the Judge needed a little time to consider who was the best person to be so appointed.

With great respect, there do seem to be a number of problems associated with this dictum. Is the judge meant to form a view as to the competence of the advocate? If yes, what are the criteria? Assuming he is not satisfied with the competence of the advocate, how is he meant to go about finding a replacement? Who is instructing the replacement? In the real world I would have thought that the advocate instructed to date by the defendant's solicitor is obviously the appropriate person to act save in very extreme cases, eg a pupil dealing with what is essentially an allegation of murder!

---

[6] Criminal Procedure and Insanity Act 1964, s 8 (as amended): 'duly approved' in relation to a registered medical practitioner means approved for the purposes of s 12 of the Mental Health Act 1983 by the Secretary of State as having special experience in the diagnosis or treatment of mental disorder.

7.7    If the issue is decided by the judge prior to any evidence as to the substance of the allegation being given, then a jury has to be empanelled to decide whether 'the defendant did the act or made the omission charged'. As to what the Crown have to prove in this connection, this is dealt with in the judgment of Judge LJ in *AG Reference (No 3 of 1998)*.[7] He said:

(a)  The Crown is required to prove the ingredients which constitute the actus reus of the crime . . . that the defendant has caused a certain event or that responsibility is to be attributed to him for the existence of a certain state of affairs, which is forbidden by the criminal law.

(b)  The Crown is not required to prove the mens rea of the crime alleged and, apart from insanity (on fitness to plead) the defendant's state of mind ceases to be relevant.

It follows from this that when the original allegation was murder, lack of intent or provocation cannot be raised on behalf of a defendant at a section 4A hearing[8] and neither can diminished responsibility.[9] If the question of fitness has been put off until the end of the prosecution case, so that a normally empanelled jury has already heard some of the evidence, then, the Judge having decided that (a) there is a case to answer and (b) the defendant is under a disability, that jury should continue to hear the matter, not to determine guilt or innocence but whether the defendant did the act charged, etc.

In *B and others*,[10] the Court of Appeal had to deal with the problem of unfitness in the context of a multi-handed trial. This was a case involving many allegations of child abuse. Prior to the trial, two of the defendants were found to be unfit to plead. The question arose as to whether the trial of the defendants who were fit to plead and the determination of the question whether the defendants who were not fit to plead did the acts alleged, should be dealt with by the same jury. Toulson LJ said:

24.  Where a jury has been empanelled to decide whether a person is guilty of a charge in the indictment, that necessarily includes finding whether he committed the actus reus. If during the trial of co-defendants one becomes unfit, the trial of the issue of his guilt comes to an end, but the proceedings continue in order for the jury to determine as a fact for the purposes of section 4A of the Act whether he committed the actus reus . . . The same principle must in our judgement apply if the unfitness occurs before the commencement of proceedings before a jury. . . .

27.  From the point of view of witnesses, the balance of advantage is obvious. A large number of complainants and other witnesses are going to have to give harrowing evidence about matters alleged to have happened to them over a span of many years. The

---

[7]  [1999] 2 Crim App R 214, 223.

[8]  *Grant* [2001] EWCA Crim 2611.

[9]  *Antoine* [2002] Crim App R 94. Lord Hutton gave the main speech, the ramifications of which have not I think yet been tested in the courts. He said (at 111): 'If there is objective evidence which raises the issue of mistake or accident or self-defence, then the jury should not find that the defendant did the act unless it is satisfied beyond reasonable doubt on all the evidence that the prosecution has negatived that defence'.

[10]  [2008] EWCA Crim 1997.

trauma of having to do so twice hardly needs to be discussed further. From the public interest again, it is obvious that, if the proceedings can fairly and justly be conducted simultaneously rather than successively they should be. We conclude in relation to D1 that the issue whether he did the acts alleged should be determined jointly with the trial of the fit defendants.

7.8    If the jury find that the defendant did the act charged, etc, then the judge must act in accordance with section 5, which provides as follows:

> 5. – (1) This section applies where
>
>      . . .
>
>      (b)   Findings are recorded that the accused is under a disability and that he did the act or made the omission charged against him.
>
> (2)   The court shall make in respect of the accused:
>      (a)   a hospital order (with or without a restriction order);
>      (b)   a supervision order; or
>      (c)   an order for his absolute discharge.

7.9    In *Hasani*,[11] the Judge determined that the defendant was not fit to plead. A jury subsequently found that he had done the acts alleged. Prior to his being dealt with pursuant to section 5, he recovered and apparently became fit to plead. The submission was made that he should still be dealt with pursuant to section 5. The Judge did not agree. He did not redetermine the question of fitness and ordered that the defendant be arraigned. On a judicial review application, Hooper LJ said:

> 14.  We think it sufficient to say that the section 4A and 5 procedures are inapplicable if, following a further section 4 hearing, the court has found the accused person fit to plead, a finding which according to section 4(6) cannot be made 'except on the written or oral evidence of two or more registered medical practitioners at least one of whom is duly approved'. That second finding obviates the need to continue with the section 4A or 5 procedures.
>
> 15.  In the light of our conclusions, we quash the order made by the Judge only because he has not held a second section 4 procedure (and indeed was not invited to do so). It is important that the procedure be followed even though the outcome seems quite clear. Having quashed the order we remit the case back to the Judge with a direction to hold a second section 4 hearing (which may only be a formality). If the Judge finds the claimant to be fit to plead, then the Judge will make the necessary order for the claimant's arraignment. If the Judge makes no such finding . . . the first finding continues in force and the Judge will then have to continue with the section 5 procedure and make the appropriate order under section 5(2).

---

[11]  [2005] EWHC 3016 (Admin).

# 8

# Vulnerable Defendants

8.1    Article 6(3)(e) of the European Convention on Human Rights (ECHR) provides that:

Everyone charged with a criminal offence has the following minimum rights

. . .

(e)  To have the free assistance of an interpreter if he cannot understand or speak the language used in court.

In *Kunagh*,[1] Lord Jauncy said:

It is an essential principle of the criminal law that a trial for an indictable offence should be conducted in the presence of the defendant . . . The basis of this principle is not simply that there should be corporeal presence but that the defendant, by reason of his presence, should be able to understand the proceedings and decide what witnesses he wishes to call, whether or not to give evidence and, if so, what matters are relevant to the case against him . . . A defendant who has not understood the conduct of the proceedings against him cannot, in the absence of express consent, be said to have had a fair trial.

Accordingly, a defendant who does not speak English should have the services of an interpreter. In *Lee Kun*,[2] Lord Reading said:

We have come to the conclusion that the safest and therefore the wisest course, when the foreigner accused is defended by counsel, is that the evidence should be interpreted to him except when he or counsel on his behalf expresses a wish to dispense with the translation and the Judge thinks fit to permit the omission: the Judge should not permit it unless he is of opinion that because of what has passed before the trial, the accused substantially understands the evidence to be given and the case to be made against him at the trial.

A more modern statement of the position is to be found in *Iqbal Begum*.[3] The case also stresses the importance of ensuring that the defendant and the interpreter can in fact understand each other. In that case, the native tongue of the appellant was Punjabi. She spoke no English. She pleaded guilty to the murder of her husband: four years later, her conviction was quashed as a nullity because she had clearly not been able to communicate with her lawyers. Watkins LJ said:

[1]  [1996] 98 Crim App R 455, 459.
[2]  [1916] 1 KB 337, 343.
[3]  (1991) 93 Crim App R 96.

No one should minimise the difficulties which sometimes occur in obtaining the services of an interpreter who is fluent not only in the language of the person who has to be interrogated but who also has knowledge of the dialect in which that language is spoken. This is merely an indication of the very great care which must be taken when a person is facing a criminal charge to ensure that he or she fully comprehends not only the nature of the charge but also the nature of the proceedings which will ensue and of the possible defences which are available having regard to the facts of the case . . . It has been said on a number of occasions that unless a person fully comprehends the charge which that person faces, the full implications of it and the ways in which a defence may be raised to it, and further is able to give full instructions to solicitor and counsel so that the court can be sure that that person has pleaded with a free and understanding mind, a proper plea has not been tendered to the court. The effect of what has happened in such a situation is that no proper trial has taken place. The trial is a nullity. It must be appreciated that the court is very much in the hands of solicitor and counsel when a plea is being tendered. The court is entitled to feel confident that before that plea has been tendered, solicitor and counsel have satisfied themselves that the person arraigned fully understands what is going on and that that person has before that time given full and intelligible instructions so that counsel has in the end been able to satisfy himself that that person is able to make a proper plea . . . Sufficient has now been said we think to cause anyone who is called upon to assist a person such as the appellant, as a first precaution to ensure that the interpreter who is engaged to perform the task of interpretation is fully competent to do so, by which we mean is fluent in the language which that person is best able to understand.

The current position in respect of the provision of interpreters is derived from a press release from the (then) Lord Chancellor's Department in 1998. The full text is set out in the standard textbooks. The salient points are as follows:

The court will be responsible for arranging the interpreter for the defendant at court . . . Normally, a separate interpreter will be arranged for each defendant. Interpretation should take place throughout the court proceedings. The prosecution and the defence will be responsible for arranging interpreters for their own witnesses. Interpreters will be expected to have knowledge of police and court procedures: ideally, they will be selected from the national register of public service interpreters.

8.2   An inability to speak the English language is but one of a number of potential disabilities from which a defendant may suffer. He may be deaf; he may be of very low intelligence. Quite apart from any special measures regime, dealt with in later paragraphs, the courts have developed a number of strategies for dealing with this by reference to the inherent jurisdiction to ensure a fair trial. There is a comprehensive statement of this power in the judgment of Kay LJ in *H*.[4] In that case he said:

25. . . . this judge has come to a conclusion in the exercise of his inherent powers that there is a need for special assistance for the appellant. He is prepared to have the equivalent of an intermediary, in the sense that he is prepared to give assistance for the defendant. As a witness he may have difficulty in understanding questions. The Judge is quite

---

[4] [2003] EWCA Crim 1208.

prepared for him to have a supporter to reassure him to be present. He is certainly prepared for there to be the equivalent of an interpreter during the course of the proceedings. We can see no reason at all why such a person in the exercise of the court's inherent powers should not, if the Judge finds it necessary and appropriate, be allowed to act in a role equivalent to an interpreter when the defendant is in the witness box as if either counsel or the Judge are having difficulty in putting questions to the defendant, because he is failing to understand their choice of language, a person with understanding of his problems may be in a position where they can act as interpreter to make clear by putting into language which he will understand, the nature of the question that he is being asked.

26. It seems to us that all those matters clearly lie within the inherent powers of the court and the court can assist the witness in that way, just as a witness who does not understand language because he speaks a foreign language can have the advantage of an interpreter to translate the question into language that he does.

27. There is the further difficulty which the Judge has addressed, which is that this defendant may have difficulty in recalling all that he wants to say to the jury because of his limitations. Again, it is not beyond the wit of the court to deal with situations such as that in the vast majority of cases and thereby to avoid the undesirable conclusion that the witness is unfit to be tried.

28. The Judge thought that this could be achieved by a very detailed defence statement being drawn and that since he had power to say what use could then be made of that defence statement, he could himself cause it to be read to the jury so that they would have that material before them and be able to hear the defendant's evidence in the light of that coherent account of what he wanted to say.

29. We can see no difficulty with that course. But we suggest as another possible course open to the Judge, which he may want to consider, the following. Any witness is entitled to refer to a document with the leave of the court if it assists them properly to give their evidence. Clearly courts are reluctant with prosecution witnesses to over-extend that facility because it may be unfair to a defendant. But where the only way in which a defendant can properly deal with a matter is by reference to some coherent account he has given in the past, then it seems to us that if the Judge thinks it necessary he can permit that course to be taken. Of course, this appellant has the difficulty that he cannot read, but we can see no problems at all, if it is necessary, with the Judge concluding that he can be asked leading questions that come from a document which he has already identified.

To like effect is the judgment of Latham LJ in *Ukpabio*.[5]
In *TP v West London Youth Court*,[6] Scott Baker LJ said:

26. It is apparent . . . that there are indeed a number of steps that can be taken during the trial. These include:

---

[5] [2007] EWCA Crim 2108; note that the actual decision, namely that the defendant could not give evidence over the live link under the special measures regime in force at that time, has now been overtaken by Youth Justice and Criminal Evidence Act 1999, s 33A by an amendment inserted by s 47 of the Police and Justice Act 2006.
[6] [2005] EWHC 2583 (Admin).

(i)    keeping the claimant's level of cognitive functioning in mind;

(ii)   using concise and simple language;

(iii)  having regular breaks;

(iv)   taking additional time to explain court proceedings;

(v)    being proactive in ensuring the defendant has access to support;

(vi)   explaining and ensuring the claimant understands the ingredients of the charge;

(vii)  explaining the possible outcome and sentence;

(viii) ensuring that cross-examination is carefully controlled so that questions are short and clear and frustration is minimised.

In *R v Camberwell Youth Court*,[7] Baroness Hale said:

> 59. The court has wide and flexible inherent powers to ensure that the accused receives a fair trial and this includes a fair opportunity of giving the best evidence he can . . . The court can allow him the equivalent of an interpreter to assist with communication, a detailed written statement could be read to the jury so that they knew what he wanted to say, and he might even be asked leading questions based upon that document, all in an attempt to enable him to give a proper and coherent account.

Most recently, there is the decision of the Divisional Court in *C v Sevenoaks Youth Court*.[8] A 12-year-old boy faced serious charges in the Youth Court. Appropriate experts agreed that he needed the services of an intermediary (the new statutory provisions not then being in force) and the Divisional Court so ordered. In an illuminating judgment, Openshaw J said:

> 12. . . . the courts have an inherent right, indeed a duty, to appoint an intermediary to help a defendant follow the proceedings and to give evidence, if without such assistance he would not be able to have a fair trial . . .

> 16. I have already made clear that there is no statutory power permitting the appointment of an intermediary for a defendant [note the position is now changed] but there may be some procedural power in the Criminal Procedure Rules. Criminal Procedure Rule 1.1 sets out the overriding objective to deal with criminal cases justly, which includes at (c) recognising the rights of a defendant, particularly under Article 6 . . . Furthermore, the court's case management powers at Rule 3.10 require the court to consider what arrangements are necessary to facilitate the participation of any person in the trial including the defendant. In an appropriate case this surely requires the appointment of an intermediary for the defendant himself.

> 17. In my judgement, when trying a young child, and most particularly a child such as [this child] who is only 12 with learning and behavioural difficulties, notwithstanding the absence of any express statutory power, the Youth Court has a duty under its inherent powers and under the Criminal Procedure Rules to take such steps as are necessary to ensure that he has a fair trial, not just during the proceedings but beforehand as he and his lawyers prepare for trial. He must be given such help as he needs to understand the case against him; he must be helped to give his own side of the story as his proof of evidence is drawn up; it may be that he needs help to speak to his lawyers, let alone to

---

[7] [2005] UKHL 4.

[8] [2009] EWHC 3088 (Admin).

the court; he will need help to follow the case as it proceeds; he would need help to decide whether to question the cadet whom he is alleged to have attacked; whether to accept his identification or to attack his credibility; he will need to decide what line to take with his co-defendant depending upon the evidence he gives; he will need particular help to decide if he is to give evidence and if so he will need help to do so. It is in the highest degree unlikely that this level of help can be given by a lawyer, however kind and sympathetic she may be. He needs someone to befriend and to help him, both during the trial itself and in preparation for it. In short, he needs an intermediary. Furthermore, if an intermediary is to be effective, he must know the intermediary and have confidence in him or her. Such trust will not be established if their first meeting is on the morning of the trial. Moreover the court would have to adapt its procedures to ensure that the hearing is fair by using simple language, by taking breaks, by taking any and all such steps as are necessary. Experienced justices sitting in Youth Courts are well able to ensure the fairness of the proceedings.

It should be noted that the case also discusses how such an intermediary is to be paid for, see paragraphs 24, 26, 27 and 33. The decision itself, in particular in its stress on the need for proper pre-trial assistance to such a youthful defendant, probably goes further than the statutory scheme now in force and referred to below, which seems largely to be confined to the trial itself.

8.3   The original statutory special measures regime did not apply to defendants. There have been recent changes. Section 33A of the Youth Justice and Criminal Evidence Act (YJCEA) 1999 now provides for the evidence of a defendant to be given via a live link. It reads as follows:

33A. – (1) This section applies to any proceedings . . . against a person for an offence.
(2) The court may, on the application of the accused, give a live link direction if it is satisfied:
    (a)   that the conditions in sub-section (4) or . . . sub-section (5) are met in relation to the accused; and
    (b)   that it is in the interests of justice for the accused to give evidence through a live link.
(3) A live link direction is a direction that any oral evidence to be given before the court by the accused is to be given through a live link.
(4) Where the accused is aged under 18 when the application is made, the conditions are that:
    (a)   his ability to participate effectively in the proceedings as a witness giving oral evidence in court is compromised by his level of intellectual ability or social functioning; and
    (b)   use of a live link would enable him to participate more effectively in the proceedings as a witness (whether by improving the quality of his evidence or otherwise).
(5) Where the accused has attained the age of 18 at that time, the conditions are that:
    (a)   he suffers from a mental disorder (within the meaning of the Mental Health Act 1983) or otherwise has a significant impairment of intelligence and social functioning;

(b)  he is for that reason unable to participate effectively in the proceedings as a witness giving oral evidence in court; and

(c)  use of a live link would enable him to participate more effectively in the proceedings as a witness (whether by improving the quality of his evidence or otherwise).

(6)  While a live link direction has effect, the accused may not give oral evidence before the court in the proceedings otherwise than through a live link.

(7)  The court may discharge a live link direction at any time before or during any hearing . . . if it appears to the court to be in the interests of justice to do so.

(8)  The court must state in open court its reasons for:

(a)  giving or discharging a live link direction; or

(b)  refusing an application for or for the discharge of a live link direction.

YJCEA 1999, section 33BA makes provision for an accused to be examined through an intermediary. The section reads as follows:

33BA. – (1) This section applies to any proceedings . . . before the Crown Court against a person for an offence.

(2)  The court may, on the application of the accused, give a direction under sub-section

(3)  if it is satisfied:

(a)  that the condition in sub-section (5) is or, as the case may be, the conditions in sub-section (6) are met in relation to the accused; and

(b)  that making the direction is necessary in order to ensure that the accused receives a fair trial.

(3)  A direction under this sub-section is a direction that provides for any examination of the accused to be conducted through an interpreter or other person approved by the court for the purposes of this section (an intermediary).

(4)  The function of an intermediary is to communicate:

(a)  to the accused, questions put to the accused; and

(b)  to any person asking such questions, the answers given by the accused in reply to them

and to explain such questions or answers so far as necessary to enable them to be understood by the accused or the person in question.

(5)  Where the accused is aged under 18 when the application is made, the condition is that the accused's ability to participate effectively in the proceedings as a witness giving oral evidence in court is compromised by the accused's level of intellectual ability or social functioning.

(6)  Where the accused has attained the age of 18 when the application is made, the conditions are that:

(a)  the accused suffers from a mental disorder (within the meaning of the Mental Health Act 1983) or otherwise has a significant impairment of intelligence and social function; and

(b)  the accused is for that reason unable to participate effectively in the proceedings as a witness giving oral evidence in court.

It should be noted that by virtue of YJCEA 1999, section 33C, the common law powers of the court in relation to assisting an accused remain unaffected by anything in the new statutory regime.

As already pointed out, the effect of the new sections seems to be confined to the defendant giving evidence in court. It does not help on the question of pre-trial assistance, when the common law may provide greater protection.

8.4    As to the procedure to be adopted in and about the making of a direction under the foregoing statutory provisions, the matter is dealt with in Part 29 of the Criminal Procedure Rules 2011 (SI 2011/1709), the relevant parts of which are as follows:

29.3 A party who wants the court to exercise its power to give or make a direction or order must:

(a)    apply in writing:

   (i)    as soon as reasonably practicable; and in any event
   (ii)   not more than 14 days after the defendant pleads not guilty, and

(b)    serve the application on:

   (i)    the court officer; and
   (ii)   each other party.

. . .

29.14 The court may decide whether to give, vary or discharge a defendant's evidence direction:

(a)    at a hearing, in public or in private, or without a hearing;
(b)    in a party's absence if that party:

   (i)    applied for the direction, variation or discharge; or
   (ii)   has had at least 14 days in which to make representations.

29.15  An applicant for a defendant's evidence direction must:

(a)    explain how the proposed direction meets the conditions prescribed by the Youth Justice and Criminal Evidence Act 1999;
(b)    in a case in which the applicant proposes that the defendant give evidence by live link:

   (i)    identify a person to accompany the defendant while the defendant gives evidence; and
   (ii)   explain why that person is appropriate;

(c)    ask for a hearing, if the applicant wants one, and explain why it is needed.

For the sake of completeness, reference may also be made to Rule 29.16 and Rule 29.17.

# 9

## Vulnerable Witnesses: Competence, Special Measures and Anonymity

9.1 The first matter to consider is the competence of the witness to give evidence. This is obviously particularly important in the case of young children. The matter is now largely governed by statute, namely section 53 of the Youth Justice and Criminal Evidence Act (YJCEA) 1999:

> 53. – (1) At every stage in criminal proceedings all persons are (whatever their age) competent to give evidence. . . .
>
> (3) A person is not competent to give evidence in criminal proceedings if it appears to the court that he is not a person who is able to:
>
> (a) understand questions put to him as a witness; and
>
> (b) give answers to them which can be understood.

It is for the court to determine questions of competence. The basic approach to such an assessment is set out in section 54 of the Act:

> 54. – (1) Any question whether a witness in criminal proceedings is competent to give evidence in the proceedings whether raised:
>
> (a) by a party to the proceedings; or
>
> (b) by the court of its own motion
>
> shall be determined by the court in accordance with this section.
>
> (2) It is for the party calling the witness to satisfy the court that, on a balance of probabilities, the witness is competent to give evidence in the proceedings.
>
> (3) In determining the question . . . the court shall treat the witness as having the benefit of any direction under section 19 (special measures).
>
> (4) Any proceedings held for the determination of the question shall take place in the absence of the jury.
>
> (5) Expert evidence may be received on the question.[1]
>
> (6) Any questioning of the witness (where the court considers that necessary) shall be conducted by the court in the presence of the parties.

---

[1] This overturns the decision of Phillips LJ (as he then was) in *Gee v DPP* [1997] 2 Crim App R 78.

In *Macpherson,*[2] dealing with the competence of a young child, Forbes J said:

> 25. In the ordinary way, that issue should be determined before the witness is sworn, usually as a preliminary issue at the start of the trial. In cases such as this, the Judge should watch the video taped interview . . . and/or ask the child appropriate questions . . . The issue raised . . . is one of understanding, that is to say: can the witness understand what is being asked and can the jury understand the witness's answers.

He went on to say that:

> 29. Questions of credibility and reliability are not relevant to competence. Those matters go to the weight of the evidence.

Although it will often be the case that the issue of competence will be resolved by the judge at the outset of the trial, this will not always be so. In *M,*[3] the trial Judge had made his ruling at the outset of the trial. In upholding his decision, Richards LJ in the Court of Appeal said:

> 23. We should stress that on the basis of the material we have seen, the members of this court think it very likely that if they had been dealing with the matter at first instance they would have allowed the boy to give evidence so as to see how things worked out in the course of cross-examination before making a final ruling on the issue of competence. It does not follow, however, that the Judge acted unreasonably in taking a different approach.

In the case of young children, the question of competence may be closely bound up with problems associated with delay. In *Powell,*[4] where the complainant was 3-and-a-half years old, Scott Baker LJ said:

> 41. However, the plain fact is that when a case depends upon the evidence of a very young child, it is absolutely essential (a) that the ABE [achieving best evidence] takes place very soon after the event, (b) that the trial (at which the child has to be cross-examined) takes place very soon thereafter. As the expert evidence in this case showed, very young children simply do not have the ability to lay down memory in a manner comparable to adults. Looking at the case with hindsight, it was completely unacceptable that the appellant should have been tried for an offence proof of which relied on the evidence of a 3-and-a-half-year-old, when the trial did not take place until over 9 months had passed from the date of the alleged offence. Competency to give evidence relates to the whole of the witness's evidence and not just to part of it.

To the same effect is the decision in *Malicki.*[5] In that case, 14 months elapsed between the initial complaint and interview of a four-year-old girl and the subsequent trial. Quashing the conviction, Richards LJ said:

> 18. The problem in such a case as it seems to us is twofold: first, the risk that a child so young does not have any accurate recollection of events 14 months previously (that is almost a quarter of his life ago): secondly, the even greater risk that if she is shown the

---

[2] [2005] EWCA Crim 3605.
[3] [2008] EWCA Crim 2751.
[4] [2006] EWCA Crim 3.
[5] [2009] EWCA Crim 365.

video of her interview just before the trial and during the trial, as she must be, all she is recollecting is what was said in the video, and that she is incapable of distinguishing between what was said on the video and the underlying events themselves. It seems to us to be a near impossible task to undertake an effective cross-examination in those circumstances where the cross-examination must depend for its effectiveness on probing what actually happened in the course of the incident itself and immediately after it, not just going over what the complainant said in her interview. These problems go beyond the normal difficulties of recollections with an adult witness or an older child.

The foregoing analysis must now be read in the light of *Barker*.[6] A girl born in November 2004 was taken into care in August 2007. In October 2007 she indicated to her foster mother something suggestive of sexual abuse. In November 2007 she told a police child protection officer that nothing had happened (and I now over-simplify) but in January 2008 during the course of a medical examination she said that the defendant had 'hurt her with his willy'. In April 2008 she gave her achieving best evidence (ABE) interview confirming the allegation of anal rape. The trial took place in April 2009. The trial Judge watched the interview and heard evidence from experts on both sides in relation to the competency question. He ruled that she was competent. When she had finished her evidence, he revisited the question and confirmed his ruling. In dismissing the appeal and giving the judgment of the court, Lord Judge said:

> 38. [dealing with section 57] The statutory provisions are not limited to the evidence of children. They apply to individuals of unsound mind. They apply to the infirm. The question in each case is whether the individual witness or, as in this case, the individual child, is competent to give evidence in the particular trial. The question is entirely witness or child specific. There are no presumptions or preconceptions. The witness need not understand the special importance that the truth should be told in court and the witness need not understand every single question or give a readily understood answer to every question. Many competent adult witnesses would fail such a competency test. Dealing with it broadly and fairly, provided the witness can understand the questions put to him and can also provide understandable answers, he or she is competent . . .

> 41. The Judge determines the competency question by distinguishing carefully between the issues of competence and credibility. At the stage when the competency question is determined, the Judge is not deciding whether a witness is or will be telling the truth and giving accurate evidence. Provided the witness is competent, the weight to be attached to the evidence is for the jury. . . .

> 43. The competency test may be re-analysed at the end of the child's evidence. This extra statutory jurisdiction is a judicial creation, clearly established in a number of decisions of this court . . . If we were inclined to do so and we are not, it would be too late to question this jurisdiction. This second test should be viewed as an element in the defendant's entitlement to a fair trial. . . .

> 50. . . . Be that as it may, in our judgement the decisions in *Powell* and *Malicki* should not be understood to establish as a matter of principle that where the complainant is a

[6] [2010] EWCA Crim 4.

young child, delay which does not constitute an abuse of process within well understood principles, can give rise to some special form of defence or that, if it does not, a submission based on unfairness within the ambit of section 78 is bound to succeed, or that there is some kind of unspecified limitation period . . . However, in cases involving very young children delay on its own does not automatically require the court to prevent or stop the evidence of the child from being considered by the jury.

51. There remains the broad question whether the conviction which is effectively dependent upon the truthfulness and accuracy of this young child is safe. In reality, what we are being asked to consider is an underlying submission that no such conviction can ever be safe. The short answer is that it is open to a properly directed jury, unequivocally directed about the dangers and difficulties of doing so, to reach a safe conclusion on the basis of the evidence of a single competent witness, whatever his or her age and whatever his or her disability. The ultimate verdict is the responsibility of the jury.

It seems to me that the following conclusions can be drawn:

(1) Every case is 'fact-specific' and 'witness-specific'.
(2) Competence and credibility are two different things and should not be conflated.
(3) The question of competence can be revisited at the end of the child's evidence – again, it is competence not credibility that is being considered.
(4) Delay of itself (not amounting to abuse of process) will not be a ground for preventing the evidence of the child from being given – this is clearly a different approach from that which informed *Powell* and *Malicki*.
(5) Even if the evidence is that of a young child, and even if there has been delay, it is still open to a jury to convict on the evidence of such a child even though there is no other evidence.

9.2   Quite apart from the statutory special measures regime, the court has certain inherent powers to protect witnesses and to assist them in giving their evidence. In *DJX*,[7] in respect of a number of child witnesses who were giving evidence in a family sex case, the trial Judge permitted the use of screens. The Court of Appeal held that he was right to do so and observed:

> We take the view . . . that what the learned Judge did here in his discretion was a perfectly proper and indeed a laudable attempt to see that there was a fair trial.

It is worth observing that in that case the Judge had given an appropriate warning to the jury to the effect that the use of screens should not prejudice them against the defendant.

9.3   It is necessary now to consider the statutory scheme usually referred to as 'special measures'. This is provided for by Part 2 of the YJCEA 1999 (as amended by the Coroners and Justice Act 2009). It may be thought that the whole scheme is unnecessarily prolix and prescriptive. There are different categories of eligibility and it is useful to bear the differences in mind.

---

[7] (1990) 91 Crim App R 36, 41.

## YJCEA 1999, Section 16 Eligibility: Age or Capacity

This section deals with witnesses who are eligible for assistance by virtue of age or incapacity:

16. – (1) . . . a witness in criminal proceedings (other than the accused) is eligible for assistance by virtue of this section:

(a) if under the age of 18 at the time of the hearing; or

(b) if the court considers that the quality of the evidence given by the witness is likely to be diminished by reason of any circumstances falling within sub-section (2).

(2) The circumstances falling within this sub-section are:

(a) that the witness:

(i) suffers from mental disorder within the meaning of the Mental Health Act 1983; or

(ii) otherwise has significant impairment of intelligence and social functioning;

(b) that the witness has a physical disability or is suffering from a physical disorder.

(3) In sub-section (1)(a), 'the time of the hearing in relation to a witness' means the time when it falls to the court to make a determination for the purpose of section 19(2) in relation to the witness.

(4) In determining whether a witness falls within sub-section (1)(b) the court must consider any views expressed by the witness.

(5) In this chapter references to the quality of a witness's evidence are to its quality in terms of completeness, coherence and accuracy: and for this purpose 'coherence' refers to a witness's ability in giving evidence to give answers which address the question put to the witness and can be understood both individually and collectively.

The particular special measures available to a witness in this category are those set out in YJCEA 1999, sections 23–30, see section 18(1)(a).

## YJCEA 1999, Section 17 Eligibility: Fears about Giving Evidence

This section deals with those witnesses who are eligible for assistance on the grounds of fear or distress in connection with testifying:

17. – (1) . . . A witness in criminal proceedings (other than the accused) is eligible for assistance by virtue of this sub-section if the court is satisfied that the quality of evidence given by the witness is likely to be diminished by reason of fear or distress on the part of the witness in connection with testifying in the proceedings.

(2) In determining whether a witness falls within sub-section (1) the court must take into account in particular:

(a) the nature and alleged circumstances of the offence to which the proceedings relate;

(b) the age of the witness;

(c) such of the following matters as appear to the court to be relevant, namely:

   (i) the social and cultural background and ethnic origins of the witness;
   (ii) the domestic and employment circumstances of the witness; and
   (iii) any religious beliefs or potential opinions of the witness;

(d) any behaviour towards the witness on the part of:

   (i) the accused;
   (ii) members of the family or associates of the accused; or
   (iii) any other person who is likely to be an accused or a witness in the proceedings.

(3) In determining that question, the court must in addition consider any views expressed by the witness.

(4) Where the complainant in respect of a sexual offence is a witness in proceedings relating to that offence . . . the witness is eligible for assistance in relation to those proceedings by virtue of this sub-section unless the witness has informed the court of the witness's wish not to be so eligible . . .

(5) A witness in proceedings relating to a relevant offence . . . is eligible for assistance in relation to those proceedings by virtue of this sub-section unless the witness has informed the court of the witness's wish not to be so eligible.

(6) For the purposes of sub-section (5) an offence is a 'relevant offence' if it is an offence described in Schedule 1A.[8]

The particular special measures available to a witness in this category are those set out in YJCEA 1999, sections 23–28, see section 18(1)(b) of the Act.

9.4   The relevant special measures available are as follows:

   (i) section 23: screening the witness from the accused;
   (ii) section 24: evidence by live link;
   (iii) section 25: evidence in private in a sex case or when intimidation is feared;
   (iv) section 26: removal of wigs and gowns;
   (v) section 27: video-recorded evidence-in-chief;
   (vi) section 28: video-recorded cross-examination or re-examination;[9]
   (vii) section 29: examination of a witness through an intermediary;
   (viii) section 30: aids to communication.

9.5   As to the making and variation of special measures directions, this is largely dealt with by YJCEA 1999, sections 19 and 20.

Section 19 of the Act is relatively straightforward. It provides as follows:

19. – (1) This section applies where in any criminal proceedings:

---

[8] Schedule 1A offences (inserted by the Coroners and Justice Act 2009) are offences where firearms or knives are used, including murder, manslaughter, grievous bodily harm, wounding and actual bodily harm.

[9] Not yet generally available.

    (a)  a party to the proceedings makes an application for the court to give a direction under this section in relation to a witness in the proceedings other than the accused; or

    (b)  the court of its own motion raises the issue whether such a direction should be given.

(2)  When the court determines that the witness is eligible for assistance by virtue of section 16 or section 17, the court must then:

    (a)  determine whether any of the special measures available in relation to the witness (or any combination of them) would in its opinion be likely to improve the quality of evidence given by the witness; and

    (b)  if so:

        (i)  determine which of those measures (or combination of them) would in its opinion be likely to maximise so far as practicable the quality of such evidence; and

        (ii)  give a direction under this section providing for the measure or measures so determined to apply to evidence given by the witness.

(3)  In determining . . . whether any special measure or measures would or would not be likely to improve or to maximise as far as practicable the quality of evidence given by the witness, the court must consider all the circumstances of the case including in particular:

    (a)  any views expressed by the witness; and

    (b)  whether the measure or measures might tend to inhibit such evidence being effectively tested by a party to the proceedings.

    . . .

(5)  'Special measures direction' means a direction under this section.

Section 20 amplifies section 19 and provides for variation of a direction. For the most part it is relatively straightforward:

20. – (1) Subject to sub-section (2) and section 21(8) a special measures direction has binding effect from the time it is made until the proceedings . . . are either:

    (a)  determined; or

    (b)  abandoned

    in relation to the accused.

(2)  The court may discharge or vary (or further vary) a special measures direction if it appears to the court to be in the interests of justice to do so and may do so either:

    (a)  on an application made by a party to the proceedings, if there has been a material change of circumstances since the relevant time; or

    (b)  of its own motion.

(3)  In sub-section (2), 'the relevant time' means:

    (a)  the time when the direction was given; or

    (b)  if a previous application has been made under that sub-section, the time when the application (or last application) was made.

    . . .

(5) The court must state in open court its reasons for:

    (a) giving or varying;

    (b) refusing an application for or for the variation or discharge of; or

    (c) discharging

    a special measures direction.

(6) Criminal Procedure Rules may make provision:

    (a) for uncontested applications to be determined by the court without a hearing;

    (b) for preventing the renewal of an unsuccessful application for a special measures direction except where there has been a material change of circumstances;

    (c) for expert evidence to be given in connection with an application for, or for varying or discharging, such a direction;

    (d) for the manner in which confidential or sensitive information is to be treated in connection with such an application and in particular as to its being disclosed to or withheld from a party to the proceedings.[10]

9.6    The relevant rule is set out in Part 29 of the Criminal Procedure Rules 2011 (SI 2011/1709) ('the Rules'):

29.1(1) This part applies:

    (a) where the court can give a direction (a special measures direction) under section 19 of the Youth Justice and Criminal Evidence Act 1999 on an application or on its own initiative (for any of the relevant measures) . . .;

    (b) where the court can vary or discharge such a direction under section 20 of the 1999 Act.

. . .

29.3 A party who wants the court to exercise its power to give or make a direction or order must:

    (a) apply in writing as soon as practicable and (in any event) not more than 14 days after the defendant pleads not guilty; and

    (b) serve the application on:

        (i)   the Court Officer;

        (ii)  each other party.

29.4 . . . (2) The court must announce at a hearing in public before the witness gives evidence the reasons for a decision:

    (a) to give, make, vary or discharge a direction or order; or

    (b) to refuse to do so.

---

[10] If the information is relevant to the credibility or capacity of a witness, it is difficult to conceive of circumstances in which it would be appropriate to keep that information from the defence. Be that as it may, there are now special provisions in the Criminal Procedure Rules 2011 to deal with this situation, see Rule 29.12 and 29.13(3).

29.5(1) The court may:

   (a)  shorten or extend (even after it has expired) a time limit under this part; and

   (b)  allow an application or representation to be made in a different form to one set out in the Practice Direction or to be made orally.

(2)  A person who wants an extension of time must:

   (a)  apply when serving the application or representations for which it is needed; and

   (b)  explain the delay.

   ...

29.8  The court may decide whether to give, vary or discharge a special measures direction:

   (a)  at a hearing, in public or in private, or without a hearing;

   (b)  in a party's absence if that party:

      (i)  applied for the direction, variation or discharge; or

      (ii)  has had at least 14 days in which to make representations.

   ...

29.10(1) An applicant for a special measures direction must:

   (a)  explain how the witness is eligible for assistance;

   (b)  explain why special measures would be likely to improve the quality of the witness's evidence;

   (c)  propose the measure or measures that in the applicant's opinion would be likely to maximise so far as practicable the quality of that evidence;

   (d)  report any views that the witness has expressed about:

      (i)  his or her eligibility for assistance;

      (ii)  the likelihood that special measures would improve the quality of his or her evidence; and

      (iii)  the measure or measures proposed by the applicant;

   (e)  in a case in which a child witness or a qualifying witness does not want the primary rule to apply, provide any information that the court may need to assess the witness's views ...

   (f)  in a case in which the applicant proposes that the witness should give evidence by live link:

      (i)  identify someone to accompany the witness while the witness gives evidence;

      (ii)  name that person if possible; and

      (iii)  explain why that witness would be an appropriate companion for the witness, including the witness's own views;

   (g)  in a case in which the applicant proposes the admission of video recorded evidence, identify:

      (i)  the date and duration of the recording;

      (ii)  which part the applicant wants the court to admit as evidence, if the applicant does not want the court to admit all of it;

(h)  attach any other material on which the applicant relies; and

(i)  if the applicant wants a hearing, ask for one and explain why it is needed.

29.11(1) A party who wants the court to vary or discharge a special measures direction must:

(a)  apply in writing as soon as practicable after becoming aware of the grounds for doing so; and

(b)  serve the application on:

(i)  the Court Officer; and

(ii)  each other party.

(2)  The applicant must:

(a)  explain what material circumstances have changed since the direction was given or last varied;

(b)  explain why the direction should be varied or discharged;

(c)  ask for a hearing if the applicant wants one and explain why it is needed.

. . .

29.13(1) This rule applies where a party wants to make representations about:

(a)  an application for a special measures direction;

(b)  an application for the variation or discharge of such a direction; or

(c)  a direction variation or discharge that the court proposes on its own initiative.

(2)  Such a party must:

(a)  serve the representations on:

(i)  the Court Officer; and

(ii)  each other party;

(b)  do so not more than 14 days after, as applicable:

(i)  service of the application; or

(ii)  notice of the direction, variation or discharge that the court proposes; and

(c)  ask for a hearing if that party wants one and explain why it is needed.

. . .

(4) Representations against a special measures direction must explain:

(a)  why the witness is not eligible for assistance;

(b)  why no special measures would be likely to improve the quality of the witness's evidence; or

(c)  why the measure or measures proposed by the applicant:

(i)  would not be likely to maximise so far as practicable the quality of the witness's evidence; or

(ii)  might tend to inhibit the effective testing of that evidence.

(5) Representations against the variation or discharge of a special measures direction must explain why it should not be made.

9.7   It might be thought that the foregoing provisions provide a relatively comprehensive and comprehensible set of rules in and about the making and granting or refusing of special measures directions and the appropriate qualifying criteria. Unfortunately, we have also to consider YJCEA 1999, sections 21, 22 and 22A and associated Criminal Procedure Rules. It has been thought necessary to make extra provision for cases involving children and cases of a sexual nature (sometimes but not always the same). The extra provisions are highly prescriptive and the language used tortuous.

Section 21 is headed 'Special Provision relating to Child Witnesses':

21. – (1) For the purposes of this section:

    (a)   a witness in criminal proceedings is a 'child witness' if he is an eligible witness by reason of section 16(1)(a);

       . . .

    (c)   a 'relevant recording' in relation to a child witness is a video recording of an interview of the witness made with a view to its admission as evidence in chief of the witness.

(2)   Where the court, in making a determination for the purposes of section 19(2) determines that a witness in criminal proceedings is a child witness, the court must:

    (a)   first have regard to sub-sections (3) to (4C) below; and
    (b)   then have regard to section 19(2),

and for the purposes of section 19(2) as it then applies to the witness, any special measures required to be applied in relation to him by virtue of this section shall be treated as if they were measures determined by the court pursuant to section 19(2) (a) and (b)(i) to be ones that . . . would be likely to maximise, so far as practicable, the quality of his evidence.

(3)   The primary rule in the case of a child witness is that the court must give a special measures direction in relation to the witness which complies with the following requirements:

    (a)   it must provide for any relevant recording to be admitted under section 27 (video recorded evidence in chief);
    (b)   it must provide for any evidence given by the witness in the proceedings which is not given by means of a video recording . . . to be given by means of a live link in accordance with section 24.

(4)   The primary rule is subject to the following limitations: [various limitations are then set out].

(4A)–(4C) . . .

(8)   Where a special measures direction is given in relation to a child witness who is an eligible witness by reason only of section 16(1)(a) and the direction provides:

      (i)   for any relevant recording to be admitted under section 27 as evidence in chief of the witness . . .

then, so far as it provides as mentioned in paragraph (a)(i) above, the direction shall continue to have effect in accordance with section 20(1) even though the witness subsequently attains that age.

To complicate matters further, we have section 22, which is headed 'Extension of Provisions of Section 21 to certain witnesses over 18'. It introduces us to the 'qualifying witness':

> 22. – (1) For the purposes of this section:
>
> > (a)  a witness in criminal proceedings . . . is a 'qualifying witness' if he:
> >
> > > (i)  is not an eligible witness at the time of the hearing (as defined by section 16(3)); but
> > > (ii)  was under the age of 18 when a relevant recording was made;
> > >
> > > . . .
> >
> > (c)  a 'relevant recording' in relation to a witness, is a video recording of an interview of the witness made with a view to its admission as evidence in chief of the witness.
>
> (2)  Sub-section (2) to (4) and (4C) of section 21, so far as relates to the giving of a direction complying with the requirement contained in section 21(3)(a) apply to a qualifying witness in respect of the relevant recording as they apply to a child witness.[11]

9.8   YJCEA 1999, section 22A is headed 'Special Provisions in relation to Sexual Offences'. It follows the same convoluted pattern as previous provisions. It could simply have provided for a rebuttable presumption in favour of the right of a complainant in a sex case to give evidence by means of a video recording. Instead, we have this:

> 22A. – (1) This section applies when in criminal proceedings relating to a sexual offence . . . the complainant in respect of that offence is a witness in the proceedings. . . .
>
> (3)  This section does not apply if the complainant is an eligible witness by reason of section 16(1)(a) . . .
>
> (4)  If a party to the proceedings makes an application under section 19(1)(a) for a special measures direction in relation to the complainant, the party may request that the direction provide for any relevant recording to be admitted under section 27 (video recorded evidence in chief).
>
> (5)  Sub-section (6) applies if:
>
> > (a)  a party to the proceedings makes a request under sub-section (4) with respect to the complainant; and
> > (b)  the court determines for the purposes of section 19(2) that the complainant is eligible for assistance by virtue of section 16(1)(b) or section 17.
>
> (6) The court must:
>
> > (a)  first have regard to sub-sections (7) to (9); and
> > (b)  then have regard to section 19(2),

---

[11]  Subject to the somewhat hedged-around discretion of the court, this seems to mean that any witness who has made what purports to be a video-recorded interview of his evidence-in-chief at a time when he was still under the age of 18 is entitled to give his evidence-in-chief by means of that recording.

and for the purposes of section 19(2) as it then applies to the complainant, any special measure required to be applied in relation to the complainant by virtue of this section is to be treated as if it were a measure determined by the court pursuant to section 19(2)(a) and (b)(i) to be one that . . . would be likely to maximise, so far as practicable, the quality of the complainant's evidence.

(7) The court must give a special measures direction in relation to the complainant that provides for any relevant recording to be admitted under section 27.

(8) The requirement in sub-section (7) has effect subject to section 27(2).

(9) The requirement in sub-section (7) does not apply to the extent that the court is satisfied that compliance with it would not be likely to maximise the quality of the complainant's evidence . . .

(10) In this section 'relevant recording' in relation to a complainant, is a video recording of an interview of the complainant made with a view to its admission as the evidence in chief of the complainant.

9.9   YJCEA 1999, sections 21 and 22 have their own Criminal Procedure Rule, namely Rule 29.9:

29.9(1) This rule applies when under section 21 or section 22 of the Youth Justice and Criminal Evidence Act 1999 the primary rule requires the court to give a direction for a special measure to assist a child witness as a qualifying witness:

(a) on an application if one is made; or
(b) on the court's own initiative in any other case.

(2) A party who wants to introduce the evidence of such a witness must as soon as practicable:

(a) notify the court that the witness is eligible for assistance;
(b) provide the court with any information that the court may need to assess the witness's views if the witness does not want the primary rule to apply; and
(c) serve any video recorded evidence on:

(i)   the Court Officer; and
(ii)  each other party.

9.10   The video-recorded evidence of the witness has therefore become a principal means by which the evidence-in-chief of the 'vulnerable' witness is to be given. It is the common experience of those who try criminal cases that the standard of interviewing and indeed the quality of the recording of the interview often leave a great deal to be desired. However, this so-called 'primary rule' is subject to section 27(2). Section 27 deals with 'video recorded evidence in chief'. It provides as follows:

27. – (1) A special measures direction may provide for a video recording of an interview of the witness to be admitted as evidence in chief of the witness.

(2) A special measures direction may, however, not provide for a video recording, or a part of such a recording, to be admitted under this section if the court is of the opinion, having regard to all the circumstances of the case, that in the interests of justice the recording, or that part of it, should not be so admitted.

(3) In considering for the purposes of sub-section (2) whether any part of a recording should not be admitted under this section, the court must consider whether any prejudice to the accused which might result from that part being so admitted is outweighed by the desirability of showing the whole, or substantially the whole, of the recorded interview.

(4) Where a special measures direction provides for a recording to be admitted under this section, the court may nevertheless subsequently direct that it is not to be so admitted if:

    (a) it appears to the court that:

        (i) the witness will not be available for cross-examination . . .; and

        (ii) the parties to the proceedings have not agreed that there is no need for the witness to be so available; or

    (b) any Criminal Procedure Rules requiring disclosure of the circumstances in which the recording was made have not been complied with to the satisfaction of the court.

(5) Where a recording is admitted under this section:

    (a) the witness must be called by the party tendering it in evidence . . .;

    (b) the witness may not without the permission of the court give evidence in chief otherwise than by means of the recording as to any matter which, in the opinion of the court, is dealt with in the witness's recorded testimony.

(6) Where in accordance with sub-section (2) a special measures direction provides for part only of a recording to be admitted . . . references in sub-sections (4) and (5) to the recording . . . are references to the part of the recording which is to be so admitted.

(7) The court may give permission for the purpose of sub-section (5)(b) if it appears to the court to be in the interests of justice to do so and may do so either:

    (a) on an application by a party to the proceedings; or

    (b) of its own motion.

Section 27 is supplemented by Part IV.40 of the Practice Direction which, in its relevant parts, provides as follows:

> 40.2 Where a court grants leave to admit a video recording in evidence, it may direct that any part of the recording be excluded. When any such direction is given, the party who made the application must edit the video recording in accordance with those directions. . . .

> 40.4 Once a trial has begun, if by reason of faulty or inadequate preparation (or some other cause) the procedures set out above have not been properly complied with and an application is made to edit the video recording, thereby making an adjournment necessary, the court may make an appropriate award of costs.

9.11 As already pointed out, many video-recorded interviews are prolix, rambling, repetitive, full of improper questions and often of poor technical quality. Necessary editing is not done. In theory, all of these matters should engage section 27. The reality seems to be somewhat otherwise.

In *G v DPP*,[12] where there had been breaches of the memorandum of good practice which then governed the interviewing of children, Philips LJ said:

> Whether the failure to comply with the memorandum of good practice should lead to the exclusion of video evidence will not necessarily be a question that can be determined by considering the nature and extent of the breaches that have occurred. It will depend upon the extent to which passages in the evidence affected by the breaches are supported by other passages in respect of which no complaint can be made. It can depend also upon other evidence in the case and the extent to which this corroborates the evidence given in the video interviews.

In *K*,[13] the Court of Appeal had to consider a case where there had been breaches of the 'achieving best evidence' guidelines. Hooper LJ said:

> 23. In *R v Hanton* [2005] EWCA Crim 2009, the Court of Appeal was concerned with a case where there were a number of alleged breaches. Having considered *G*, it adopted as the test 'could a reasonable jury properly directed be sure that the witness has given a credible and accurate account on the videotape notwithstanding any breaches'. If yes, it was a matter for the jury. If no, the interview would be inadmissible. The test could also be expressed in this way. 'Were the breaches such that a reasonable jury properly directed could not be sure that the witness gave a credible and accurate account in the video interview' . . . Read as a whole, *G* indicates that the prime consideration is the reliability of the video evidence which will normally be assessed by reference to the interview itself, the condition under which it was held, the age of the child and the nature and extent of any breach of the code.

Dealing with the reference in *G* to 'other evidence', Hooper LJ went on to say:

> 29. We should only add that our reading of *G* is that the court considered it possible, rather than necessary or desirable, for a court to have regard to other evidence in the case. It may not sufficiently have emphasised, though we do, that any such reference to other evidence should be undertaken with considerable caution, since it may not be often that other evidence can assist as to the credibility, accuracy and completeness of a video interview.

It often happens that the only way of following the evidence on the video is by reference to the written transcript of what had been said. In *Welstead*,[14] the trial Judge allowed the jury to have copies of the transcript. In the Court of Appeal, Evans LJ said:

> In our judgement he was entitled to do that, provided that certain conditions were met. First that the transcripts would in fact be likely to assist them in following the evidence . . . secondly, that he made it clear to them that the transcripts were made available only for that limited purpose and that they should concentrate primarily on the oral evidence. The transcript was not the child's evidence in the case. Thirdly, that he give them such directions, both at the time and in the summing up, as would be likely to be an effective safeguard against the risk of disproportionate weight being given to the transcript.

[12] [1997] 2 Crim App R 78, 87.
[13] [2006] EWCA Crim 472.
[14] [1996] 1 Crim App R 59, 69.

In the above case, the jury gave the transcripts back when they retired to consider their verdict. In *Morris*,[15] the jury took the transcript with them when they retired. The Court of Appeal disapproved. They said it was rarely that a jury should be permitted to retire with the transcript even when the defence consented.

The authorities were reviewed in *Popescu*.[16] Giving the judgment of the Court of Appeal, Aikens LJ said:

> 35. The general rule must be that great care must be taken before a jury is given transcripts of an ABE interview at all, even whilst the video is being shown. It should only be given to the jury after there has been a discussion of the issue between the Judge and Counsel in the absence of the jury and it should only be done if there is a very good reason for it, eg the evidence would be difficult to follow on the screen or the audio quality is very poor.

> 36. Secondly, if the transcript is given to the jury, we suggest that the Judge must warn the jury then and there to examine the video as it is shown, not least because of the importance of the demeanour of the witness in giving evidence. Thirdly, the transcript should, save perhaps in very exceptional circumstances, be withdrawn from the jury once the ABE video evidence in chief has been given. Again, if the jury is to retain the transcripts during the cross-examination, this possibility must be given positive thought before it is done . . . If the jury are to retain the transcripts, the reasons why they are being permitted to do so should be explained to them.

> 37. Fourthly, if the transcripts are retained during cross-examination, then they should be recovered once the witness has finished his or her evidence. The general rule must be that the jury should not thereafter have the transcript again.

> 38. . . . Sixthly, the jury should not, except perhaps in exceptional circumstances, be permitted to retire with the transcripts. Those exceptional circumstances will usually only be present if the defence positively wants the jury to have the transcript and the Judge is satisfied that there are very good reasons why the jury should retire with the transcripts.

> 39. If the jury is to do so, it must again be subject to discussion with Counsel and a specific ruling from the Judge. The Judge must explain to the jury, in the course of his summing up, why they are being allowed the transcripts and the limited use to which they must be put, viz to aid them to understand the evidence in chief of the relevant witness and, if it be the case, that the defence want the jury to retain the transcripts. If this course is adopted, then it is incumbent upon the Judge to ensure that the cross-examination and re-examination of the witness is fully summed up to the jury and the jury must be specifically reminded that they must take all that evidence into consideration in their deliberation and must not be over-reliant upon the evidence in chief.

Given the inadequacies already referred to of many of the videos of child witnesses, jurors often want to see part or all of the video again. The proper approach to such a request is dealt with at some length in the judgment of Lord Taylor in *Rawlings*.[17] He said:

---

[15] [1998] Crim LR 416.
[16] [2010] EWCA Crim 1230.
[17] [1995] 2 Crim App R 222, 237.

In our judgement, it is a matter for the Judge's discretion as to whether the jury's request for the video to be replayed should be granted or refused . . . Usually, if the jury simply wish to be reminded of what the witness said, it would be sufficient and most expeditious to remind them from his own note. If however the circumstances suggest or the jury indicate that how the words were spoken is of importance to them, the Judge may in his discretion allow the video, or the relevant part thereof, to be replayed. It would be prudent where the reason for the request is not stated or obvious for the Judge to ask whether the jury wish to be reminded of something said, which he may be able to give them from his note, or whether they wish to be reminded of how the words were said. If the Judge does allow the video to be replayed he should comply with the following three requirements:

(a)  the replay should be in court with Judge, Counsel and the defendant present;
(b)  the Judge should warn the jury that because they are hearing the evidence in chief of the complainant for a second time, they should guard against the risk of giving it disproportionate weight simply for that reason and should bear well in mind the other evidence in the case;
(c)  to assist in maintaining a fair balance, he should, after the replay of the video, remind the jury of the cross-examination and re-examination of the complainant from his notes whether the jury asked him to do so or not.

9.12    It is worth remembering YJCEA 1999, section 32:

Where on a trial on indictment with a jury evidence has been given in accordance with a special measures direction, the Judge must give the jury such warning (if any) as the Judge considers necessary to ensure that the fact that the direction was given in relation to the witness does not prejudice the accused.

See also at 9.2 above.


## Witness Anonymity

9.13    In *Davis*[18] (in the Court of Appeal), the court was dealing with a case where gangsters were on trial and the witnesses were terrified. The trial Judge had permitted those witnesses to give their evidence anonymously. Having held that there was clear jurisdiction at common law to admit the incriminating evidence of an anonymous witness and having gone on to review the European human rights jurisprudence, the President said:

51. The court accepted that the Convention rights of witnesses included, where necessary, the preservation of their anonymity, and in our judgement decided that the concealment of the identity of witnesses is not inconsistent with the right to a fair trial, provided first the need for anonymity is clearly established, second that cross-examination of the witness by an advocate for the defendant is permitted, and finally the ultimate test, that the trial should be fair.

---

[18]  [2006] EWCA Crim 1155.

This decision was reversed by the House of Lords.[19] In turn their decision was overturned by the speedy enactment of the Criminal Evidence (Witness Anonymity) Act 2008, the relevant provisions of which are now set out in sections 86–93 of the Coroners and Justice Act 2009. The relevant provisions are as follows:

> 86. – (1) In this chapter a 'witness anonymity order' is an order made by a court that requires such specified measures to be taken in relation to a witness in criminal proceedings as the court considers appropriate to ensure that the identity of the witness is not disclosed in or in connection with the proceedings.
>
> (2) The kinds of measures that may be required to be taken in relation to a witness include measures for securing one or more of the following:
>
>> (a) that the witness's name and other identifying details may be:
>>
>>> (i) withheld;
>>> (ii) removed from materials disclosed to any party to the proceedings;
>>
>> (b) that the witness may use a pseudonym;
>> (c) that the witness is not asked questions of any specified description that might lead to the identification of the witness;
>> (d) that the witness is screened to any specified extent;
>> (e) that the witness's voice is subjected to modulation to any specified extent. . . .
>
> 87. – (1) An application for a witness anonymity order to be made in relation to a witness in criminal proceedings may be made to the court by the prosecutor or the defendant.
>
> (2) Where an application is made by the prosecutor, the prosecutor:
>
>> (a) must (unless the court directs otherwise) inform the court of the identity of the witness; but
>> (b) is not required to disclose in connection with the application:
>>
>>> (i) the identity of the witness; or
>>> (ii) any information that might enable the witness to be identified to any other party to the proceedings or his or her legal representatives;
>
>> . . .
>
> (6) The court must give every party to the proceedings the opportunity to be heard on an application under this section.
>
> (7) But sub-section (6) does not prevent the court from hearing one or more parties in the absence of a defendant and his or her legal representatives if it appears to the court to be appropriate to do so in the circumstances of the case.
>
> 88. – (1) This section applies where an application is made for a witness anonymity order to be made in relation to a witness in criminal proceedings.
>
> (2) The court may make such an order only if it is satisfied that conditions A to C below are met.
>
> (3) Condition A is that the proposed order is necessary:
>
>> (a) in order to protect the safety of the witness or another person or to prevent any serious damage to property; or

---

[19] [2008] UKHL 36.

(b)  in order to prevent real harm to the public interest (whether affecting the carrying on of any activities in the public interest or the safety of a person involved in carrying on such activities, or otherwise).

(4)  Condition B is that, having regard to all the circumstances, the effect of the proposed order would be consistent with the defendant receiving a fair trial.

(5)  Condition C is that the importance of the witness's testimony is such that in the interests of justice the witness ought to testify, and

(a)  the witness would not testify if the proposed order were not made; or

(b)  there would be real harm to the public interest if the witness were to testify without the proposed order being made.

(6)  In determining whether the proposed order is necessary for the purpose mentioned in sub-section (3)(a), the court must have regard (in particular) to any reasonable fear on the part of the witness:

(a)  that the witness or another person would suffer death or injury; or

(b)  that there would be serious damage to the property,

if the witness were to be identified.

89. – (1) When deciding whether conditions A to C in section 88 are met in the case of an application for a witness anonymity order, the court must have regard to:

(a)  the considerations mentioned in sub-section (2) below; and

(b)  such other matters as the court considers relevant.

(2)  The considerations are:

(a)  the general right of a defendant in criminal proceedings to know the identity of a witness in the proceedings;

(b)  the extent to which the credibility of the witness concerned would be a relevant factor when the weight of his or her evidence comes to be assessed;

(c)  whether evidence given by the witness might be the sole or decisive evidence implicating the defendant;

(d)  whether the witness's evidence could be properly tested (whether on grounds of credibility or otherwise) without his or her identity being disclosed;

(e)  whether there is any reason to believe that the witness:

(i)  has a tendency to be dishonest; or

(ii)  has any motive to be dishonest in the circumstances of the case,

having regard (in particular) to any previous convictions of the witness and to any relationship between the witness and the defendant or any associates of the defendant;

(f)  whether it would be reasonably practicable to protect the witness by any means other than by making a witness anonymity order specifying the measures that are under consideration by the court.

90. – (1) . . .

(2)  The Judge must give the jury such warning as the Judge considers appropriate to ensure that the fact that the order was made in relation to the witness does not prejudice the defendant.

Applications for such orders must be made in accordance with Rule 29 of the Rules:

29.18(1) The court must decide whether to make, vary or discharge a witness anonymity order:

    (a)  at a hearing (which will be in private unless the court otherwise directs) or without a hearing (unless any party asks for one);

    (b)  in the absence of a defendant.

(2)  The court must not exercise its power to make, vary or discharge a witness anonymity order or to refuse to do so:

    (a)  before or during the trial, unless each party has had an opportunity to make representations;

    . . .

29.19(1)  An applicant for a witness anonymity order must:

    (a)  include in the application nothing that might reveal the witness's identity;

    (b)  describe the measures proposed by the applicant;

    (c)  explain how the proposed order meets the conditions prescribed by section 88 of the Coroners and Justice Act 2009;

    (d)  explain why no measures other than those proposed will suffice, such as:

        (i)   an admission of the facts that would be proved by the witness;

        (ii)  an order restricting public access to the trial;

        (iii) reporting restrictions;

        (iv) a direction for a special measure . . .;

        (v)  introduction of the witness's written statement as hearsay evidence under section 116 of the Criminal Justice Act 2003; or

        (vi) arrangements for the protection of the witness;

    (e)  attach to the application:

        (i)   a witness statement setting out the proposed evidence, edited in such a way as not to reveal the witness's identity;

        (ii)  where the prosecutor is the applicant, any further prosecution evidence to be served, and any further prosecution material to be disclosed under the Criminal Procedure and Investigations Act 1996, similarly edited; and

        (iii) any defence statement that has been served or as much information as may be available to the applicant that gives particulars of the defence; and

    (f)  ask for a hearing, if the applicant wants one.

(2)  At any hearing of the application, the applicant must:

    (a)  identify the witness to the court, unless at the prosecutor's request the court otherwise directs; and

    (b)  present to the court, unless it otherwise directs:

        (i)   the unedited witness statement from which the edited version has been prepared;

> (ii)   where the prosecutor is the applicant, the unedited version of any further prosecution evidence or material from which an edited version has been prepared; and
>
> (iii)   such further material as the applicant relies on to establish that the proposed order meets the conditions prescribed by section 88 of the 2009 Act.

(3) At any such hearing:

> (a)   the general rule is that the court will receive, in the following sequence:
>
> > (i)   representations first by the applicant and then by each other party in all the parties' presence; and then
> >
> > (ii)   information withheld from a defendant and further representations by the applicant in the absence of any (or any other) defendant; but
>
> (b)   the court may direct other arrangements for the hearing.

(4) Before the witness gives evidence, the applicant must identify the witness to the court:

> (a)   if not already done;
>
> (b)   without revealing the witness's identity to any other party or person; and
>
> (c)   unless at the prosecutor's request the court otherwise directs.

Although perhaps technically superseded by the above Rules, amendment 21 to the Consolidated Criminal Practice Direction at paragraphs 1.15.1 and following should also be noted.

Guidance as to the proper approach to the making of such an order was given by the Court of Appeal in *Myers*:[20]

> 8. The Act creates what may fairly be regarded as a new statutory special measure . . . It is however clear that an anonymity order should be regarded as the special measure of last practicable resort. . . .
>
> 10. For the avoidance of doubt, common law principles relating to public interest immunity when such issues arise in the context of witness anonymity are expressly preserved . . . Our approach to this issue enables us to highlight that the obligations of the prosecution in the context of a witness anonymity application go much further than the ordinary duties of disclosure. As we shall see when we examine the statutory considerations, a detailed investigation into the background of each potential anonymous witness will almost inevitably be required. . . .
>
> 12. As we have explained, all the processes are subject to existing principles, not least that the Crown must comply with its existing duties in relation to full and frank disclosure (save as expressly permitted by the Act in relation to withholding of information on the basis of public interest immunity). The process as a whole must be fair. Disclosure must be complete, in accordance with principles laid down in this court and the structured proactive approach indicated by the guidance of the Director of Public Prosecutions and the guidelines provided by the Attorney General. At the same time the defence statement . . . which provides for broader identification by the defence of the

---

[20]   [2008] EWCA Crim 2989.

issues, is a crucial document, which must help inform and focus the disclosure process. The disclosure process cannot be circumscribed by a minute analysis of the text of the defence statement and some of the considerations identified in section [89], such as for example the possibility of collusion between intended anonymous witnesses, where there is more than one, should be specifically investigated and addressed in the context of disclosure not least because the defence may be ignorant of material which could or would be included in the case statement if it was known to the defendant. In short, the Crown must be proactive, focusing closely on the credibility of the anonymous witness and the interests of justice.

13. Nothing in the Act diminishes the overriding responsibility of the trial Judge to ensure that the proceedings are conducted fairly. Well understood principles relating not only to the admission of evidence, including the powers of the court under section 78 of the Police and Criminal Evidence Act [1984] to exclude evidence, are unchanged. Beyond that, the Judge is entitled and normally should reflect both at the close of the prosecution case and indeed if the defendant has given evidence, when the defence evidence is concluded, whether properly directed, notwithstanding the crucial incriminating evidence was given by an anonymous witness or witnesses, and in the light of the evidence as a whole, the case can safely be left to the jury . . .

17. [After setting out the statutory conditions which have to be established in section 88] . . . we immediately emphasise that all three conditions A, B and C must be met before the jurisdiction to make a witness anonymity order arises. Each is mandatory. Each is distinct. However clearly two of the three conditions are met, the jurisdiction to make an order does not arise unless the third condition is also satisfied. When all three conditions are met, but not until they are met, the jurisdiction to make a witness anonymity order arises . . .

21. [After considering the statutory considerations in section 89] . . . the considerations in sub-sections (2)(b), (d) and (e) are linked in the broad sense that they relate to the weight to be attached to the evidence of the anonymous witness and the safeguarding of the process by which his credibility may, so far as practicable, be objectively verified and then tested in cross-examination. They can and indeed should apply to every witness in respect of whom an anonymity order is sought. In this context the process of investigation and disclosure is crucial, not simply in relation to previous occasions when the witness may have been dishonest in general, but also whether there may be any reason to question his honesty or motivation in the particular case. The defence statement provides the benchmark against which the disclosure process must be examined. So for example, a defendant who believes that he may be the victim of a malevolent plot to incriminate him when he is innocent should normally be able to give some indication of his concerns in his defence statement and to indicate the identity of anyone who he believes may have a malign motive to incriminate him. It can then, if raised by him, be the subject of further enquiries, perhaps indeed with the use of special Counsel . . .

23. [Dealing with section 89] . . . sub-section (2)(c) directly addresses the jurisprudence of the European Court, highlighted by the observations of Lord Mance on this topic in *Davis*. Taken on its own, the fact that a witness provides the sole or decisive evidence against the defendant is not, of itself, conclusive whether conditions A to C are met . . . If the evidence of the anonymous witness may be either the sole or the decisive

evidence incriminating the defendant, that consideration must be addressed and taken into account when the court is deciding whether condition B has been satisfied . . .

26. [Considering the statutory condition in section 88] . . . in most cases, the most helpful approach would probably be to address condition C first; the interests of justice are undefined . . . The order should not be made where the oral testimony of the witness realistically analysed, is not potentially important or where the proposed anonymous evidence could be addressed by admissions or agreed facts or, subject to proper editing, capable of being read. It must in any event also be clear that notwithstanding, for example, the powers vested in the court in relation to contempt in an appropriate case, the witness will not testify. The test is stark. That the witness might prefer not to testify or would be reluctant or unhappy at the prospect, is not enough. Condition C is expressly directed to oral testimony and the evidence envisaged in its provisions is the evidence to be given by a witness who will be called . . .

27. We should perhaps add that it is open to the court to reach the conclusion that the witness would not testify if the circumstances of the offence itself justified the inference, for example, where it is apparent that the witness was present when a gun was fired or the circumstances of the killing show the kind of outrageous arrogance displayed by the killer in *Davis*. Unhappily the challenge to the rule of law itself posed by gun and weapon carrying individuals or members of gangs of criminals and the legitimate fears which this engenders in the public, particularly where an attack is carried out in public, is undiminished.

28. It was suggested in argument that unless the risk to the safety of the witness was attributable to the actions of the defendant personally, condition A could not be established. We disagree. The problem arises if and when the safety of the witness is under threat: the threat may come from any source.

29. Condition A is linked to sub-section (6). The order must be necessary . . . Condition A is not fulfilled unless the order is necessary for the protection of the safety of the witness or any other person or to prevent serious damage to property or alternatively to prevent real harm to the public interest. In relation to human beings, the issue is unembellished by adjectives. The question is safety and this may encompass the risk of personal injury or death or a reasonable fear of either. In relation to property, however, the risk must be serious and any harm to the public interest must be real.

Recent illustrations of the practical operation of these provisions are provided by *Powar*[21] and *Taylor*.[22]

---

[21] [2009] EWCA Crim 594.
[22] [2010] EWCA Crim 830.

# 10

## The Reluctant Witness

10.1  In respect of cases committed or sent to the Crown Court, both prosecution and defence will have copies of the witness statements. So far as 'sent' cases are concerned, the prosecution must serve those papers within 50 days of sending in respect of defendants in custody, and within 70 days in respect of defendants who are on bail.[1] So far as committed cases are concerned, the statements would have been served in the Magistrates' Court. Ignoring the unreal provisions of section 9 of the Criminal Justice Act 1967 (proof by written statements),[2] by the time of the PCMH the defence should indicate which of the prosecution witnesses they require to attend to give evidence. Likewise, the Crown will have decided those whom they wish to call in any event. The police and the appropriate witness care units usually arrange for those witnesses who are required to attend to be warned that their attendance will be required on the day of trial. At this stage no compulsion is involved.

10.2  Sometimes prior to trial, a witness indicates a reluctance to attend or does not acknowledge the notification that he is required to attend. In those circumstances, the procedures set out in the Criminal Procedure (Attendance of Witnesses) Act (CP(AW)A) 1965 may be utilised.[3] The first step involves the 'summons' stage. The relevant parts of section 2 of the Act are as follows:

2. – (1) This section applies when the Crown Court is satisfied that:

    (a)   a person is likely to be able to give . . . material evidence . . . for the purpose of any criminal proceedings before the Crown Court; and

    (b)   it is in the interests of justice to issue a summons under this section to secure the attendance of that person to give evidence.

(2)  In such a case, the Crown Court shall . . . issue a summons (a witness summons) directed to the person concerned and requiring him to:

    (a)   attend before the Crown Court at the time and place stated in the summons; and

    (b)   give the evidence . . .

---

[1] Crime and Disorder Act 1998 (Service of Prosecution Evidence) Regulations 2005 (SI 2005/902). In practice, in most ordinary cases, the papers are served within a shorter period of time.

[2] Which provides that a written statement is admissible in evidence unless within 7 days the defence indicate that they require the witness to give evidence (subject to judicial discretion to extend).

[3] The provisions of the CP(AW)A 1965 relating to the attendance of witnesses to produce documents are dealt with in chapter four on disclosure.

(3)  A witness summons may only be issued under this section on an application and the Crown Court may refuse to issue the summons if any requirement relating to the application is not fulfilled.

(4)  [A paraphrase because of the uncertainties surrounding the continued existence of committal proceedings: the application must be made as soon as is reasonably practicable after committal or, in a section 51 'sent' case, as soon as reasonably practicable after service of the papers.] . . .

(7)  An application must be made in accordance with Criminal Procedure Rules.

The appropriate procedure is set out in Part 28 of the Criminal Procedure Rules 2011. The relevant points are as follows:

28.2(1)  The court may issue or withdraw a witness summons . . . with or without a hearing.

(2)  A hearing under this part must be in private unless the court otherwise directs.

28.3(1)  A party who wants the court to issue a witness summons . . . must apply as soon as practicable after becoming aware of the grounds for doing so.

(2)  The party applying must:

(a)  identify the proposed witness;

(b)  explain:

(i)  what evidence the proposed witness can give;

(ii)  why it is likely to be material evidence; and

(iii)  why it would be in the interests of justice to issue a summons.

(3)  The application may be made orally unless:

. . .

(b)  the court otherwise directs.

10.3   Sometimes it would only be apparent at the trial itself that a witness has not attended and is unlikely to attend. The court has power of its own motion to issue a witness summons. This derives from CP(AW)A 1965, section 2D, which is as follows:

2D. For the purposes of any criminal proceedings before it, the Crown Court may of its own motion issue a summons (a witness summons) directed to a person and requiring him to:

(a)  attend before the court at the time and place stated in the summons; and

(b)  give evidence . . .

10.4   So far, we have dealt with the 'summons' procedure. We now move on to the 'arrest' scenario. This is provided for by section 4 of the Act:

4. – (1) If a judge of the . . . Crown Court is satisfied by evidence on oath that a witness in respect of whom a . . . witness summons is in force is unlikely to comply with . . . the summons, the judge may issue a warrant to arrest the witness and bring him before the court before which he is required to attend. Provided that a warrant shall not be issued under this sub-section . . . unless the judge is satisfied

by such evidence aforesaid that the witness is likely to be able to give . . . material evidence.[4]

The foregoing sub-section therefore deals with the situation where prior to trial it is known that a witness in respect of whom a witness summons has been issued is unlikely to comply with it. Section 4(2) deals with the situation where a person who is subject to a witness summons fails to attend the trial. It provides as follows:

> 4. . . . (2) Where a witness who is required to attend before the Crown Court by virtue of . . . a witness summons fails to attend in compliance with the summons, that court may:
>
> (a) in any case, cause to be served on him a notice requiring him to attend the court forthwith or at such time as may be specified in the order;
> (b) if the court is satisfied that there are reasonable grounds for believing that he has failed to attend without just cause, or if he has failed to comply with a notice under paragraph (a) above, issue a warrant to arrest him and bring him before the court.

In either of the arrest scenarios above, there is a power in the court to remand the person concerned in custody. This derives from section 4(3) of the Act, which provides:

> 4. . . . (3) A witness brought before the court in pursuance of a warrant under this section may be remanded by that court in custody or on bail until such time as the court may appoint for receiving his evidence or dealing with him under section 3.[5]

In *H v Wood Green Crown Court*,[6] the appellant (who had been arrested after non-compliance with a witness summons) turned hostile in the witness box. After he had finished giving his evidence, the judge remanded him in custody pursuant to section 4(3) on the basis that he might be required to answer further questions later in the trial. The legality of this step was one of the issues dealt with in the Divisional Court. Wilkie J said:

> 29. There is no dispute but that the judge lawfully remanded the claimant in custody overnight on more than one occasion during the course of his giving evidence . . . The power to remand continued for as long as it was anticipated that the claimant may be required to give evidence on subsequent days. It is a commonplace of the conduct of criminal trials that whenever a witness has given his evidence . . . the question arises whether that witness can be released from further attendance at court. In the vast majority of cases the witness is released but in some cases it may be that there is some outstanding issue . . . and accordingly he is told that he may be required to attend on that further occasion . . . In the very rare case such as the present, the court has power to remand a witness in custody pursuant to section 4(3). That power does not expire until such time as he is released from further attendance at court.

---

[4] The appropriate procedure is set out in Rule 28.3 of the Criminal Procedure Rules 2011 (SI 2011/1709), already set out at 10.2 above.
[5] For 'dealing with him under section 3' see at 10.5 below.
[6] [2006] EWHC 2683 (Admin).

When considering the issue of a warrant of arrest, it is important to bear in mind what was said by Hughes LJ in *Popat*:[7]

> 14. We should add that it is the common experience of judges sitting in the Crown Court that where a witness is reluctant and has failed to appear in response to a summons, very often the mere issue of a warrant for arrest is enough to achieve attendance. Knowing that, it is very common for Crown Court judges to give a direction at the time of issuing a warrant for arrest which is designed in the interests of the witness to avoid the witness having to be locked up overnight or perhaps for longer. We do not wish to discourage that humane exercise of the Crown Court jurisdiction but we do point out that, as this case demonstrates, a direction not to execute a warrant except at the Crown Court means that if the witness chooses not to come, the warrant can never be executed. Accordingly, a different form of humane direction is required. We have no doubt that there are several possibilities. One which is sometimes adopted is to direct that the police officers need not execute the warrant if satisfied that the witness is going to attend voluntarily, or need not execute it if the witness agrees to come with the officer. Another may in some circumstances be to issue a warrant backed for bail.

10.5   By CP(AW)A 1965, section 3, disobedience to a witness summons is punishable as a contempt of court. The section provides:

> 3. – (1) Any person who, without just excuse, disobeys a witness summons requiring him to attend before any court shall be guilty of contempt of that court and may be punished summarily by that court as if this contempt had been committed in the face of the court.
>
> (2) No person shall by reason of any disobedience mentioned in sub-section (1) above be liable to imprisonment for a period exceeding three months.

Such a contempt is to be treated seriously. In *Yusuf*,[8] Rose LJ said:

> 16. The role of the courts in seeking to protect the public . . . can only properly be performed if members of the public cooperate with the courts. That cooperation includes participation in the trial process . . . as a witness. Witnesses who may have important evidence to give must come to court if they are summoned . . . If they choose to ignore a summons, they are in contempt of court and can expect to be punished because their failure to attend is likely to disrupt the trial process and in some cases to undermine it entirely.

Normally, in order for the contempt to be proved, the summons must actually have been served. In *Wang*,[9] the Court of Appeal left open the question of whether section 3 bites when a witness knows that a summons is to be applied for and then deliberately evades service.

---

[7] [2008] EWCA Crim 1921. The case is also useful as a reminder of the difference between the summons and the warrant: the warrant is directed to the police officer, the summons is directed to the witness. The offence of contempt (see 10.5 below) is the disobedience to the summons rather than disobedience to the warrant – the warrant is issued as an aid to the power to punish for contempt for non-compliance with the warrant.

[8] [2003] 2 Crim App R 32. See also *Lennock* (1993) 97 Crim App R 228, where it was said that culpable forgetfulness could not amount to a 'just excuse' for not attending in response to a summons.

[9] [2005] EWCA Crim 476.

10.6   The witness who attends but who refuses to be sworn or give evidence after he has been sworn is likewise in contempt of court and liable to be dealt with as such. As in all contempt cases 'in the face of the court' a degree of care is required on the part of the judge. If the witness wants to give evidence to explain why he refuses or refused to testify at a trial, for example because of duress, he should be allowed to do so.[10] In *K*,[11] the appellant, who was a serving prisoner, refused to give evidence against a defendant who was also a serving prisoner. In committing him for contempt, the trial judge failed to offer him the opportunity of legal representation and prevented him from explaining why he was refusing to testify. Watkins LJ said that duress could be a defence to an allegation of contempt. He went on to say:

> The court is well aware of the difficulties confronting judges who from time to time are faced with an obdurate and stubborn person who refuses to give evidence . . . There are many ways of dealing with a situation of that kind. Sometimes . . . inaction . . . at other times, stern measures . . . What is always wise is that no action be taken in haste . . . The appellant was denied his basic right to defend himself . . . Moreover, it is of the highest importance that an appellant, before he is punished . . . is given the opportunity of seeking and taking legal advice, in other words of being represented.

Not only should a recalcitrant witness be given the opportunity of providing an explanation and of being represented, but also any hasty action by the judge is to be avoided. In *Philips*,[12] a witness was brought back at the end of the day, found to be in contempt and sent to prison for four months. Watkins LJ said:

> The judge was we think unnecessarily precipitous . . . in proceeding to deal with this appellant at the time he did. We think it advisable in circumstances of this kind to punish at the conclusion of the trial or, at the very soonest, at the end of the prosecution case. The witness who refuses to testify may have at his disposal evidence of great importance . . . or he may be one whose evidence adds little or nothing . . . Such a person . . . when his significance or otherwise could be properly assessed may be very likely punished or . . . his contempt disregarded altogether.

The proper approach to punishment in this type of case is set out in *Montgomery*[13] in the judgment of Potter J. He said:

> It is perhaps useful to set out the principles which emerge from the cases. First, an immediate custodial sentence is the only appropriate sentence to impose upon a person who interferes with the administration of justice . . . unless the circumstances are wholly exceptional . . . Second, whilst review of the authorities suggests that interference with or threats made to jurors are usually visited with higher sentences than in the case of a witness who refuses to give evidence, there is no rule or established practice to that effect, the circumstances of each case being all-important. Third, whilst it is legitimate in the case of a witness refusing to testify, to have regard to the fact that the maximum

---

[10]  *Lewis* (1993) 96 Crim App R 412.
[11]  (1984) 78 Crim App R 82.
[12]  (1984) 78 Crim App R 85, 93.
[13]  [1995] 2 Crim App R 23, 27, approved and applied in *Robinson* [2006] EWCA Crim 613.

sentence for failing to comply with a witness order is three months, that should not inhibit the court from imposing a sentence substantially longer than three months for a blatant contempt in the face of the court by a witness who has refused to testify, fully realising what he was refusing to do . . . Fourth, the principal matters affecting sentence are as follows:

(a) the gravity of the offence being tried;
(b) the effect upon the trial;
(c) the contemnor's reasons for failing to give evidence;
(d) whether or not the contempt is aggravated by impertinent defiance of the judge, rather than simple or stubborn refusal to answer;
(e) the scale of sentences in similar cases, albeit each case must turn on its own facts;
(f) the antecedents, personal circumstances and characteristics of the contemnor;
(g) whether or not a special deterrent is needed.

# 11

## Adjournments

11.1    This chapter will not deal with adjournments rendered necessary by amendments/severance of the indictment. These are governed by section 5 of the Indictments Act 1915 (as amended). The relevant authorities are *Smith*[1] and *Johal*.[2]

11.2    We are concerned with applications to adjourn fixed hearings either on the day of the hearing or shortly before. Most such applications will be because witnesses have not turned up or some hoped-for piece of evidence is not available. In dealing with such an application, the court, in the final analysis, is making a judgement. It was expressed thus by the President in *Clarke*,[3] in dealing with an interlocutory appeal by the Crown against a decision of the trial judge to refuse their application for an adjournment, the ruling effectively terminating the proceedings. He said:

> 29.    Time and again in this court emphasis has been laid on the simple proposition that case management decisions are made by trial judges, not by this court. Adjournments are sought and refused or granted on very many grounds: sometimes at the behest of the prosecution, sometimes the defence. Sometimes the decision is insignificant. At other times, as here, it is critical to the outcome of the case. But the decision is a decision for what is usually described as the discretion of the Judge, but in fact is a decision which reflects his or her judgement on an overall balance of all the material as it stands before him at the time when the decision has to be made.

11.3    The approach to such applications is set out in the authorities referred to in this paragraph. In *R v Hereford Magistrates*,[4] Bingham LCJ said:

> The decision whether to grant an adjournment does not depend on a mechanical exercise of comparing previous delays in other cases with the delay in the instant application. It is not possible nor desirable to identify hard and fast rules as to when adjournments should or should not be granted. The guiding principle must be that Justices should fully examine the circumstances leading to applications for delay, the reasons for those applications and the consequences both to the prosecution and the defence. Ultimately they must decide what is fair in the light of all those circumstances.

[1]  34 Crim App R 168.
[2]  (1972) 56 Crim App R 348.
[3]  [2007] EWCA Crim 2532.
[4]  [1997] 2 Crim App R 340, 353.

This court will only interfere with the exercise of the Justices' discretion whether to grant an adjournment in cases when it is plain that a refusal will cause substantial unfairness to one of the parties. Such unfairness may arise when a defendant is denied a full opportunity to present his case . . . Applications for adjournment must be subjected to rigorous scrutiny.

A full checklist is set out in the judgment of Jack J in *Picton*,[5] in a passage which has subsequently been approved in cases such as *Taylor*,[6] *Nadour*,[7] and *Visvaratnam*.[8] He said:

9.(a)  A decision whether to adjourn is a decision within the discretion of the trial court. An appellate court will interfere only if very clear grounds for doing so are shown.

(b)  Magistrates should pay great attention to the need for expedition in the prosecution of criminal proceedings; delays are scandalous; they bring the law into disrepute; summary justice should be speedy justice; an application for an adjournment should be rigorously scrutinised.

(c)  Where an adjournment is sought by the prosecution, Magistrates must consider both the interest of the defendant in getting the matter dealt with and the interest of the public that criminal charges should be adjudicated upon, and the guilty convicted as well as the innocent acquitted. With a more serious charge the public interest that there be a trial will carry greater weight.

(d)  Where an adjournment is sought by the accused, the Magistrates must consider whether, if it is not granted, he will be able fully to present his defence and, if he will not be able to do so, the degree to which his ability to do so is compromised.

(e)  In considering the competing interests of the parties, the Magistrates should examine the likely consequences of the proposed adjournment, in particular its likely length and the need to decide the facts whilst recollections are fresh.

(f)  The reason that the adjournment is required should be examined and, if it arises through the fault of the party asking for the adjournment, that is a factor against granting the adjournment, carrying weight according to the gravity of the fault. If that party was not at fault that may favour an adjournment. Likewise, if the party opposing the adjournment has been at fault, that will favour an adjournment.

(g)  The Magistrates should take appropriate account of the history of the case and whether there have been earlier adjournments and at whose request and why.

(h)  Lastly of course, the factors to be considered cannot be comprehensively stated but depend upon the particular circumstances of each case and they will often overlap. The court's duty is to do justice between the parties in the circumstances as they have arisen.

11.4    Although cases are 'fact-specific', a number of authorities do illustrate how the concept of 'fault' operates in this context. In *R v Bradford Justices*,[9] crucial defence witnesses had failed to turn up on two occasions. The Justices refused to issue warrants, the case went ahead and the defendant was convicted. Mann LJ said:

[5]  [2006] EWHC 1108 (Admin).
[6]  [2008] EWHC 3006 (Admin).
[7]  [2009] EWHC 1505 (Admin).
[8]  [2009] EWHC 3017 (Admin).
[9]  (1990) 91 Crim App R 390, 392.

The Justices have a duty to hear a case which a defendant wishes to advance. These witnesses were plainly material . . . Whether they would have been adequate witnesses or cogent witnesses, I do not know, but it appears to me that the power to grant a witness warrant is one which ought to be exercised when evidence is crucial.

It might be thought that in this case the defendants were slightly lucky since after the non-attendance on the first occasion an application might have been made then for the witness summons.

In *R v Ealing Justices*,[10] after defence witnesses had failed to turn up, the Justices refused an adjournment because they felt that the defendant should have taken steps prior to the hearing to obtain witness summonses for their attendance. Quashing the conviction, the Divisional Court held that when witnesses were persons who were apparently willing to attend voluntarily, the fact that the defence had failed to apply for a summons was irrelevant. The Justices should not have focused upon the perceived irresponsibility of the witness but on the question of whether, on the material before them, there was proper room for the conclusion that the applicant was himself the author of the difficulties in question. The fundamental point was whether, in all the circumstances of the case, including the legitimate interests of the prosecution and the court, it was fair to continue the hearing. The overriding consideration had to be the fairness of the proceedings.

In *North East Hertfordshire Justices*,[11] the Justices had refused to grant a prosecution application for an adjournment where a witness, who was clearly a willing witness, had been unable to attend the hearing because of heavy snow. This decision was quashed in strong terms. Cook J said:

27. In my judgement, the Justices' decision can fairly be characterised as irrational and perverse. Whilst I have every sympathy with the desire of Magistrates to ensure that cases come on quickly . . . the fundamental issue with which any court must grapple when an adjournment is sought is the question of justice for all those involved. It is clear . . . that the prosecution should not be shut out as a form of punishment for the inefficiency of the CPS let alone the supposed default of a witness.

28. In this case the CPS were not at fault and nor was the witness . . . Whilst the interests of the defendant must always be borne in mind, including his legitimate expectation to be dealt with promptly, a proper balance must be struck between the interests of the parties and the general public interest in prosecuting and convicting offenders.

In *Lappin v HM Customs*,[12] the need for the adjournment arose entirely as a result of the defendant's own persistent failure to comply with the timetable laid down by the court in respect of the obtaining of expert evidence. Dismissing his application to quash, based on the refusal of an adjournment, Gouldring J said:

23. I of course accept that the appellant was entitled to a fair trial in the determination of his civil rights and obligations. Whether he received one depends on all the circumstances of the case. In assessing those circumstances, a court is entitled to take into

[10] [1999] Crim LR 840.
[11] [2008] EWHC 103 (Admin).
[12] [2004] EWHC 953 (Admin).

account the desirability of his having an expert report, but the reasons for his failure to do so at the time of trial. If the reality is that he did not have such a report because of his persistent failure to obtain one over a period of time, it cannot be said that the resulting trial was unfair and in breach of his Article 6 rights.

24. In my view, the reason for the absence of the report was the appellant's persistent failure to obtain one. It cannot be said in the light of that failure, that the action of the Crown Court in insisting on the hearing going ahead was in any sense disproportionate or unfair.

In *Visvaratnam*,[13] the non-attendance of a doctor who was a vital prosecution witness was due to the fault of either the police or the CPS or a combination of both. The only other witness, a forensic scientist, had told the CPS well in advance of the trial date that he would not be available – nothing had been done about this. It follows that on the day fixed for trial, the prosecutor turned up without any witnesses. The defence were ready. The prosecutor asked for and obtained an adjournment. The Divisional Court quashed their decision and ordered the acquittal of the defendant. Openshaw J said:

14. In considering the competing interests of the parties, Magistrates should examine the likely consequences of the proposed adjournment and its likely length . . . The reason that the adjournment is required should be examined and if it arises through the fault of the party seeking the adjournment, that is a factor against granting the adjournment, carrying weight in accordance with the gravity of the fault. . . .

19. So these are the competing considerations. I have no doubt there is a high public interest in trials taking place on the date for trial and that trials should not be adjourned unless there is good and compelling reason to do so. The sooner the prosecution understand this, that they cannot rely on their own serious failures to warn witnesses, the sooner the efficiency in the Magistrates' Court system will improve. An improvement in timeliness and the achievement of a more effective and efficient system of criminal justice in the Magistrates' Court will bring about great benefits to victims and to witnesses and huge savings in time and money.

11.5    Any application to adjourn in the circumstances dealt with in this chapter has to be subjected to 'rigorous scrutiny'.[14] Where the application is based on the absence of what is said to be an important witness, the court is entitled to enquire as to the nature of the evidence that the witness may be able to give. In *R v Bracknell Justices*,[15] the Divisional Court said that if the legal representative does not himself volunteer sufficient information about the nature of the proposed evidence, then the court itself should ascertain what sort of support to the defence case that absent witness could give.

11.6    It is worth considering separately the position that arises when a manipulative defendant recognises that the case is going badly for him and seeks to bring

[13] See n 8 above.
[14] *Belogun v DPP* [2010] EWHC 799 (Admin) and *Hereford Magistrates*, see n 4 above.
[15] [1990] Crim LR 266.

about a situation whereby the existing trial has to be aborted and a new trial held. Such a situation can arise when the defendant, for no objectively good reason, sacks his existing team or so changes his instructions that his existing team feel obliged to withdraw. This was the position in *Ulcay*.[16] Having brought about a situation where those then representing him felt obliged to withdraw, the Judge granted a short adjournment to enable fresh lawyers to take over. To (over)simplify a complicated situation, the second set of lawyers requested a further two weeks' adjournment which the trial judge refused, because to grant it would have the effect of completely derailing the trial. Upholding the decision of the trial Judge not to grant that adjournment, the President said:

> 24. It is, however, equally elementary that the processes designed to ensure the fairness of his trial cannot be manipulated or abused by the defendant as to derail it and a trial is not to be stigmatised as unfair when the defendant seeking to derail it is prevented from doing so by robust judicial control. Such a defendant must face the self-inflicted consequences of his actions. . . .

> 36. In all these circumstances, the Judge was entitled to exercise his discretion to refuse the lengthy adjournment sought by Counsel . . . A lengthy adjournment would have produced either an inordinate delay in the trial of all the defendants, in which case the jury would have been discharged and a new trial started again at huge public inconvenience and cost, and possibly prejudice to the remaining defendants as well as the prosecution, or alternatively,. that which the appellant was seeking, for the trial of the remaining defendants to continue with the jury discharged from giving a verdict in his case and the subsequent trial of the appellant on his own. That would have been contrary to the interests of justice overall. The fact that the Judge was prepared to transfer the legal aid certificate does not mean that he was saying that, whatever the consequences to the trial, new representatives must be obtained and that thereafter he would conduct the trial in accordance with whatever applications were made by new counsel.

[16] [2007] EWCA Crim 2379.

# 12

## Trial in the Absence of the Defendant

12.1   This chapter is concerned with the situation which arises when a defendant absents himself from his trial, either at the outset or during its course. Sometimes the absence will be for good reason such as illness; at other times it may be because the defendant has decided simply to abscond or not show up.

12.2   In *Jones*,[1] Lord Bingham said:

> 16. For very many years the law of England and Wales has recognised the right of a defendant to attend his trial and, in trials on indictment, has imposed an obligation upon him so to do . . . But, for many years, problems have arisen in cases where, although the defendant is present at the beginning of the trial, it cannot be continued to the end in his presence. This may be because of genuine but intermittent illness of the defendant . . . or misbehaviour . . . or because the defendant has voluntarily absconded. In all these cases the court has been recognised as having a discretion . . . whether to continue the trial or to order that the jury be discharged . . . The existence of such a discretion is well established but it is of course a discretion to be exercised with great caution and with close regard to the overall fairness of the proceedings: a defendant affected by involuntary illness or incapacity would have much stronger grounds for resisting the continuance of the trial over one who has voluntarily chosen to abscond.

He went on to say:

> 10. and 11. In turning to general principle, I find it hard to discern any principle distinction between continuing a trial in the absence, for whatever reason, of a defendant and beginning a trial which is not in law commenced . . . One who voluntarily chooses not to exercise a right cannot be heard to complain that he has lost the benefits which he might have expected to enjoy had he exercised it . . . If he voluntarily chooses not to exercise his right to appear, he cannot impugn the fairness of the trial on the ground that it followed a course different from that which it would have followed had he been present and represented.

12.3   It follows, therefore, that a discretion is vested in the trial judge to continue the trial or indeed start the trial in the absence of the defendant. In *Jones*, Lord Bingham said:

> 13. The discretion to commence a trial in the absence of a defendant should be exercised with the utmost care and caution. If the absence of the defendant is attributable to involuntary illness or incapacity, it would very rarely, if ever, be right to exercise the

[1] [2002] UKHL 5.

discretion in favour of commencing the trial, at any rate unless the defendant is represented and asks that the trial should begin.

Subject to two points referred to hereafter, he approved the checklist set out in the judgment of Rose LJ in the court below:[2]

22. In our judgement, in the light of the submissions which we have heard . . . the principles which should guide the English courts in relation to the trial of a defendant in his absence are these:

(1) A defendant has, in general, a right to be present at his trial and a right to be legally represented.

(2) These rights can be waived, separately or together, wholly or in part, by the defendant himself. They may be wholly waived if, knowing, or having the means of knowledge as to when and where his trial is to take place, he deliberately and voluntarily absents himself and/or withdraws instructions from those representing him. They may be waived in part if, being present and represented at the outset, the defendant, during the course of his trial, behaves in such a way as to obstruct the proper course of the proceedings and/or withdraws his instructions from those representing him.

(3) The trial judge has a discretion as to whether a trial should take place or continue in the absence of a defendant and/or his legal representatives.

(4) That discretion must be exercised with great care and it is only in rare and exceptional cases that it should be exercised in favour of a trial taking place or continuing, particularly if the defendant is unrepresented.

(5) In exercising that discretion, fairness to the defence is of prime importance, but fairness to the prosecution must also be taken into account. The Judge must have regard to all the circumstances of the case including in particular:

   (i) the nature and circumstances of the defendant's behaviour in absenting himself from the trial or disrupting it . . . and in particular, whether his behaviour was deliberate, voluntary and as such has plainly waived his right to appear;

   (ii) whether an adjournment might result in the defendant being called or attending voluntarily and/or not disrupting the proceedings;

   (iii) the likely length of such an adjournment;

   (iv) whether the defendant, though absent, is or wishes to be legally represented at the time or has, by his conduct, waived his right to representation;

   (v) whether an absent defendant's legal representatives are able to receive instructions from him during the trial and the extent to which they are able to present his defence;

   (vi) the extent of the disadvantage to the defendant in not being able to give his account of events, having regard to the nature of the evidence against him;

   (vii) the risk of the jury reaching an improper conclusion about the absence of the defendant;

   (viii) the seriousness of the offence, which affects the defendant, victims and public;

   (ix) the general public interest and the particular interest of victims and witnesses that a trial should take place within a reasonable time of the events to which it relates;

---

[2] *Hayward* [2001] EWCA Crim 168.

(x)   the effect of delay on the memories of witnesses;

(xi)   where there is more than one defendant, and not all have absconded, the undesirability of separate trials and the prospects of a fair trial for the defendants who are present.

(6) If the Judge decides that a trial should take place or continue in the absence of an unrepresented defendant, he must ensure that the trial is as fair as the circumstances permit. He must, in particular, take reasonable steps, both during the giving of evidence and in the summing up, to expose weaknesses in the prosecution case and to make such points on behalf of the defendant as the evidence permits. In his summing up he must warn the jury that absence is not an admission of guilt and adds nothing to the prosecution case.

The two reservations or modifications indicated by Lord Bingham in *Jones* were as follows:

14. and 15.  First I do not think the seriousness of the offence which affects defendants, victim and public listed in paragraph (viii), as a matter relevant to the exercise of the discretion, is a matter which should be considered . . . secondly it is generally desirable that a defendant be represented even if he has voluntarily absconded.

Reference should also be made to the consolidated Criminal Practice Direction, the relevant parts of which are as follows:

1.13.17  A defendant has a right, in general, to be present and to be represented at his trial. However, a defendant may choose not to exercise those rights by voluntarily absenting himself and failing to instruct his lawyer adequately so that they can represent him . . . in such circumstances, the court has a discretion whether the trial should take place in his/her absence.

1.13.18  The court must exercise its discretion to proceed in the absence of the defendant with the utmost care and caution. The overriding concern must be to ensure that such a trial is as fair as circumstances permit and leads to a just outcome.

1.13.19  Due regard should be had to the judgment of Lord Bingham in *R v Jones* in which Lord Bingham identified circumstances to be taken into account before proceeding, which include: the conduct of the defendant, the disadvantage to the defendant, public interest, the effect of any delay and whether the attendance of the defendant could be secured at a later hearing. Other relevant considerations are the seriousness of the offence and likely outcome if the defendant is found guilty. [Author's note: it is not clear to me how the last sentence is compatible with what Lord Bingham said in paragraphs 14 and 15 of *Jones*.]

A practical illustration as to when it is appropriate to conduct a trial in the absence of the defendant is provided by *Smith*.[3] For no good reason at all, the defendant had sacked his legal team. He was given ample opportunity to reinstruct them. At trial, he refused to come out of his cell. He was convicted by the jury. One of the grounds of appeal was that the Judge was wrong to allow the trial to proceed in the absence of the defendant, it having emerged subsequently that

[3]   [2006] EWCA Crim 2307.

the defendant was of low intelligence, albeit perfectly fit to plead. In dismissing the appeal, Hallett LJ said:

36. As far as the appellant's absence from trial was concerned, this was his choice. It was one over which the Judge had no control. The appellant had the right to be present at his trial, but despite repeated invitations to attend, he declined to exercise that right. In our judgement . . . he clearly and unequivocally waived his right to attend . . . He was offered numerous opportunities to change his mind, but adjournments failed to resolve the situation. Another adjournment was undesirable. It was clearly in the public interest and the interests of the prosecution witnesses for the trial to proceed as soon as possible . . . The Judge was entitled to bear in mind the effect upon the prosecution and their witnesses of yet another period of delay, at the end of which there could be no guarantee, given the appellant's behaviour to date, that he would cooperate . . .

42. It is of course an extreme case when a trial will proceed in the absence of an accused and when he is unrepresented. In our judgement, in this case, unless the Judge was to give in to the appellant's attempt at blackmailing the court, he had no option but to proceed as he did.

*Smith* was an illustration of when the court had bent over backwards to assist the defendant. But, the court should not be too hasty in allowing the trial to proceed in the absence of a recalcitrant defendant. In *Armrouchi*,[4] the appellant was in prison at the time of his trial. On the day of his trial, the prison reported that he was refusing to come out of his cell. The Judge refused an adjournment of 24 hours to see whether he was really refusing to attend and the trial went ahead in the defendant's absence. The Court of Appeal held that this was unfair. Hughes LJ said:

10. To proceed in the absence of a defendant is sometimes necessary. It is accepted in this case that one of the situations in which it is necessary . . . is when a defendant has deliberately absented himself. If the Trial Judge is sure (a) that the defendant has deliberately absented himself and (b) that there are no reasonable steps that can be taken to get him to court, then a trial in his absence is permitted by law. It is however a serious step to take . . . It is a step which ought normally to be taken only if it is unavoidable.

11. The practical consequences for a defendant who wishes to contest the allegation, whether for good, bad or indifferent reasons, are enormous. He cannot give evidence and he cannot even respond to changes or subtleties in the evidence as it comes out. The jury, however carefully directed, is at least at risk of concluding that if he is not attending it must be because he has no confidence in his case . . .

15. My universal experience is that in this kind of situation, the proper course is to adjourn for 24 hours and to ensure that an explicit warning is delivered to the defendant that his trial is going to take place without him if he is not there tomorrow . . . We would suggest that most Crown Court Judges would require written confirmation from the prison that the warning has been delivered and preferably in writing.

---

[4] [2007] EWCA Crim 3019. To similar effect is the decision in *Farrell* [2008] EWCA Crim 2748.

12.4   The observation of Lord Bingham in *Jones* to the effect that it is generally desirable that a defendant be represented even if he has voluntarily absconded, has the capacity to create some difficulty for the lawyers concerned. The full quotation is as follows:

> 15.  The task of representing at trial a defendant who is not present and who may well be out of touch, is of course rendered much more difficult and unsatisfactory and there is no possible ground for criticising the legal representatives who withdrew from representing at trial in this case. But the presence throughout the trial of legal representatives, in receipt of instructions from the client at some earlier stage and with no object other than to protect the interests of that client, does provide a valuable safeguard against the possibility of error and oversight. For this reason, Trial Judges routinely ask Counsel to continue to represent a defendant who has absconded during the trial and Counsel in practice accede to such an invitation and defend their absent client as best they properly can in these circumstances.

In *O'Hare*,[5] which involved the trial of an absent defendant, the Judge asked if his legal representatives were going to stay and counsel explained that they were not and both he and his instructing solicitor withdrew. The solicitor had taken advice from the Law Society and felt she had to withdraw because she was without instructions. Counsel withdrew because the solicitor had withdrawn and he likewise felt that he was without instructions and could not be of any use. In respect of that withdrawal, Thomas LJ said:

> 37.  In the light of these provisions [semble – The Rules of Professional Conduct] no possible criticism can be made of Counsel or of the solicitor withdrawing.

However, he went on to say:

> 34.  We must assume that these provisions have been carefully considered by the Bar Council and the Law Society in the light of the speeches in *Jones*. Although we do appreciate the difficulties that legal representatives are put in if a client absconds, we consider that in the light of paragraph 15 of the speech of Lord Bingham in *Jones* and the circumstances of this case, that the Law Society and the Bar Council should reconsider their rules of conduct. The attendance of legal representatives who have received instructions at an earlier stage provides . . . a valuable safeguard.

The Court of Appeal returned to this subject in *Ulcay*.[6] They heard submissions from the Bar Council and the Law Society (as to the position of lawyers who may be in professional difficulties or perceived difficulties). In fact, the case was not concerned with the position of lawyers who are faced with an absconding or absent client: it concerned the situation faced by lawyers who were instructed during the course of a trial, the defendant having sacked his previous team. The

---

[5]  [2006] EWCA Crim 471. If counsel does stay, he is entitled to ask questions of witnesses for the prosecution in as much detail as he wishes, based on his written instructions. A ruling which prevents counsel doing this renders nugatory the benefits of having counsel remain to represent the absent defendant, see *Kepple* [2007] EWCA Crim 1339.

[6]  [2007] EWCA Crim 2379.

new lawyers declined to act on the grounds that they had insufficient time to prepare. Their Lordships made clear that:

> 30. The court cannot oblige the lawyers to continue to act when he has made a professional judgement that he is obliged, for compelling reasons, to withdraw from the case.

But, so far as the newly instructed lawyers were concerned, the court felt that they had been wrong to decline to act. In his judgment, the President (as he then was) said:

> 41. In our judgement, the barrister faced with the problem which faced new Counsel in the present trial was professionally required ... 'to soldier on and do the best she could' ... And, perhaps we should add that in circumstances when Counsel is soldiering on, doing his or her best, an order for wasted costs, or a successful action for professional negligence against Counsel who has taken on this burdensome responsibility in such an awkward situation, could not realistically be in contemplation in the absence of some remarkable subsequent developments.

Dealing specifically with the position of a solicitor and the Law Society rules (and in particular Rule 2.01(b)) the President said:

> 44. In our judgement, the answer is that Rule 2.01 of the Law Society Rules is not directed to, and the solicitor is not prevented from acting nor required to cease to act where, an order of the court creates difficulties and makes it that much harder for him to discharge his professional obligation to his client. These difficulties arise because of the Judge's ruling, not the absence of appropriate resources or necessary competence. The ruling, however, is binding on him as it is on the barrister, and indeed everyone else involved in the conduct of the case. In the situation currently under consideration, the conduct of criminal litigation, the solicitor is an officer of the court. He has an obligation to the court to comply with its order and to do his best for his client in the light of those orders. We can see no reason why the professional position of the barrister and solicitor can or should be distinguished. Both owe a duty to the court. Both should comply with it. Both must soldier on. Neither is in breach of the rules of his profession nor acting improperly or negligently ...

An almost perfect example of how a judge should not behave when faced with an absent defendant and solicitor and counsel who felt they could not continue to act, is provided by *Boodhou*.[7] The defendant had indicated that he had no intention of attending the trial. The Judge made strong comments about solicitor and counsel remaining. Having considered their position and (pre-*Ulcay*) consulted their professional bodies, both said they were withdrawing. The Judge made a wasted costs order against the solicitor! Happily, this was quashed by the Court of Appeal who said that the Recorder was entirely wrong.

---

[7] [2007] EWCA Crim 14.

# 13

## Basis of Plea, *Newton* Hearings and *Goodyear* Indications

13.1    Where a defendant accepts that he is guilty of the offence charged but disputes some of the details in the prosecution case, he may put forward a basis of plea. The acceptability or otherwise of this basis by the court and the prosecution is or may be crucial to the sentencing decision and is likewise vital in the context of a *Goodyear* indication (see below).

13.2    In considering the basis of plea, the starting point is the decision of the Court of Appeal in *Underwood*.[1] Judge LJ gave general guidance about the procedure to be adopted when the defendant pleads guilty on a factual basis different from that which appears on the Crown's case or on a study of the papers. I can do no better than set out the following paragraphs from his judgment:

> 3.  The starting point has to be the defendant's instructions. His advocate will appreciate whether any significant facts about the prosecution evidence are disputed and the factual basis on which the defendant intends to plead guilty. If the resolution of the facts in dispute may matter to the sentencing decision, the responsibility for taking any initiative and alerting the prosecutor to the areas of dispute rests with the defence. The Crown should not be taken by surprise and if it is suddenly faced with a proposed basis of plea of guilty where important facts are disputed, it should, if necessary, take time for proper reflection and consultation to consider its position and the interests of justice. In any event, whatever view may be formed by the Crown on any proposed basis of plea, it is deemed to be conditional on the Judge's acceptance of it.
>
> 4.  The Crown may accept and agree the defendant's account of the disputed facts. If so, the agreement should be reduced into writing and signed by both advocates. It should then be made available to the Judge before the start of the Crown's opening and, if possible, before he is entitled to approve the acceptance of any plea or pleas. If, however, pleas have already been accepted and approved, then it should be available before the sentencing hearing begins. If the agreed basis of plea is not signed by the advocate for both sides, the Judge is entitled to ignore it: similarly, if the document is not legible. The Crown may reject the defendant's version. If so, the areas of dispute should be identified in writing and the document should focus the court's attention on the precise fact or facts which are in dispute.

---

[1]  [2004] EWCA Crim 2256.

5. The third and most difficult situation arises when the Crown may lack the evidence positively to dispute the defendant's account. In many cases an issue raised by the defence is outside the knowledge of the prosecution. The prosecution's position may well be that they had no evidence to contradict the defence assertion. This does not mean that the truth of matters outside their own knowledge should be agreed. In these circumstances, particularly if the facts relied upon by the defendant arise from his personal knowledge and depend on his own account of the fact, the Crown should not normally agree the defendant's account unless it is supported by other material. Neither the prosecution nor the Judge is bound to agree facts merely because . . . the prosecutor cannot 'gainsay' the defendant's account. Again, the court should be notified at the outset in writing of the points in issue and the Crown's responses.

6. . . . We emphasise that whether or not the basis of plea is 'agreed', the Judge is not bound by any such agreement and is entitled of his own motion to insist that any evidence relevant to the facts in dispute should be called before him . . . At the risk of stating the obvious, the Judge is responsible for the sentencing decision and he may therefore order a *Newton* hearing to ascertain the truth about disputed facts.

7. The prosecuting advocate should assist him by calling any appropriate evidence and testing the evidence advanced by the defence. The defence advocate should similarly call any relevant evidence and, in particular, where the issue arises from facts which are within the exclusive knowledge of the defendant and the defendant is willing to give evidence in support of his case, be prepared to call him. If he is not, and subject to any explanation which may be proffered, the Judge may draw such inferences he thinks fit from that fact.

8. The Judge must then make up his mind about the facts in dispute. He may of course reject evidence called by the prosecution. It is sometimes overlooked that he may equally reject assertions advanced by the defendant, or his witnesses, even if the Crown does not offer positive contradictory evidence. . . .

10. Again, by way of reminder, we must explain some of the limitations on the *Newton* hearing procedure:

> . . .

> (f) The Judge is entitled to decline to hear evidence about disputed facts if the case advanced on the defendant's behalf is, for good reason, to be regarded as absurd or obviously untenable. If so, however, he should explain why he has reached this conclusion.

13.3   The matter is also dealt with in amendment no 22 to the Consolidated Criminal Practice Direction.[2] Again, I simply set out the relevant provisions:

> IV.45.10 The prosecution may reach an agreement with the defendant as to the factual basis on which the defendant will plead guilty, often known as an 'agreed basis of plea'. It is always subject to the approval of the court, which will consider whether it is fair and in the interests of justice.

---

[2] May 2009.

IV.45.11 *R v Underwood* outlines the principles to be applied where the defendant admits that he or she is guilty, but disputes the basis of offending alleged by the prosecution:

(a) The prosecution may accept and agree the defendant's account of the disputed facts or reject it in its entirety. If the prosecution accepts the defendant's basis of plea, it must ensure that the basis of plea is factually accurate and enables the sentencing judge to impose a sentence appropriate to reflect the justice of the case.
(b) In resolving any disputed factual matters, the prosecution must consider its primary duty to the court and must not agree with or acquiesce in an agreement which contains material factual disputes.
(c) If the prosecution does accept the defendant's basis of plea, it must be reduced to writing, be signed by advocates for both sides, and made available to the Judge prior to the prosecution's opening.
(d) An agreed basis of plea that has been reached between the parties must not contain any matters which are in dispute.
(e) On occasion the prosecution may lack the evidence positively to dispute the defendant's account, for example where the defendant asserts a matter outside the knowledge of the prosecution. Simply because the prosecution does not have evidence to contradict the defendant's assertions does not mean those assertions should be agreed. In such a case, the prosecution should test the defendant's evidence and submissions by requesting a *Newton* hearing following the procedure set out in paragraph IV.45.13 below.
(f) If it is not possible for the parties to resolve a factual dispute when attempting to reach a plea agreement under this part, it is the responsibility of the prosecution to consider whether the matter should proceed to trial, or to invite the court to hold a *Newton* hearing as necessary.
(g) Subject to paragraph IV.45.12, where the prosecution has not invited the court to hold a *Newton* hearing, and where the factual dispute between the prosecution and the defence is likely to have a material impact on the sentence, if the defence does not invite the court to hold a *Newton* hearing, the court is entitled to reach its own conclusion of the facts on the evidence before it.

IV.45.12 *Underwood* emphasises that whether or not pleas have been 'agreed', the Judge is not bound by any such agreement and is entitled of his or her own motion to insist that any evidence relevant to the facts in dispute (or upon which the Judge requires further evidence for whatever reason) should be called. Any view formed by the prosecution on a proposed basis of plea is deemed to be conditional on the Judge's acceptance of the basis of plea.

IV.45.13 Where the defendant pleads guilty but disputes the basis of offending alleged by the prosecution, the following procedure should be followed:

(a) the defendant's basis of plea must be set out in writing, identifying what is in dispute;
(b) the court may invite the parties to make representations about whether the dispute is material to sentence; and
(c) if the court decides that it is a material dispute, the court will invite such further representations or evidence as it may require and decide the dispute in accordance with the principles set out in *Newton*.

IV.45.14 Where the disputed issue arises from facts which are within the exclusive knowledge of the defendant and the defendant is willing to give evidence in support of his case, the defence advocate should be prepared to call the defendant. If the defendant is not willing to testify, and subject to any explanation which may be given, the Judge may draw such inferences as appear appropriate. Paragraphs 6 to 10 of *Underwood* provide additional guidance regarding the *Newton* hearing procedure.

13.4    The mechanism for resolving disputed issues of fact relating to a basis of plea is the *Newton* hearing.[3] The appropriate procedure is set out in the quotations from *Underwood* above. The burden of proof still rests on the Crown. Save in the case of manifest absurdity, a finding adverse to a defendant should not be made without the hearing of evidence, with the defendant having the opportunity to challenge that evidence and make appropriate submissions.

13.5    In the real world, many defendants simply want to know what their likely sentence will be in the event of their pleading guilty. The position of such a defendant, and indeed the position of the judge who may be asked for an indication of sentence, is now governed by the case of *Goodyear*.[4] There is no purpose in attempting to summarise the case; accordingly there is set out below extensive extracts from the judgment of Judge LJ. These passages spell out what the approach should be:

> 30. The starting point is fundamental. The defendant is personally and exclusively responsible for his plea. When he enters it, it must be entered voluntarily, without improper pressure. There is to be no bargaining with or by the Judge. . . .

> 49. In our judgement there is a significant distinction between a sentence indication given to a defendant who has deliberately chosen to seek it from the Judge, and an unsolicited indication directed at him from the Judge and conveyed to him by his Counsel. We do not see why a judicial response to a request for information from the defendant should automatically be deemed to constitute improper pressure on him. The Judge is simply acceding to the defendant's wish to be fully informed before making his decision . . .

> 51. We have further reflected whether there should continue to be an absolute prohibition against the Judge making any observations at all which may trigger this process. The Judge is expected to check whether the defendant has been advised about the advantages which would follow an early guilty plea. Equally, he is required to ascertain whether appropriate steps have been taken by both sides to enable the case to be disposed of without a trial . . . We do not believe it would be logical, and it would run contrary to the modern views of the Judge's obligations to manage the case from the outset, to maintain as a matter of absolute prohibition that the Judge is always and invariably precluded from reminding Counsel in open court, in the presence of the defendant, of the defendant's right to seek an advance indication of sentence . . . If, notwithstanding any observation by the Judge, the defendant does not seek an indica-

---

[3] *Newton* (1983) 77 Crim App R 13: 'The second method which could be adopted by the Judge in the circumstances is himself to hear the evidence on one side and another and come to his own conclusion, acting so to speak as his own jury on the issue which is the root of the problem'.
[4] [2005] EWCA Crim 888.

tion of sentence, then . . . it would not be appropriate for the Judge to give or insist on giving an indication of sentence, unless in any event he would be prepared to give the indication permitted by *Turner* (1970) 54 Crim App R 72 that the sentence will or will not take a particular form. . . .

54. In our judgement, any advance indication of sentence to be given by the Judge should normally be confined to the maximum sentence if a plea of guilty were tendered at the stage at which the indication is sought.

55. The Judge should not give an advance indication of sentence unless one has been sought by the defendant.

56. He remains entitled . . . to exercise the power recognised in *Turner* to indicate that the sentence, or type of sentence, on the defendant would be the same whether the case proceeded as a plea of guilty or went to trial with a resulting conviction . . . He is also entitled in an appropriate case to remind the defence advocate that the defendant is entitled to seek an advance indication of sentence.

57. In whatever circumstances an advance indication of sentence is sought, the Judge retains an unfettered discretion to refuse to give one. . . .

61. Once an indication has been given, it is binding and remains binding on the Judge who has given it and it also binds any other Judge who becomes responsible for the case. In principle, the Judge who has given an indication should, when possible, deal with the case immediately, and if that is not possible, any subsequent hearing should be listed before him . . . If, after a reasonable opportunity to consider his position in the light of the indication, the defendant does not plead guilty, the indication will cease to have effect.

62. . . . an indication should not be sought on a basis of hypothetical facts. When appropriate, there must be an agreed written basis of plea. Unless there is, the Judge should refuse to give an indication. . . .

64. Whether or not the Judge has given an appropriate reminder, the defence advocate should not seek an indication without written authority, signed by his client, that he, the client, wishes to seek an indication.

65. The advocate is personally responsible for ensuring that his client fully appreciates that: . . .

> (b) any sentence indication given by the Judge remains subject to the entitlement of the Attorney General to refer an unduly lenient sentence to the Court of Appeal;
> (c) any indication given by the Judge reflects the situation at the time when it is given and if a guilty plea is not tendered in the light of that indication, the indication ceases to have effect.

66. An indication should not be sought while there is any uncertainty between the prosecution and the defence about an acceptable plea . . . or any factual basis relating to that plea. Any agreed basis should be reduced into writing before an indication is sought. . . .

74. The Judge is most unlikely to be able to give an indication . . . in complicated or difficult cases, unless issues between the prosecution and the defence have been

addressed and resolved. Therefore in such cases, no less than seven days' notice in writing of an intention to seek an indication should normally be given . . . to the prosecution and to the court. If an application has been made without notice when it should have been given, the Judge may conclude that any inevitable adjournment should have been avoided and that the discount for the guilty plea should be reduced accordingly. It may be that in due course the Criminal Procedure Rules Committee will wish to consider the question of notice, and its length.

75.  The hearing should normally take place in open court with a full recording of the entire proceedings, and both sides represented, in the defendant's presence.

The matter is also dealt with in amendment no 22 to the Consolidated Criminal Practice Direction. The relevant parts read as follows:

IV.45.29 Prior to pleading guilty by any of the above routes, it is open to a defendant in the Crown Court to request from the Judge an indication of the maximum sentence likely to be imposed if a guilty plea is tendered at that stage in the proceedings, in accordance with the guidance in *Goodyear*.

IV.45.30 Attention is drawn to the guidance set out in paragraph 53 and following of *Goodyear*. During the sentence indication process and during the actual sentencing hearing, the prosecution advocate is expected to assist the court in sentencing by providing, where appropriate, references to the relevant statutory powers of the court, relevant sentencing guidelines and authorities and such assistance as the court is likely to require.

IV.45.31 Whether to give such an indication is a matter for the discretion of the Judge, to be exercised in accordance with the principles outlined by the Court of Appeal in *Goodyear*. Such indication should normally not be given if there is a dispute as to the basis of plea unless the Judge concludes that he or she can properly deal with the case without the need for a *Newton* hearing. In cases where a dispute arises, the procedure in *Underwood* should be followed prior to the court considering a sentencing indication further . . . Following an indication of sentence, if a defendant does not plead guilty, the indication will not bind the court.

IV.45.32 Attention is drawn to paragraph 70(d) of *Goodyear* which emphasises that the prosecution 'should not say anything which may create the impression that the sentence indication has the support or approval of the Crown'. This prohibition against the Crown indicating its approval of a particular sentence applies in all circumstances when a defendant is being sentenced.

IV.45.33 A *Goodyear* indication should be given in open court in the presence of the defendant but any reference to the hearing is not admissible in any subsequent trial; and reporting restrictions should normally be imposed.

13.6  Most of the problems that have arisen in respect of *Goodyear* indications have done so in the context of the public protection provisions of the Criminal Justice Act 2003. In *AG's Reference no 112 of 2006*,[5] the defendant pleaded guilty on the day of trial to an offence of wounding with intent, a specified serious

[5] [2006] EWCA Crim 2396.

violence offence. He did so after the Judge had given a *Goodyear* indication that the sentence would be three years' imprisonment. The defendant had previous convictions for specified offences. Quashing the sentence and imposing a sentence of imprisonment for public protection, Hughes LJ said:

> 8. There is no sign, either at the stage when he was asked to give a *Goodyear* indication or when he came to sentence, that the Judge considered the question of significant risk of serious harm and the various statutory steps which are required by section 224 and following of the Criminal Justice Act 2003. There is no sign . . . that the Judge ever addressed the question of whether or not this was an offence which required the passing of a sentence of imprisonment for public protection . . . He was obliged by statute to consider those provisions.

An authority to the contrary, *McDonald,*[6] must now be regarded as wrong. In *Seddon,*[7] the Judge had given an indication as to the notional determinate sentence that he would pass but had made it plain that he could not rule out the possibility of an indeterminate sentence until he had seen the appropriate reports. When the matter came back before him, the reports clearly raised the question of dangerousness so far as the defendant was concerned. The Judge passed a sentence of imprisonment for public protection. New counsel on both sides thought that the Judge had previously indicated a maximum sentence of four years, though no one had the transcript at that stage. Repeating what had been said in *Kulah,*[8] Hughes LJ said:

> 12. If the Judge decides to give an indication when an assessment of future risk remains to be made, he should make the following matters clear:
>
> (a) The offence . . . is a specified offence.
> (b) The information and materials necessary to undertake the assessment of future risk which is required by those provisions are not available and that that assessment remains to be concluded.
> (c) If the defendant is later assessed as dangerous the sentence mandated by the provisions . . . will be imposed.
> (d) If the defendant is not later assessed as dangerous, the indication relates in the ordinary way to the maximum determinate sentence which will be imposed.
> (e) If the offender is later assessed as dangerous, the indication can only relate to the notional determinate term which will be used in the calculation of the minimum specified period the offender would have to serve before he may apply to the Parole Board to direct his release . . .
>
> But if . . . the assessment of dangerousness falls to be dealt with at the second hearing, the Judge at that hearing cannot shirk it. If the evidence should drive him to the conclusion that the dangerousness condition is met, the mandatory sentence . . . must be passed notwithstanding any previous indication. The indication, in short, cannot relieve the Judge of the statutory obligation to pass the indefinite or extended sentence if the statutory conditions for doing so are met.

[6] [2007] EWCA Crim 1117.
[7] [2007] EWCA Crim 3022.
[8] [2007] EWCA Crim 1701.

The most recent authority is *Newman*.[9] In January 2010, the Judge gave a *Goodyear* indication suggesting that the maximum sentence would be one of three years' imprisonment. The matter came back before the Judge in March 2010 and he explained that he had made a mistake in giving that indication, particularly now that he had seen a pre-sentence report which raised a number of matters highly pertinent to the matter of dangerousness for the purposes of sentencing and the Criminal Justice Act 2003. He expressed a revised view. He told counsel that he would give leave to the defendant to vacate his plea if he so desired. Although 'disappointed', the defendant said he was prepared to be sentenced and the Judge duly passed a sentence more severe than that indicated in January. The Court of Appeal dismissed the appeal. Gross J said:

18. Counsel submitted . . . that the indication was binding once acted upon. With respect, we are unable to agree . . . His submission is couched in terms of private rights, where such concepts are valid and will prevail. But we are not dealing with that situation here. The public interest in an appropriate sentence must trump any question of disappointment in the rare cases where such a situation might arise. It goes without saying however . . . that revisions to *Goodyear* indications should be very much the exception and, as it seems to us, they can only be made in a manner which is fair to the defendant: in other words, where the matter can be revised without the defendant sustaining any prejudice other than mere disappointment.

19. In the present case, the Judge was plainly in error, as he himself acknowledged, with regard to the guidelines category in which he placed the offence. The Judge was understandably anxious about the facts he had subsequently discovered in the pre-sentence report and the questions which then arose as to whether the case merited a determinate or some other sentence. Had the Judge left the matter as set out in the *Goodyear* indication, first there would have been the unfortunate consequence of an inadequate sentence being passed contrary to the public interest and, secondly, there would have been a risk of an Attorney General's reference to the benefit of no one.

20. The course the Judge adopted, namely offering the appellant the chance of vacating his plea, was one which was entirely fair to the appellant. The appellant realistically and prudently chose not to vacate his plea but he maintained his plea knowing full well that the Judge would no longer be bound by the initial *Goodyear* indication. In these circumstances, we are not persuaded that any injustice resulted or that the appellant now has any legitimate grounds of complaint.

13.7    It is important to remember that an indication is only binding for the time at which it is given. This is clearly set out in *Patel*.[10] In that case, Hughes LJ said:

20. The import of *Goodyear* is very clear. If the Judge accedes to an application to give an indication, he and any other Judge is bound by it but only if the defendant thereupon pleads guilty. If there is any doubt about that, it needs to be laid to rest.

[9] [2010] EWCA Crim 1566.
[10] [2009] EWCA Crim 67.

He went on to say that this was so even where, in calculating the appropriate *Goodyear* sentence, the judge had expressed himself in terms of what the likely sentence would be after trial. He said:

21. We wish to make it clear that *Goodyear* means what it says. If the indication is not accepted by pleading guilty, it lapses and is thereafter irrelevant. In particular, the reasons why a Judge may subsequently perfectly properly form the view that his hypothetical thoughts at the time of the indication about sentence after trial were too low, certainly include the case where the evidence has worsened for the defendant, but also extend to the case where the Judge has simply had time to apply his mind with greater care and having heard the evidence to the proper balance of sentence between defendants.

# 14

## Changing a Plea of Guilty

14.1   The procedure to be followed when a defendant wishes to change a previously entered guilty plea to one of not guilty is now set out in the Criminal Procedure Rules 2011 (SI 2011/1709). Rule 39.3 provides as follows:

> 39.3(1) The defendant must apply as soon as practicable after becoming aware of the grounds for making an application to change a plea of guilty, and may only do so before the final disposal of the case, by sentence or otherwise.
>
> (2) Unless the court otherwise directs, the application must be in writing and it must:
>
> (a) set out the reasons why it would be unjust for the guilty plea to remain unchanged;
>
> (b) indicate what, if any, evidence the defendant wishes to call;
>
> (c) identify any proposed witness; and
>
> (d) indicate whether legal professional privilege is waived, specifying any material name and date.
>
> (3) The defendant must serve the written application on:
>
> (a) the Court Officer; and
>
> (b) the prosecutor.

14.2   In *S v Recorder of Manchester*,[1] Lord Reid said (at 448):

> It has long been the law that when a man pleads guilty to an indictment, the trial Judge can permit him to change his plea to not guilty at any time before the case is finally disposed of by sentence or otherwise.

He went on to say (at 449):

> It is always for the court's discretion whether to allow the accused to change his plea.

Accordingly, the principle is relatively easy to state. The judge has a discretion to allow a defendant to withdraw his plea of guilty at any time prior to sentence.

14.3   The difficulty arises in defining the nature and extent of the discretion and how it should be exercised. It seems fairly clear that normally it should be exercised against allowing the change of plea. In *Drew*,[2] Lord Lane said (at 199):

---

[1]   [1971] AC 481.
[2]   (1985) 81 Crim App R 190.

In our judgement only rarely would it be appropriate for the trial Judge to exercise his undoubted discretion in favour of an accused person wishing to change an unequivocal plea of guilty to one of not guilty. Particularly, this is so in cases where, as here, the accused has throughout been advised by experienced Counsel and when after full consultation with his Counsel he has already changed his plea to one of guilty at an earlier stage of the proceedings.

In *Sayed*,[3] Scott Baker LJ said:

32. The Judge has a discretion, but it is only in very rare cases that it would be right for that discretion to be exercised in favour of an accused who has been appropriately and competently advised and allow him to change an unequivocal plea of guilty to not guilty.

The fundamental question appears to be whether the judge hearing the application is satisfied that the plea represented a genuine acknowledgement of guilt. In *Sheikh*,[4] Mantell LJ said:

16. It is well accepted that quite apart from cases where the plea of guilty is equivocal or ambiguous, the court retains a residual discretion to allow the withdrawal of a guilty plea when not to do so might work an injustice. Examples might be when a defendant has been misinformed about the nature of the charge or the availability of a defence, or where he has been put under pressure to plead guilty in circumstances where he is not truly admitting guilt. It is not possible to attempt a comprehensive catalogue of the circumstances in which the discretion might be exercised. Commonly however, it is reserved for cases where there is doubt that the plea represents a genuine acknowledgement of guilt.

*Surhaindo*[5] is an example of a plea entered on the basis of erroneous advice and where the Court of Appeal said that the Judge was wrong in not letting the defendant change it.

The latest word on the subject is to be found in the judgment of Lord Phillips in *Revitt v DPP*.[6] In that case, unrepresented defendants, having declined to seek legal advice, pleaded guilty to dangerous driving. After retiring to consider sentence but before announcing it, the Magistrates came back into court. The defendants now had a solicitor representing them. He applied to withdraw the guilty pleas on the basis that the defendants had not understood the charge. The Magistrates refused to allow a change of plea. The defendants were sentenced to imprisonment. Lord Phillips said:

17. If, after an unequivocal plea of guilty has been made, it becomes apparent that the defendant did not appreciate the elements of the offence to which he was pleading guilty, then it is likely to be appropriate to permit him to withdraw his plea . . . Such a situation should be rare, for it is unlikely to arise when the defendant is represented and, when he is not, it is the duty of the court to make sure that the nature of the offence is made clear to him before a plea of guilty is accepted.

[3] [2005] EWCA Crim 2386.
[4] [2004] EWCA Crim 492.
[5] [2006] EWCA Crim 1429.
[6] [2006] EWHC 2226 (Admin).

18. It may happen, and again this is likely to be rare, that the court hearing an application to withdraw a guilty plea will or should appreciate that the facts relied upon by the prosecutor do not add up to the offence charged. In such circumstances justice will normally demand that the defendant be permitted to withdraw his plea.

19. The onus lies on the party seeking to vacate a guilty plea to demonstrate that justice requires that this should be permitted.

# 15

## Submission of No Case to Answer

15.1   The approach of a judge faced with a submission at the close of the prosecution case that the defendant has 'no case to answer' is governed by what was said by Lord Lane in *Galbraith*.[1] He said:

(1) If there is no evidence that the crime alleged has been committed by the defendant, there is no difficulty – the Judge will stop the case.

(2) The difficulty arises where there is some evidence, but it is of a tenuous character, for example because of inherent weakness or vagueness or because it is inconsistent with other evidence.

   (a) Where the Judge concludes that the prosecution evidence, taken at its highest, is such that a jury properly directed could not properly convict on it, it is his duty, on a submission being made, to stop the case.

   (b) Where, however, the prosecution evidence is such that its strength or weakness depends on the view to be taken of a witness's reliability, or other matters which are generally speaking within the province of the jury and where on one possible view of the facts there is evidence on which the jury could properly come to the conclusion that the defendant is guilty, then the Judge should allow the matter to be tried by the jury.

In *Broadhead*,[2] Keene LJ said:

37.  One of the most overworked phrases used by defence advocates at trial when making a submission of no case is that derived from the decision in *Shippey* [1988] Crim LR 767 about not 'picking out all the plum and leaving the duff behind'. Overused it may be, but Turner J's celebrated words in that case embody a valid and important point . . . The Judge's task in considering such a submission at the end of the prosecution case is to assess the prosecution evidence as a whole. He has to take account of the weaknesses of the evidence as well as such strengths as there are. He needs to look at the evidence at that stage in the trial in the round therefore.

To like effect is the following paragraph from the judgment of Moses LJ in *Robson*.[3] That was a case involving historic allegations of physical abuse. He said:

6.  As this court has repeatedly emphasised, the dangers inherent in such cases require the Judge carefully to scrutinise the evidence himself in order to see whether it is safe to leave the case to the jury . . . This scrutiny requires the Judge to consider not only the

[1] (1981) 73 Crim App R 124, 127.
[2] [2006] EWCA Crim 1705.
[3] [2006] EWCA Crim 2754.

nature and quality of the evidence but also inconsistencies, either within the evidence of one witness or between a number of witnesses. It is not sufficient for a Judge merely to remark that inconsistencies are a matter for the jury. So they may be in many cases. But in cases where the complaints are of events many years ago, it is the responsibility of the Judge to consider whether the inconsistencies are such that no jury, even when properly directed as to the significance of such inconsistencies, could safely convict.

15.2    At one time it was thought that if counsel did not make a submission of no case that was open to him, no subsequent appeal could be brought based on that omission. The responsibility of the trial judge did not require or entitle him to interfere.[4] That position has changed. In *Brown,*[5] it was held that a judge has a responsibility not to allow a jury to consider evidence on which they could not safely convict. If, at the conclusion of the prosecution evidence, the trial judge was of the opinion that no reasonable jury, properly directed, could safely convict, he should raise the matter for discussion with counsel, even if no submission of no case has been made. If, having heard submissions, he was still of the same opinion, he should withdraw the case from the jury. This was confirmed in another case, also *Brown,*[6] where Longmore LJ said:

> No doubt, this is a power which should be very sparingly exercised and only if the Judge really is satisfied that no reasonable jury, properly directed, could on the evidence safely convict.

15.3    The submission should normally be made in the absence of the jury.[7] In *Crosdale,*[8] Lord Steyn said:

> The important point is that the jury cannot assist the Judge in his decision as to whether there is sufficient evidence for the Judge to place before the jury. That part of the proceedings is concluded by the Judge alone . . . There is no sensible reason why the jury should witness that part of the proceedings. On the contrary, there are substantial reasons why, in the interests of an effective and fair determination of the issue . . . the jury should be asked to retire. If the jury do not withdraw, there is a risk they will be influenced by what they hear . . . Irrespective of whether the defence ask the jury to withdraw or not, the Judge should invite the jury to withdraw during submissions that a defendant does not have a case to answer.

15.4    Subject only to what is set out hereafter, a judge has no power to rule on an application that there is no case to answer until the close of the prosecution case. This emerges very clearly from the judgment of the Court of Appeal in *N Limited.*[9] Having listened to extensive argument prior to the jury being sworn, the judge ruled that the defendant in a health and safety prosecution had no case to answer.

---

[4]  *Jewett* [1981] Crim LR 113.
[5]  [1998] Crim LR 196.
[6]  [2002] 1 Crim App R 5.
[7]  *Falconer-Attlee* (1974) 58 Crim App R 348.
[8]  [1995] 2 All ER 500, 507.
[9]  [2008] EWCA Crim 1223.

The prosecution appealed pursuant to section 58 of the Criminal Justice Act 2003. Allowing the appeal, Hughes LJ said:

26. There is sound reason for the jurisdiction to entertain a submission that there is no case to answer to be exercised at the close of the Crown case. It is then that it is known for certain what the evidence actually is. Until then, the most that can be known is what it is expected to be. In the present case, whilst it was known what the witness statement said, it could not be known exactly how the evidence would come out. Not every relevant question has necessarily (or even usually) been asked of witnesses at the stage of taking their statements . . . In any event, we do not see how there can be identified the 'exceptional' or 'rare' cases in which it is contended by these defendants that the Judge can exercise the discretionary power claimed, and the suggestion that it can only be undertaken on judicial initiative risks blurring the proper distinction between the function of the Crown and the Judge, and the Judge being seen to make decisions which are, at that stage, properly for the Crown.

An exception to this general rule is set out in paragraphs 27 and 28 of the judgment of Hughes LJ in *N*. He said:

27. That does not mean that it may not sometimes be appropriate and convenient for the parties to agree to ask the Judge to rule as a matter of law whether on agreed or admitted facts the offence charged is made out. A simple practical example is the situation where the end of the Crown case is nigh, subject only to outstanding evidence which it can be known will take a particular form, for example the police interviews. It may be administratively convenient for the parties to ask, or for the Judge to suggest, that an expected submission of no case be made then rather than half a day later . . . The key point is that the outstanding evidence is known for certain: it is admitted or agreed what it will be. Similarly, it may often happen that in advance of the calling of any evidence at all, the parties may agree that it would be helpful for the Judge to rule upon the question whether, on agreed or admitted or assumed facts, the offence charged would be made out. That may well be done with a view to the Crown accepting that it may offer no evidence if the ruling is against it, just as it may be done with a view to a defendant considering whether to plead guilty if the ruling is otherwise. The difference from the power here claimed is that the Judge is invited to proceed upon established or assumed and agreed facts, and has no power to compel acquittal until the end of the Crown evidence . . .

28. Nor do we in the least discourage beneficial active case management by the Judge which, in some cases, include judiciously expressed views designed to encourage, within proper limits, a course of action by one side or the other, just as it may include direction as to the manner in which evidence will be given. We have no doubt that it is open to the Judge, in a proper case, to suggest to the parties that he be invited to rule on agreed or admitted facts in the manner set out . . . Provided that the Judge is scrupulous to avoid descent into the arena and any claim to control either side's case, such case management is desirable and necessary in pursuit of the overriding objective set out in the Criminal Procedure Rules.

# 16

## Bad Character and Proof of Previous Convictions or Previous Misconduct

16.1 Bad character, for the purposes of sections 98 and 112 of the Criminal Justice Act (CJA) 2003, includes both the previous convictions of a defendant, a co-defendant or a witness and other instances of reprehensible behaviour on their part. So far as the bad character of a defendant is concerned, the evidence is only admissible if one or more of the provisions of section 101 of the Act are capable of being complied with. It should be noted that amongst those provisions is that the evidence 'has substantial probative value in relation to an important matter in issue between the defendant and a co-defendant'. In respect of persons other than a defendant (usually a witness) matters are governed by section 100 of the Act.

16.2 CJA 2003, section 111 is as follows:

111. – (1) Rules of court may make such provision as appear to the appropriate authority to be necessary or expedient for the purposes of this Act: and the appropriate authority is the authority entitled to make the rules.
(2) The rules may, and, where the party in question is the prosecution, must, contain provision requiring a party who –

(a) proposes to adduce evidence of a defendant's bad character, or
(b) proposes to cross-examine a witness with a view to eliciting such evidence,

to serve on the defendant such notice and such particulars of or relating to the evidence as may be prescribed.
(3) The rules may provide that the court or the defendant may, in such circumstances as may be prescribed, dispense with a requirement imposed by virtue of sub-section (2).
(4) In considering the exercise of its powers with respect to costs, the court may take into account any failure by a party to comply with a requirement imposed by virtue of sub-section (2) and not dispensed with by virtue of sub-section (3).[1]

The relevant rules are set out in Part 35 of the Criminal Procedure Rules 2011 (SI 2011/1709).

---

[1] This is the only sanction for non-compliance expressly set out in the CJA 2003.

Applications generally

35.2(1) A party who wants to introduce evidence of bad character must:

    (a) make an application under Rule 35.3, where it is evidence of a non-defendant's bad character;

    (b) give notice under Rule 35.4 where it is evidence of a defendant's bad character.

(2) An application or notice must:

    (a) set out the facts of the misconduct on which that party relies;

    (b) explain how that party will prove those facts (whether by certificate of conviction, other official record or other evidence) if another party disputes them; and

    (c) explain why the evidence is admissible.

Bad character of person other than the defendant

35.3(1) This rule applies where a party wants to introduce evidence of the bad character of a person other than the defendant.

(2) That party must serve an application to do so on:

    (a) the Court Officer; and

    (b) each other party.

(3) The applicant must serve the application:

    (a) as soon as reasonably practicable; and in any event

    (b) not more than 14 days after the prosecutor discloses material on which the application is based (if the prosecutor is not the applicant).

(4) A party who objects to the introduction of the evidence must:

    (a) serve notice on:

        (i) the Court Officer; and

        (ii) each other party

    not more than 14 days after service of the application; and

    (b) in the notice explain, as applicable:

        (i) which, if any, facts of the misconduct set out in the application that party disputes;

        (ii) what, if any, facts of the misconduct that party admits instead;

        (iii) why the evidence is not admissible; and

        (iv) any other objection to the application.

(5) . . .

Bad character of defendant

35.4(1) This rule applies where a party wants to introduce evidence of a defendant's bad character.

(2) That party must serve notice on:

    (a) the Court Officer; and

    (b) each other party.

(3) A prosecutor who wants to introduce such evidence must serve the notice not more than 14 days after the defendant pleads not guilty.

(4) A co-defendant who wants to introduce such evidence must serve the notice:

(a) as soon as reasonably practicable; and in any event

(b) not more than 14 days after the prosecutor discloses material on which the notice is based.

(5) A party who objects to the introduction of the evidence must:

(a) apply to the court to determine the objection;

(b) serve the application on:

(i) the Court Officer; and

(ii) each other party,

not more than 14 days after service of the notice; and

(c) in the application explain, as applicable:

(i) which, if any, facts of the misconduct set out in the notice that party disputes;

(ii) what, if any, facts of the misconduct that party admits instead;

(iii) why the evidence is not admissible;

(iv) why it would be unfair to admit the evidence; and

(v) any other objection to the notice.

(6) . . .

Court's power to vary

35.6(1) The court may:

(a) shorten or extend (even after it has expired) a time limit under this part;

(b) allow an application or notice to be in a different form to one set out in the Practice Direction or to be made or given orally;

(c) dispense with a requirement for notice to introduce evidence of a defendant's bad character.

(2) A party who wants an extension of time must:

(a) apply when serving the application or notice for which it is needed; and

(b) explain the delay.

# Summary of Time Limits

(1) Prosecution application to introduce the bad character of a defendant: not more than 14 days after the defendant pleads not guilty. This does not preclude the prosecution serving a notice prior to that time – any response in opposition not more than 14 days after service of the notice.

(2) Defendant application to introduce the bad character of a co-defendant: as soon as reasonably practicable and in any event not more than 14 days after the prosecution discloses material on which the notice is based – any response in opposition not more than 14 days after service of the application.

(3) Prosecution or defendant application to introduce the bad character of a witness or some other person: as soon as reasonably practicable and in any event, on a defendant application, not more than 14 days after the prosecutor discloses material on which the application is based – any response in opposition within 14 days of service of the application.

16.3    The 'dispensing power' in Rule 35.5 has been widely used. In *Robinson v Sutton Coldfield Magistrates*,[2] there had been abject failures by the prosecution to serve a bad character application within the time limits laid down. In spite of this, the Justices allowed the evidence of bad character to be given. Owen J made some general observations as to the proper approach of a court in those circumstances:

> 14. The first point to make is that time limits must be observed. The objective of the Criminal Procedure Rules . . . depends upon adherence to the timetable set out in the Rules. Secondly, Parliament has given the court a discretionary power to shorten a time limit or extend it even after it has expired. In the exercise of that discretion, the court will take account of all the relevant considerations, including the furtherance of the overriding objective. I am not persuaded that the discretion should be fettered in the manner for which the claimant contends, namely that time should only be extended in exceptional circumstances.

> 15.  In this case there were two principal material considerations: first the reason for the failure to comply with the rules. As to that, a party seeking an extension must plainly explain the reasons for its failure. Secondly, there was the question of whether the claimant's position was prejudiced by the failure.

> 16.  . . . Any application for an extension will be closely scrutinised by the court. A party seeking an extension cannot expect the indulgence of the court unless he clearly sets out the reasons why it is seeking the indulgence.

It would seem that in order for a defendant to succeed on appeal where he challenges the admissibility of bad character evidence which was admitted at trial and where notice periods had not been complied with or notices not properly served, he must show some special prejudice to him arising from the decision (assuming the evidence was otherwise admissible).

In *Culhane*,[3] on the first day of the trial the prosecution sought to introduce the previous convictions of both defendants. No notice had been given pursuant to Rule 35.4. Refusing leave to appeal on this ground, Rix LJ said:

> 25.  . . . Ultimately the question for the court is whether there could be any conceivable prejudice involved . . . The court has specific power under [Rule 35.6] . . . to waive the time limit or the giving of notice.

In *Chapman*,[4] having written a letter to the defence indicating that they were not going to make a bad character application, the Crown had a change of heart

---

[2] [2006] EWHC 307 (Admin).
[3] [2006] EWCA Crim 1053.
[4] [2006] EWCA Crim 2545.

shortly before trial. The Judge admitted the evidence and the defendant was convicted. In the Court of Appeal, Hooper LJ said:

> 20. Counsel was not able to point out to the trial Judge or to us any particular prejudice
> which was suffered by this appellant as a result of the late application.

16.4    Assuming prima facie admissibility and assuming no problem with proof,
the question arises as to when the judge should make a ruling on admissibility. In
*Gyima*,[5] Gage LJ said:

> 40. We can entirely understand the practical reason for inviting a Judge at the outset of
> a trial to rule whether a defendant's previous convictions are or are not admissible.
> There are plainly good reasons for this, for the purposes of the administration of justice
> where there is a prospect that, once the ruling to admit the conviction is made, the
> defendant will plead guilty. However, in our judgement, judges and practitioners
> should be astute to recognise that there may be cases where it is important to defer such
> a ruling until the whole of the evidence of the prosecution has been adduced. In such
> cases, where it appears that there may be weaknesses or potential weaknesses in the
> prosecution case, it is unwise to rule on the admission of previous convictions until the
> court is able to make a better assessment of the strength or weakness of the prosecution
> case.

16.5    In *Hanson*,[6] Rose LJ said:

> 17. . . . It follows from what we have already said that, in a conviction case, the Crown
> needs to decide, at the time of giving notice of the application, whether it proposes to
> rely simply upon the fact of conviction or also upon the circumstances of it. The former
> may be enough where the circumstances of the conviction are sufficiently apparent
> from its description to justify a finding that it can establish propensity . . . But where, as
> will often be the case, the Crown needs and proposes to rely on the circumstances of the
> previous conviction, those circumstances and the manner in which they are to be
> proved, must be set out in the application.

In *Lamaletie*,[7] Underhill J said:

> 14. Contrary to what appears to have been thought, there is no rule that full details are
> necessary in every case where the Crown seeks to rely on a previous conviction as estab-
> lishing propensity . . . We certainly accept that it is good practice for such details to be
> available in case they are required: but whether they are necessary in order for the jury
> fairly to assess their relevance to propensity will depend upon the facts of the particular
> case. In the present case it is at least strongly arguable that the jury could draw a relevant
> conclusion from the simple fact, without more, that the defendant had no fewer than
> six convictions for offences of violence over a period of as many years.

---

[5]  [2007] EWCA Crim 429.
[6]  [2005] EWCA Crim 824.
[7]  [2008] EWCA Crim 314.

16.6    If the party seeking to rely upon bad character evidence simply wishes to prove the fact of the conviction, but the conviction is not admitted, the starting point is section 73 of the Police and Criminal Evidence Act (PACE) 1984 (as amended by Coroners and Juries Act 2009, section 144 and Schedule 17). The amendment effectively equates convictions in EU countries with domestic convictions. The relevant parts are as follows:

> s.73 – (1) Where in any proceedings, the fact that a person has in the United Kingdom or any other member state been convicted . . . of an offence . . . is admissible in evidence, it may be proved by producing a certificate of conviction . . . relating to that offence and proving that the person named in the certificate . . . is the person whose conviction is to be proved.
>
> (2) For the purposes of this section, a certificate of conviction:
>
>> (a) shall, as regards a conviction . . . on indictment, consist of a certificate, signed by the proper officer of the court where the conviction . . . took place, giving the substance and effect . . . of the indictment and of the conviction . . . and a document purporting to be a duly signed certificate of conviction . . . under this section shall be taken to be such a certificate unless the contrary is proved, and
>>
>> . . .
>>
>> (c) shall, as regards a conviction . . . by a court in a member state (other than the United Kingdom) consist of a certificate, signed by a proper officer of the court where the conviction . . . took place, giving details of the offence, of the conviction . . . and of any sentence.
>
> . . .
>
> (4) The method of proving a conviction . . . authorised by this section shall be in addition to and not to the exclusion of any other authorised manner of proving a conviction.

PACE 1984, section 73 therefore deals with convictions both in the United Kingdom and within the European Union.

So far as 'foreign convictions' are concerned, there are also the provisions of section 7 of the Evidence Act 1851 which provides as follows:

> All judgments, decrees, orders and other judicial proceedings of any court of justice in any foreign state . . . may be proved in any court of justice . . . either by examined copies or by copies authenticated as hereinafter mentioned: that is to say . . . if the document sought to be proved be a judgment, decree, order, or other judicial proceedings of any foreign court . . . the authenticated copy to be admissible in evidence must purport either to be sealed with the seal of the foreign . . . court to which the original document belongs, or, in the event of such court having no seal, to be signed by the Judge.

The section continues:

> If any of the aforesaid authenticated copies shall purport to be sealed or signed as hereinbefore respectively directed, the same shall respectively be admitted in evidence in every case in which the original document could have been received in evidence without any proof of the seal where a seal is necessary, or of the signature.

16.7   In respect of any conviction, whether domestic or foreign, which it is sought to rely upon, it has to be proved that the relevant memorandum or certificate relates to the defendant before the court. In *Burns*,[8] the prosecution produced a memorandum of conviction relating to a person with the same name and the same date of birth as the defendant. The trial Judge ruled that the memorandum was sufficient to prove that the person identified therein was the defendant. The defendant did not give evidence, nor did he adduce any positive evidence that the memorandum did not relate to him. Giving judgment in the Court of Appeal, Rose LJ said that ultimately, whether it had been proved that the memorandum related to the defendant was a matter of fact for the jury. He said:

> 17. It cannot . . . be a matter of law as to what is capable of giving rise to prima facie evidence of identification in this context. Similarity in name and date of birth between a memorandum and a defendant may or may not amount to prima facie proof . . . Everything must depend upon the circumstances of the particular case.

In *Pattison v DPP*,[9] the appellant had been convicted by the Justices of driving whilst disqualified. He gave his name at the time of his arrest but in interview declined to say whether he was a disqualified driver. At the hearing, the prosecution produced a certificate of conviction to prove the previous disqualification and the defendant did not give or call any evidence. Referring to section 73, Newman J said:

> 12. It is clear that proof according to the provisions of section 73 involves two evidential stages: (i) the production of the certificate of conviction and (ii) proof to the criminal standard that the person to whom the certificate relates is the accused. As to (ii), the proof contemplated by the sub-section is not limited to particular defined methods of proof, for example, proof by an admission by or on behalf of the accused or by the evidence of fingerprints or by someone who was present in court at the time that the person was convicted and disqualified being present to give evidence. The evidential issue is at large: proof to the criminal standard will be required that the person to whom the certificate relates is the person there and then before the court.

He went on to say:

> 26: In my judgement the following principles can be distilled from the cases:
>
> (a) As with any other essential element of an offence, the prosecution must prove to the criminal standard that the person accused was a disqualified driver.
> (b) It can be proved by any admissible means such as an admission (even a non-formal one) by the accused that he was a disqualified driver.
> (c) If a certificate of conviction is relied upon pursuant to section 73, then it is an essential element of the prosecution case that the accused is proved to the criminal standard to be the person named in the certificate.
>
> . . .

---

[8] [2006] EWCA Crim 617.
[9] [2005] EWHC 2938 (Admin).

(e)  There is, however, no prescribed way that this must be proved. It can be proved by any admissible means.
(f)  An example of such means is a match between the personal details of the accused on the one hand and the personal detail recorded on the certificate of conviction.
(g)  Even in a case where the personal details such as the name of the accused are not uncommon, a match will be sufficient for a prima facie case.
(h)  In the absence of any evidence contradicting this prima facie case, the evidence will be sufficient for the court to convict.
(i)  The failure of the accused to give any contradictory evidence in rebuttal will be a matter to take into account.

A good practical illustration as to the manner of proving a foreign conviction (though the reasoning is applicable to a UK conviction as well) is provided by *Mauricia*.[10] The defendant disputed that a Dutch conviction related to him. The Crown called a liaison officer with the Rotterdam police. He produced certified certificates of judgment from the Netherlands which indicated that a man with the defendant's name, born on the day that the defendant was born, had been convicted of offences of dishonesty. He also produced fingerprint records relating to those convictions. The prosecution called further evidence showing that the fingerprints matched those of the defendant. In the Court of Appeal, Longmore LJ said:

> 33. The Crown still has to prove that the examined copies of the conviction relate to the defendant who is currently before the court . . . that can be proved by any admissible evidence in the ordinary way. It is just a matter of proving that the person mentioned in the certificate and the defendant in court are one and the same person. Evidence of fingerprints is easily the most sensible way in which to proceed and there is nothing in the Evidence Act 1851 to suggest that proceedings by way of fingerprint evidence is in any way inadmissible.

In *Kordasinski*,[11] the letter of request procedure pursuant to sections 7 and 8 of the Crime (International Cooperation) Act 2003 had been utilised to obtain details of the Polish convictions of the defendant. These convictions were then provable against the defendant by virtue of section 7 of the Evidence Act 1851 and became admissible pursuant to the provisions of CJA 2003, section 101.

16.8  Sometimes, mere proof of the fact of a previous conviction will not be sufficient. As Rose LJ said in *Hanson* (above):

> 17. But when, as will often be the case, the Crown needs and proposes to rely on the circumstances of the previous conviction, those circumstances and the manner in which they are to be proved must be set out in the application . . . We would expect the relevant circumstances of previous convictions generally to be capable of agreement and that . . . they will be put before the jury by way of admission. Even when the circumstances are genuinely in dispute, we would expect the minimum indisputable facts

[10]  [2002] EWCA Crim 678.
[11]  [2006] EWCA Crim 2981.

to be thus admitted. It will be very rare indeed for it to be necessary for the Judge to hear evidence before ruling on admissibility under the Act.

If one dare say this in the context of any ruling by Rose LJ, it may be that he slightly under-estimated the obduracy of some defendants as well as the fact that, in the final analysis, the burden of proof rests on the prosecution. Set out below are some of the methods which prosecutors have used or attempted to use when they wish to introduce more than the mere fact of conviction.

## Criminal Justice Act 2003, Section 117

It is worth setting out the relevant parts of the section:

117. – (1) In criminal proceedings a statement contained in a document is admissible as evidence of any matters stated if:

(a) oral evidence given in the proceedings would be admissible as evidence of that matter;

(b) the requirements of sub-section (2) are satisfied; and

(c) the requirements of sub-section (5) are satisfied in a case where sub-section (4) requires them to be.

(2) The requirements of this sub-section are satisfied if:

(a) the document . . . was created or received by a person in the course of a trade, business, profession or other occupation or as the holder of a paid or unpaid office;

(b) the person who supplied the information contained in the statement (the relevant person) had or may reasonably be supposed to have had personal knowledge of the matters dealt with; and

(c) each person (if any) through whom the information was supplied from the relevant person to the person mentioned in paragraph (a) received the information in the course of a trade, business, profession or other occupation or as the holder of a paid or unpaid office.

. . .

(4) The additional requirements of sub-section (5) must be satisfied if the statement:

(a) was prepared for the purposes of pending or contemplated criminal proceedings or for a criminal investigation;

. . .

(5) The requirements of this sub-section are satisfied if:

(a) any of the five conditions mentioned in section 116(2) is satisfied . . .; or

(b) the relevant person cannot reasonably be expected to have any recollection of the matters dealt with in the statement (having regard to the length of time since he supplied the information and all other circumstances).

It follows that the relevant person must be a person with actual or presumed knowledge of the matters dealt with in the statement and that he or she supplied the information either directly or indirectly to the creator of the document which is to be given in evidence, that creator acting at the time in the course of a trade or business, etc. This was the problem in *Humphriss*.[12] The Crown sought to prove not only the facts of previous convictions but details of the methods used by the defendant in and about the commission of those offences which gave rise to the convictions. An officer of the Essex police retrieved the relevant records from the police computer. Those records derived from information supplied by employees of the Essex police who had a duty to record information supplied by other relevant persons or organisations. It was successfully argued in the Court of Appeal that 'the relevant persons' in that case, ie the ones who had actual or presumed knowledge, were the complainants in the earlier cases and that there was no evidence that those complainants had initially supplied the information which was then inputted into the computer system. Accordingly, section 117(2)(b) had not been complied with. Two passages from the judgment of Lord Woolf are relevant:

> 15. Accordingly it is submitted, the right course to have adopted was that which was adopted prior to the Criminal Justice Act. A statement should have been obtained from the complainant. If that had been done, it may or may not have been possible to rely on the circumstances in section 116(2) which allows statements to be adduced before a jury when a witness is unavailable.[13] . . .

> 21. . . . It emphasises the importance of the Crown deciding that if they want more than the evidence of the conviction . . . they must ensure that they have available the necessary evidence to support what they require. That will normally require the availability of either a statement by the complainant relating to the previous conviction in a sexual case or the complainant to be available to give first-hand evidence of what happened.

Ignoring the difficulties referred to in note 13, there are other problems with the 'statement' solution. In *Bovell*,[14] Rose LJ said:

> 2. It is worth mentioning that the basis of plea in relation to an earlier conviction may be relevant where it demonstrates differences from the way in which the prosecution initially put the case. In other words, a mere reference to the statement of a complainant in an earlier case may not provide the later court with the material needed to make a decision as to the admissibility of the earlier conviction.

It has to be remembered that the basis of plea is not recorded in the certificate of conviction from a Crown Court. These difficulties were highlighted in *Ainscough*.[15] A police officer gave evidence about the defendant's previous conviction, including details of the offence. His information was derived entirely from the police national computer. The defendant did not dispute the fact of the conviction but he did not accept the accuracy of the detail. Giving judgment in the Court of Appeal, Maurice Kay LJ said:

---

[12] [2005] EWCA Crim 2030.

[13] It is respectfully submitted that there may be problems with this suggestion unless in fact the maker of the statement is dead, unfit, outside the United Kingdom or cannot be found; absent those conditions, s 116 cannot be used.

[14] [2005] EWCA Crim 1091.

[15] [2006] EWCA Crim 694.

18. . . . Where there is a dispute between the prosecution and the defence about the facts which support previous convictions, it is not enough for the prosecution simply to rely on the police national computer.

He went on to say:

19. However, we appreciate that there may be cases where the position is simply too complicated. Whatever the complainant may have said in a statement at the time of the earlier conviction, or may say now in evidence to the court, it may be that a current defendant was sentenced on a different basis as a result of a basis of plea proffered and accepted by the prosecution and the Judge. In other words, where these matters are in dispute, there is a need for caution, there is a need to have regard to what was said in *Humphriss* and there is a need to ensure that a current trial does not give rise to numerous satellite issues about what did or did not happen in some case many years ago.

It might be argued that it would be an abuse of process for the prosecution to seek to call a witness to give evidence which directly goes against the basis of plea accepted in the earlier case, even if what the witness is likely to say was in line with the original witness statement.

In certain circumstances though, a basic 'statement' may be both admissible and sufficient to prove a particular fact. In *Wellington v DPP*,[16] the prosecution in the Magistrates' Court had put in evidence an extract from the police national computer. This extract showed the name and address of the defendant and details of an alias used by him, this alias being the name given when the man alleged to be the defendant had been stopped in connection with the current offence. Dismissing an argument that the evidence was inadmissible because CJA 2003, section 117 was not complied with, the Judge said:

31. It should be noted that this was a standard print-out. It does not contain any additional details of the kind which featured in *Humphriss* . . . In my judgement, the inescapable inference from the document is that the police officer who supplied the information 'had or may reasonably be supposed to have had personal knowledge' of the fact that the defendant was using the alias.

In *Hogart*,[17] the defendant was charged with defrauding a French woman. The prosecution wished to introduce (largely on a similar fact basis) the judgment of the trial Judge in an earlier unrelated civil case, involving another woman. During the course of that judgment, the Judge had made a number of findings of fact which were highly relevant to the current case. In the Court of Appeal, Longmore LJ said:

20. . . . The reasons for the judgment would come within section 117 of the Criminal Justice Act.

[16] [2007] EWHC 1061 (Admin).
[17] [2007] EWCA Crim 338.

## Criminal Justice Act 2003, Section 114(1)(d)

This section provides for the admissibility of hearsay evidence in statement form where 'the court is satisfied that it is in the interests of justice for it to be admissible'. The only reported decision in respect of its use in the context of the proving of past misconduct is *Steen*.[18] The facts were unusual and it is respectfully submitted that it provides no general warrant for the use of section 114(1)(d) in this context. The defendant was charged with fraud. He had previously been convicted of an almost identical fraud. He refused to agree the circumstances of the previous conviction. The Crown had produced a transcript of his evidence in the earlier proceedings as well as copies of his police interviews. They wanted to put in evidence a summary of what had been said in the evidence and in the interviews, simply in order to make that evidence more manageable. The Judge ruled the summary admissible 'in the interests of justice'. Approving the Judge's decision, though regretting that he had apparently paid little regard to the factors set out in section 114(2), Latham LJ said:

> 18. It is clearly in the interests of justice that the document should go before the jury. The underlying material, namely the evidence of the appellant and his interviews with the police, could be put without difficulty before the jury in unredacted form. We see no reason why the jury should be encumbered with any more of the material contained within those pieces of evidence than is necessary for a sensible understanding of the way in which the prosecution put their case in relation to the charge that the appellant faces in the present trial and such material from those documents as the appellant himself considers will assist his defence.

---

[18] [2007] EWCA Crim 335.

# 17

---

# Hearsay

---

17.1  The substantive law in relation to the admissibility of hearsay evidence is now set out in Chapter 2 of the Criminal Justice Act (CJA) 2003. Section 114 provides as follows:

> 114. – (1) In criminal proceedings a statement not made in oral evidence in the proceedings is admissible as evidence of any matter stated if, but only if:
>
> > (a) any provision of this chapter or any other statutory provision makes it admissible;
> >
> > (b) any rule of law preserved by section 118 makes it admissible;
> >
> > (c) all parties to the proceedings agree to it being admissible; or
> >
> > (d) the court is satisfied that it is in the interests of justice for it to be admissible.

In *Johnson*[1] (a case concerning social service documents and where the parties had disregarded an order of the Judge), Thomas LJ said:

> 21.  We would add that it is in any event essential when hearsay or bad character evidence will be put before the jury by agreement and the order of the court is not required (in contra-distinction to the position in this case) that the court is informed at the outset of the trial what has been agreed and how the advocates propose that the agreed evidence is to be placed before the jury. If the agreement is made during the trial, then the Judge should be told immediately after the agreement.

So far as procedure is concerned, CJA 2003, section 132(1) provides for the making of rules by the Criminal Procedure Rules Committee. The section continues as follows:

> 132.  . . . (2) The Rules may make provision for the procedure to be followed and other conditions to be fulfilled by a party proposing to tender a statement in evidence under any provision of this chapter.
>
> (3) The Rules may require a party proposing to tender the evidence to serve on each party to the proceedings such notice and such particulars of or relating to the evidence as may be prescribed.
>
> (4) The Rules may provide that the evidence is to be treated as admissible by agreement of the parties if:
>
> > (a) a notice has been served in accordance with provisions made under sub-section (3); and

---

[1]  [2010] EWCA Crim 385.

(b) no counter-notice in the prescribed form objecting to the admission of the evidence has been served by a party.

(5) If a party proposing to tender evidence fails to comply with a prescribed requirement applicable to it:

    (a) the evidence is not admissible except with the court's leave;

    (b) when leave is given the court or jury may draw such inferences from the failure as appear proper;

    (c) the failure may be taken into account by the court in considering the exercise of the court's powers with respect to costs.

(6) In considering whether or how to exercise any of its powers under sub-section (5), the court shall have regard to whether there is any justification for the failure to comply with the requirement.

(7) A person shall not be convicted of an offence solely on an inference drawn under sub-section (5)(b).[2]

It is clear that section 132(5)(b) gives the court power to refuse leave to admit hearsay evidence where the appropriate procedures have not been gone through – a rare illustration of statute providing an express sanction for non-compliance with procedural requirements. In *McKewan*,[3] a criminal damage trial in the Magistrates' Court had taken 10 months to come to trial. There had been nine pre-trial reviews and one vacated trial date. On the day of trial, the prosecution wanted a further adjournment because a witness was said to be ill. No adequate steps had been taken to justify the admission of the statement of that witness pursuant to CJA 2003, section 116, namely, that the witness was unfit to give evidence. Rejecting the application for an adjournment, the Magistrates had then acceded to a prosecution request to admit the statement pursuant to section 114(1)(d), then commonly (though erroneously) called 'the safety valve'. Quashing the ensuing conviction, Gross J said:

> 18. For my part, the safety valve is there to prevent injustice. It would have to be an exceptional case for it to be relied upon . . . to rescue the prosecution from the consequences of its own failures.

However, later authorities suggest that although justified in that case because of the appalling prosecution failures, the case lays down no proposition of general application. In *Sak*,[4] an important prosecution witness became unexpectedly unavailable. Refusing a prosecution application to adjourn, the Magistrates allowed the evidence to be admitted pursuant to section 114(1)(d). Upholding the conviction and referring specifically to *McKenna*, Thomas LJ said:

> 25. In my view, the observations must be seen as observations made in the context of that case, where the prosecution had made many mistakes and been guilty of many

---

[2] So far as I am aware, no guidance has been given by the Court of Appeal as to the approach to drawing adverse inferences pursuant to CJA 2003, s 132(5) and (7). It is difficult to conceive of circumstances where a jury could be invited to infer guilt from a failure to serve a hearsay notice in time. No doubt, if leave has been given in respect of a late application, comment might be made as to its reliability.

[3] [2007] EWHC 740 (Admin).

[4] [2007] EWHC 2886 (Admin).

failures. It is not in my view an observation of general application. It is applicable solely to the facts of that case . . .

26. Section 114 sets out the way in which the court may exercise the power to admit hearsay evidence, and in my view no general gloss, such as describing it as 'a safety valve' or any other term, is appropriate. The section is part of a chapter. It must be read in its entirety in the context of that chapter; no further gloss is necessary.

17.2    The rules are set out in Part 34 of the Criminal Procedure Rules 2011 (SI 2011/1709) (the Rules'). The relevant parts are as follows:

34.2(1) This rule applies where a party wants to introduce hearsay evidence for admission under any of the following sections of the Criminal Justice Act 2003:

(a)  section 114(1)(d) (evidence admissible in the interests of justice);
(b)  section 116 (evidence where a witness is unavailable);
(c)  section 121 (multiple hearsay).

(2)  That party must:

(a)  serve notice on:

(i)    the Court Officer; and
(ii)   each other party.

(b)  in the notice:

(i)    identify the evidence that is hearsay;
(ii)   set out any facts on which that party relies to make the evidence admissible;
(iii)  explain how that party will prove those facts if another party disputes them; and
(iv)  explain why the evidence is admissible; and

(c)  attach to the notice any statement or other document containing the evidence that has not already been served.

(3)  A prosecutor who wants to introduce such evidence must serve the notice not more than 14 days after the defendant pleads not guilty.
(4)  A defendant who wants to introduce such evidence must serve the notice as soon as reasonably practicable.
(5)  A party entitled to receive a notice under this rule may waive that entitlement by so informing:

(a)  the party who would have served it; and
(b)  the court.

It is worth mentioning here the note to the rule which spells out that:

This rule does not require notice of hearsay evidence that is admissible under any of the following sections of the 2003 Act:

(a)  section 117 (business and other documents);
(b)  section 118 (preservation of certain common law categories of admissibility);
(c)  section 119 (inconsistent statements);
(d)  section 120 (other previous statements of witnesses); or
(e)  section 127 (expert evidence – preparatory work).

34.3(1) This rule applies where a party objects to the introduction of hearsay evidence.

(2) That party must:

(a) apply to the court to determine the objection;

(b) serve the application on:

(i)   the Court Officer; and

(ii)  each other party;

(c) serve the application as soon as reasonably practicable, and in any event not more than 14 days after:

(i)   service of notice to introduce the evidence under Rule 34.2;

(ii)  service of the evidence to which that party objects, if no notice is required by that rule; or

(iii) the defendant pleads not guilty;

whichever of those events happens last, and

(d) in the application explain:

(i)   which, if any, facts set out in a notice under Rule 34.2 that party disputes;

(ii)  why the evidence is not admissible;

(iii) any other objection to the application.

(3) The court:

(a) may determine an application:

(i)   at a hearing, in public or in private; or

(ii)  without a hearing;

(b) must not determine the application unless the party who served the notice:

(i)   is present; or

(ii)  has had a reasonable opportunity to respond;

(c) may adjourn the application; and

(d) . . .

34.4(1) This rule applies where:

(a) a party has served notice to introduce hearsay evidence under Rule 34.2; and

(b) no other party has applied to the court to determine an objection to the introduction of the evidence.

(2) The court will treat the evidence as if it were admissible by agreement.

34.5(1) The court may:

(a) shorten or extend (even after it has expired) a time limit under this part;

(b) allow an application on notice to be in a different form to one set out in the Practice Direction, or to be made or given orally;

(c) dispense with the requirement for notice to introduce hearsay evidence.

(2) A party who wants an extension of time must:

(a) apply when serving the application on notice with which it is needed; and

(b) explain the delay.

17.3    Both the CJA 2003 and the Rules clearly contemplate a situation where hearsay evidence would be deemed to be admissible by agreement where a party who has received a notice has not given a counter notice. In *Williams of Portmadog v Vehicle and Operator Services Agency*,[5] some hearsay evidence was admitted during the course of the trial with no notice or counter notice having been served and no objection was taken at the time. The issue for the Divisional Court was whether the defendant had 'agreed' to the evidence going in for the purposes of section 114(1)(c). Treacy J said:

> 13. . . . However, what I am quite clear about is that 'agreement' for these purposes does not necessarily require some contract law analysis of 'offer' and 'acceptance' nor does it require some formal recording of the position by the court, nor does it necessarily require express agreement between the parties in all circumstances.
>
> 14. Those experienced in criminal litigation are familiar with the situation whereby something is done in the course of a hearing by one party without a demur from the other side. Judges and justices up and down the country regularly hear evidence admitted without anything formal being said by the parties to the court. The Tribunal, in the absence of objection or submission, that there is no objection to the admissibility of the evidence and thus that there is agreement to its admissibility. In effect, the agreement is implicit, or capable of being implicit, in the circumstances pertaining before the court, and particularly in circumstances where the appellant has the benefit of legal representation. . . .
>
> 16. I have come to the conclusion that the Justices, in the circumstances which obtained, were entitled to treat the agreement as to the adducing of hearsay evidence as one which arose from the circumstances as they presented themselves before the court, and I do not think the Justices were wrong in so acting.

However, the caveat entered by Keene LJ should be noted. He said:

> 19. I would emphasise that agreement to the admission of hearsay evidence under that particular provision is not to be inferred automatically or in all circumstances from an absence of objection at the time the evidence is given. It depends on all the circumstances. In particular, if a defendant is unrepresented, it would be very difficult indeed for such an inference to be drawn. In most cases it would be impossible. But such an inference may be open to the court where the defendant is legally represented and no objection to admissibility is taken. Even then the court is not obliged to draw such an inference, but it may, in appropriate circumstances, do so.

17.4    Although this book is concerned with procedure and does not purport to deal with the substantive law, there is another aspect of the current hearsay provisions which has procedural overtones. CJA 2003, section 116 allows for the admission of hearsay evidence if certain conditions are satisfied. One of those conditions derives from section 116(2)(d) which provides that 'the relevant person cannot be found although such steps as it is reasonably practicable to take to find him have been taken'. This sub-section has been considered by the Court of Appeal.

---

[5] [2008] EWHC 849 (Admin).

In *Adams*,[6] a nightclub bouncer had given a statement for the prosecution. He was required by the defence to attend the trial. At the PCMH a trial date had been fixed. On the day of the trial, the witness did not appear and the Recorder admitted the statement pursuant to section 116(2)(d). On appeal, Hughes LJ said:

> 13. . . . leaving contact with a witness such as this until the last working day before the trial is not good enough and it is certainly not such steps as it is reasonably practicable to take to find him.

In *T*,[7] an important witness gave a statement to the police but indicated in that statement that he was leaving the area and had no intention of attending the trial. A trial date was fixed at the PCMH. About two weeks before trial, a witness summons was issued. An attempt was made to serve it about 10 days before trial. The officer who attempted to serve it was told that the witness had moved. A mobile phone number was available but when called was switched to 'off'. At trial the statement was admitted. No evidence was called in relation to the steps taken to find the witness. The position was simply outlined by prosecuting counsel. Quashing the conviction, Thomas LJ said:

> 29. It seems to us that in a case of this kind, unless there is a written agreed statement of facts, it is simply not possible to proceed to consider an application without evidence as to the steps taken to find the witness . . .

> 31. There was, because matters proceeded so informally before the Judge, no attempt to try and establish what steps the police had taken through the well-known programme established for witness care to keep contact with her, to explain to her her duty to attend, and to try and find where she had gone in the months before the PCMH . . . Nor was there any evidence when enquiries came to be made in the early part of 2008 and in the month or two before trial as to what information the witness's mother had about her location, no evidence as to what enquiries had been made of social security . . . She had been on the telephone. There is no evidence as to whether any attempt had been made to trace her through cell site analysis. It is said that all of this might be expensive. It may be. We do not know because there was no evidence about that.

> 32. It seems to us . . . that there must be a suspicion that this kind of application is being dealt with far too informally. Given the importance of the right to confrontation under our law, it is quite impermissible to proceed with an application of this kind informally.

> 33. It is to be hoped in applications of this kind that the facts can be agreed, but, if not, evidence must be called and the Judge must make findings of fact.

---

[6] [2007] EWCA Crim 3025.
[7] [2009] EWCA Crim 1213.

# 18

## Applications in Respect of the Previous Sexual History of a Complainant

18.1   The relevant parts of sections 41 and 42 of the Youth Justice and Criminal Evidence Act (YJCEA) 1999 are as follows:

41. – (1) If at trial a person is charged with a sexual offence then, except with the leave of the court:

(a)  no evidence may be adduced; and
(b)  no question may be asked in cross-examination

by or on behalf of any accused . . . about any sexual behaviour of the complainant.

(2)  The court may give leave in relation to any evidence or question only on an application made by or on behalf of an accused, and may not give such leave unless it is satisfied:

(a)  that sub-section (3) or (5) applies; and
(b)  that a refusal of leave might have the result of rendering unsafe a conclusion of the jury . . . on any relevant issue in the case.

(3)  This sub-section applies if the evidence or question relates to a relevant issue in the case and either:

(a)  that issue is not an issue of consent; or
(b)  it is an issue of consent and the sexual behaviour of the complainant to which the evidence or question relates is alleged to have taken place at or about the same time as the event which is the subject-matter of the charge against the accused; or
(c)  it is an issue of consent and the sexual behaviour of the complainant to which the evidence or question relates is alleged to have been, in any respect, so similar:

(i)  to any sexual behaviour of the complainant which (according to evidence adduced or to be adduced by or on behalf of the accused) took place as part of the event which is the subject-matter of the charge against the accused; or
(ii)  to any other sexual behaviour of the complainant which (according to such evidence) took place at or about the same time as that event,

that the similarity cannot reasonably be explained as coincidence.

(4)  For the purposes of sub-section (3) no evidence or question shall be regarded as relating to a relevant issue in the case if it appears to the court to be reasonable to

assume that the purpose (or main purpose) for which it would be adduced or asked is to establish or elicit material for impugning the credibility of the complainant as a witness.

(5) This sub-section applies if the evidence or question:

    (a) relates to any evidence adduced by the prosecution about any sexual behaviour of the complainant; and

    (b) in the opinion of the court would go no further than is necessary to enable the evidence adduced by the prosecution to be rebutted or explained by or on behalf of the accused.

(6) For the purposes of sub-sections (3) and (5), the evidence or question must relate to a specific instance (or specific instances) of alleged sexual behaviour on the part of the complainant (and accordingly nothing in those sub-sections is capable of applying in relation to the evidence or question to the extent that it does not so relate).

42. – (1) In section 41:

    (a) 'relevant issue in the case' means any issue falling to be proved by the prosecution or defence in the trial of the accused;

    (b) 'issue of consent' means any issue whether the complainant in fact consented to the conduct constituting the offence with which the accused is charged (and accordingly does not include any issue as to the belief of the accused that the complainant so consented).

18.2   Section 3 of the Human Rights Act 1998 provides that:

3. So far as is possible to do so, primary legislation ... must be read and given effect to in a way which is compatible with the Convention of rights.

The House of Lords in *A*[1] were able to utilise the provisions of section 3 in order that the highly restrictive terms of YJCEA 1999, section 41 could be interpreted in such a way as to ensure that a defendant's right to a fair trial was not irreparably damaged. The following paragraphs from the speeches of Lord Steyn and Lord Hutton are very relevant. Lord Steyn said:

45. It is therefore possible under section 3 to read section 41 and in particular section 41(3)(c) as subject to the implied provision that evidence or questioning which is required to ensure a fair trial under Article 6 ... should not be treated as inadmissible. The result of such a reading would be that sometimes logically relevant sexual experience between a complainant and an accused may be admitted under section 41(3)(c). On the other hand, there will be cases where previous sexual experience between a complainant and an accused will be irrelevant ... Where the line is to be drawn must be left to the judgement of trial judges.

46. The effect of the decision today is that under section 41(3)(c) ... the test of admissibility is whether the evidence (and questioning in relation to it) is nevertheless so relevant to the issue of consent that to exclude it would endanger the fairness of the trial under Article 6 ... If the test is satisfied then evidence should not be excluded.

[1] [2001] UKHL 25.

Lord Hutton said:

> 152. Where there has been a recent close and affectionate relationship between the complainant and the defendant, it is probable that the evidence will be relevant, not to advance the bare assertion that because she consented in the past she consented on the occasion in question, but . . . that evidence of such a relationship will show the complainant's specific mindset towards the defendant, namely her affection for him. . . .

> 163. . . . I consider that section 41(3)(c) should be read as including evidence of such previous behaviour by the complainant because the defendant claims that her sexual behaviour on previous occasions was similar, and the similarity was not a coincidence because there was a causal connection which was her affection for and feelings of attraction towards the defendant. It follows that I am in full agreement with the test of admissibility stated by . . . Lord Steyn in paragraph 46 of his speech.

Although of little or no assistance on the general approach to section 41, it is worth mentioning the speech of Lord Hope in connection with section 41(3)(a), namely, that the issue is not one of consent (though note that leave is still required). He said:

> 79. Paragraph (a) of sub-section (3) sets out the first qualifying condition. That is that the issue to which the evidence or question relates is not an issue of consent . . . Examples of issues which fall within this paragraph because the evidence of sexual behaviour is proffered for specific reasons are (a) the defence of honest belief . . .; (b) that the complainant was biased against the accused or had a motive to fabricate the evidence; (c) that there is an alternative explanation for the physical conditions on which the Crown rely to establish that intercourse took place; and (d) especially in the case of young complainants . . . that the detail of their account must have come from some other sexual activity before or after the event which provides an explanation for their knowledge of that activity.

18.3   This and the following paragraph deal with the procedural requirements surrounding an application to introduce the previous sexual history of the complainant. It is somewhat complicated. The YJCEA 1999 itself contains relevant provisions:

> 41. . . . (6) For the purposes of sub-sections (3) and (5) the evidence or question must relate to a specific instance (or specific instances) of alleged sexual behaviour on the part of the complainant (and accordingly nothing in this sub-section is capable of applying in relation to the evidence or question to the extent that it does not so relate).
> . . .
> 43. – (1) An application for leave shall be heard in private and in the absence of the complainant . . .
> (2) Where such an application has been determined, the court must state in open court
>    . . .
>    (a) its reasons for giving or refusing leave; and
>    (b) if it gives leave, the extent to which evidence may be adduced or questions asked in pursuance of the leave . . .

(3) Criminal Procedure Rules may make provision:

    (a) requiring applications for leave to specify, in relation to each item of evidence or question to which they relate, particulars of the grounds on which it is asserted that leave should be given by virtue of sub-section (3) or (5) of section 41;

    (b) enabling the court to request a party to the proceedings to provide the court with information which it considers would assist it in determining an application for leave;

    (c) ...

18.4   Part 36 of the Criminal Procedure Rules 2011 (SI 2011/1709) (as conditioned by the above-mentioned statutory provisions) govern the making of a section 41 application:

36.2  The defendant must apply for permission to do so:

    (a) in writing; and

    (b) not more than 28 days after the prosecutor has complied or purported to comply with section 3 of the Criminal Procedure and Investigations Act 1996 (disclosure by prosecutor).

36.3  The application must:

    (a) identify the issue to which the defendant says the complainant's sexual behaviour is relevant;

    (b) give particulars of:

        (i)  any evidence that the defendant wants to introduce; and

        (ii) any questions that the defendant wants to ask;

    (c) identify the exception to the prohibition in section 41 of the Youth Justice and Criminal Evidence Act 1999 on which the defendant relies; and

    (d) give the name and date of birth of any witness whose evidence about the complainant's sexual behaviour the defendant wants to introduce.[2]

36.4  The defendant must serve the application on the Court Officer and all other parties.

36.5  A party who wants to make representations about an application under Rule 36.2 must:

    (a) do so in writing not more than 14 days after receiving it; and

    (b) serve those representations on the Court Officer and all other parties.

36.7  The court may shorten or extend (even after it has expired) a time limit under this part.

---

[2] Presumably, the legality of this requirement derives from YJCEA 1999, s 43(3)(b). The argument has now been rendered somewhat academic in any event by virtue of the new provisions in the defence disclosure regulations requiring a defendant to identify which witnesses he proposes calling.

# 19

## Expert Evidence

19.1   Matters relating both to the content of and the disclosure of expert evidence are set out in Part 33 of the Criminal Procedure Rules 2011 (SI 2011/1709) ('the Rules'). This rule-making authority is in part derived from section 81 of the Police and Criminal Evidence Act 1984 and section 20(3) of the Criminal Procedure and Investigations Act 1996.

19.2   So far as service and use of an expert report is concerned, this is dealt with by Rules 33.4 and 33.5:

33.4(1) A party who wants to introduce expert evidence must:

(a)   serve it on:

(i)   the Court Officer; and
(ii)   each other party;

(b)   serve it:

(i)   as soon as practicable;

(c)   if another party so requires, give the party a copy of, or a reasonable opportunity to inspect:

(i)   a record of any examination, measurement, test or experiment on which the expert's findings and opinions are based or that were carried out in the course of reaching those findings and opinions;
(ii)   anything on which any such examination, measurement, test or experiment was carried out.

(2) A party may not introduce expert evidence if that party has not complied with this rule unless:

(a)   every other party agrees; or
(b)   the court gives permission.

33.5 A party who serves on another party or on the court a report by an expert must, at once, inform that expert of that fact.

It should be noted that Rule 33.4(2) is one of those rare instances which spells out a possible sanction for non-compliance with the Rules, namely a refusal to allow the evidence to be given. This power, of course, derives from the statutes set out at 19.1 above.

19.3    Quite apart from the Rules, the common law had evolved quite detailed requirements as to the nature of the duty of an expert and what should be contained in his report. The classic account derives from the judgment of Cresswell J in the *Ikarian Reefer*.[1] In summary:

(1)    Expert evidence presented to the court should be, and should be seen to be, the independent product of the expert uninfluenced as to form or content by the exigencies of litigation.

(2)    An expert witness should provide independent assistance to the court by way of objective and unbiased opinion, in relation to matters within his experience. An expert witness should never assume the role of an advocate.

(3)    An expert witness should state the facts or assumptions on which his opinion is based. He should not omit to consider material facts which could detract from his concluded opinion.

(4)    An expert witness should make it clear when a particular question or issue falls outside his expertise.

(5)    If an expert opinion is not properly researched because he considers that insufficient data are available, then this must be stated, with an indication that the opinion is no more than a provisional one. In cases where an expert who has prepared a report could not assert that the report contained the truth, the whole truth and nothing but the truth without some qualification, that qualification should be stated in the report.

(6)    If after exchange of reports, an expert witness changes his view, having read the report of the other side or for any other reason, such change of view should be communicated (through legal representatives) to the other side without delay.

(7)    Where expert evidence refers to photographs and suchlike these must be provided to the other side at the same time as the exchange of reports.

In *Harris*,[2] the Court of Appeal stressed that the guidelines given by Cresswell J were very relevant to criminal proceedings:

> 273: They should be kept well in mind by both prosecution and defence. The new Criminal Procedure Rules provide wide powers of case management to the court . . . In cases involving allegations of child abuse, the Judge should be prepared to give directions in respect of expert evidence . . . it ought to be possible to narrow the areas of dispute before trial and limit the volume of expert evidence which the jury will have to consider.

In *B*,[3] the Court of Appeal gave further guidance. Gage LJ said:

> 177.    In addition to the specific features referred to by Cresswell J, we add the following as necessary inclusions in an expert report:

---

[1]    [1993] 2 Lloyds Reports 68, 81 and 82.
[2]    [2006] 1 Crim App R 5.
[3]    [2006] EWCA Crim 417.

(1) details of the expert's academic and professional qualifications, experience and accreditation relevant to the opinion expressed in the report and the range and extent of the expertise and any limitation upon the expertise;

(2) a statement setting out the substance of all the instructions received, questions upon which an opinion is sought, the materials provided and considered, and the documents, statements, evidence, information or assumptions which are material to the opinion expressed or upon which those opinions are based;

(3) information relating to who has carried out measurements, examinations, tests, etc and the methodology used and whether or not such measurements, etc were carried out under the expert's supervision;

(4) where there is a range of opinion in the matters dealt with in the report, a summary of the range of opinions and the reason for the opinion given. In this connection, any material facts or matters which detract from the expert's opinion, and any points which could fairly be made against any opinion expressed, should be set out;

(5) relevant extracts of literature or any other material which might assist the court;

(6) a statement to the effect that the expert has complied with his or her duty to the court to provide independent assistance by way of objective and unbiased opinion in relation to matters within his or her expertise and an acknowledgement that the expert will inform all parties and where appropriate the court, in the event that his or opinion changes on any material issues;

(7) where on an exchange of expert reports matters arise which require a further or supplemental report, the above guidelines should of course be complied with.

The foregoing provisions are now substantially codified in the Rules. The relevant parts in relation to the duties of the expert and the contents of any report are set out in Rule 33.2 and 33.3:

33.2(1) An expert must help the court to achieve the overriding objective by giving objective and unbiased opinion on matters within his expertise.

(2) This duty overrides any obligation to the person from whom he receives instructions or by whom he is paid.

(3) This duty includes an obligation to inform all parties and the court if the expert's opinion changes from that contained in a report served as evidence or given in a statement.

33.3(1) An expert's report must:

    (a) give details of the expert's qualifications and relevant experience and accreditation;

    (b) give details of any literature or other information which the expert has relied on in making the report;

    (c) contain a statement setting out the substance of all facts given to the expert, which are material to the opinions expressed in the report or upon which those opinions are based;

    (d) make clear which of the facts stated in the report are within the expert's own knowledge;

    (e) say who carried out any examination, measurement, test or experiment which the expert has used for the report; and

        (i) give the qualifications, relevant experience and accreditation of that person;

      (ii)   state whether or not the examination, measurement, test or experiment was carried out under the expert's supervision; and

      (iii)  summarise the findings on which the expert relies;

(f)   where there is a range of opinion on the matters dealt with in the report:

      (i)   summarise the range of opinion; and

      (ii)  give reasons for his own opinion;

(g)  if the expert is not able to give his own opinion without qualification, state the qualification;

(h)  contain a summary of the conclusions reached;

(i)   contain a statement that the expert understands his duty to the court and has complied and will continue to comply with that duty;

(j)   contain the same declaration of truth as a witness statement.

19.4    The decisions referred to above are now substantially codified in Rule 33.3:

33.3(1)  An expert's report must:

(a)  give details of the expert's qualifications, relevant experience and accreditation;

(b)  give details of any literature or other information which the expert relied on in making the report;

(c)  contain a statement setting out the substance or giving all facts given to the expert which are material to the opinion expressed in the report or upon which those opinions are based;

(d)  make clear which of the facts stated in the report are within the expert's own knowledge;

(e)  say who carried out any examination, measurement, test or experiment which the expert has used for the report; and:

      (i)   give the qualifications, relevant experience and accreditation of that person;

      (ii)  say whether or not the examination, measurement, test or experiment was carried out under the expert's supervision; and

      (iii)  summarise the findings on which the expert relies;

(f)   where there is a range of opinion on the matters dealt with in the report:

      (i)   summarise the range of opinion; and

      (ii)  give reasons for his own opinion;

(g)  if the expert is not able to give his opinion without qualification, state the qualification;

(h)  contain a summary of the conclusions reached;

(i)   contain a statement that the expert understands his duty to the court and has complied and will continue to comply with that duty;

(j)   contain the same declaration of truth as a witness statement.

19.5    Rule 33 also contains provisions which are important both in terms of case management and in terms of endeavouring to avoid a plethora of expert reports in multi-handed cases:

33.6(1) This Rule applies where more than one party wants to introduce expert evidence.

(2) The court may direct the experts to:

    (a) discuss the expert issues in the proceedings; and

    (b) prepare a statement for the court on the matters on which they agree and disagree, giving their reasons.

(3) Except for that statement, the content of that discussion must not be referred to without court permission.

(4) A party may not introduce expert evidence without the court's permission if the expert has not complied with a direction under this rule.

33.7(1) Where more than one defendant wants to introduce expert evidence on an issue at trial, the court may direct that the evidence on that issue is to be given by one expert only.

(2) Where the co-defendants cannot agree who should be the expert, the court may:

    (a) select the expert from a list prepared or identified by them; or

    (b) direct that the expert be selected in another way.

33.8(1) Where the court gives a direction under 33.7 for a single joint expert to be used, each of the co-defendants may give instructions to the expert.

(2) When a co-defendant gives instructions to the expert, he must at the same time send a copy of the instructions to the other co-defendants.

(3) The court may give directions about:

    (a) the payment of the expert's fees and expenses; and

    (b) any examination, measurement, test or experiment which the expert wishes to carry out.

(4) The court may, before an expert is instructed, limit the amount that can be paid by way of fees and expenses to the expert.

(5) Unless the court otherwise directs, the instructing co-defendants are jointly and severally liable for the payment of the expert's fees and expenses.

19.6 The court has a power to vary the requirements of Part 33. This derives from Rule 33.9 which provides:

33.9(1) The court may:

    (a) extend (even after it has expired) the time limit under this Part;

    (b) allow the introduction of expert evidence which omits a detail required by this part.

(2) A party who wants an extension of time must:

    (a) apply when serving the expert evidence of which it is required;

    (b) explain the delay.

# 20

## Contempt

20.1 This chapter is concerned with contempt in the face of the court, or activities closely connected with court proceedings and where swift action is required. It does not deal with those activities such as press reporting which may lead to action being taken by the Attorney General in the Divisional Court and which are outwith the day-to-day functions of those who sit in the Crown Court. Likewise, it does not deal with contempt arising from a disobedience to an order of the Crown Court, for example in connection with restraint proceedings.

20.2 Aside from any considerations of an inherent jurisdiction, the power to commit for contempt has a number of statutory sources. The relevant part of section 45 of the Senior Courts Act 1981 provides as follows:

> 45. . . . (4) . . . The Crown Court shall, in relation to the attendance and examination of witnesses, any contempt of court, the enforcement of its orders and all other matters incidental to its jurisdiction, have the like powers, rights, privileges and authority of the High Court.

Order 52 of the Rules of the Supreme Court (now to be found in Schedule 1 to the Civil Procedure Rules) expressly preserves the power of the Crown Court to send to prison those who commit contempt in the face of the court or who disobey its orders. The Rule also gives a power to suspend any prison sentence; this derives from Order 52 Rule 7(1).

Section 14(1) of the Contempt of Court Act 1981 requires that any order for committal to prison must be for a fixed term and in any event cannot exceed two years.

20.3 It is necessary to consider what in fact constitutes a contempt of court. In *Attorney General v Leveller Magazine*,[1] Lord Diplock said:

> Although criminal contempts of court take a variety of forms, they all share a common characteristic: they involve an interference with the due administration of justice either in a particular case or more generally as a continuing process. It is justice itself that is flouted by contempt of court, not the individual court or Judge who is attempting to administer it.

---

[1] [1979] AC 440, 449.

However, as Staughton LJ said in *Powell*,[2] referring to what Lord Diplock had said:

> We accept those observations . . . But when one comes to the task of carrying them into effect, there is we think more guidance to be found in section 12 of the Contempt of Court Act 1981. That was an enactment providing for the first time power for a Magistrates' Court to commit for contempt.

Section 12 is as follows:

> 12. – (1) A Magistrates' Court has jurisdiction under this section to deal with any person who:
>
> (a) wilfully insults the justice or justices, any witness before or officer of the court or any solicitor or Counsel having business in the court, during his or their sitting or attendance in court or in going to or returning from court; or
> (b) wilfully interrupts the proceedings of the court or otherwise misbehaves in court.

In *Griffin*,[3] Mustill LJ said:

> It is beyond doubt that activities taking place either before or after the trial and away from the precinct, are capable of amounting to contempt if they constitute an interference with the course of justice in pending proceedings.

The jurisdiction persists when the trial has ended. In *Huggins*,[4] whilst the jury were still present just after the contemnor's mother had been sentenced, he shouted at the jury. Moses LJ said:

> 13. The close of a trial is a moment of particular sensitivity and stress for a jury. Their anxieties in sitting in judgement on a fellow citizen can only be heightened if they are shouted at or, worse, abused or threatened. We reject any notion that there can be no contempt where the trial has finished.

The jurisdiction also extends to acts committed outside the courtroom but in the near vicinity thereof, eg threatening a witness who has given evidence where that witness is in a nearby café,[5] or at a bus stop.[6]

20.4    This paragraph and those that follow are concerned with the exercise of the jurisdiction to commit for contempt. Although immediate action may be required to restore order, the decision to commit to prison should never be taken hastily. This is a message running through any number of authorities. Coupled with the need to avoid hasty action is the equally compelling need to ensure that the contempt proceedings are fair. This is particularly so because it is a summary process and until very recently no rules had been laid down in statute or statutory instrument as to the procedures to be followed.

---

[2] (1994) 98 Crim App R 224, 236.
[3] (1989) 88 Crim App R 63, 67.
[4] [2007] EWCA Crim 732.
[5] *Moore v Clerk of Bristol Assize* [1971] 1 WLR 1669.
[6] *AS* [2008] EWCA Crim 138.

The starting point is the judgment of Lawton LJ in *Moran*,[7] though his comments about legal advice have been superseded by subsequent cases. He said:

> The following principles should be borne in mind. First a decision to imprison a man for contempt of court should never be taken too quickly. The Judge should give himself time for reflection as to what is the best course to take. Secondly, he should consider whether that time for reflection should not extend to a different day because overnight thoughts are sometimes better than thoughts on the spur of the moment. Thirdly, the Judge should consider whether the seeming contemnor should have some advice . . . Justice does not require a contemnor in the face of the court to have a right to legal advice. But if the circumstances are such that it is possible for the contemnor to have advice, he should be given the opportunity of having it . . . Giving an opportunity to apologise is one of the most important aspects of this summary procedure which in many ways is draconian.

To like effect is a passage in the judgment of Staughton LJ in *Powell* (see at 20.3 above). He said:

> Jurisdiction to deal with contempt in the face of the court . . . has to be exercised with great caution. The court is the victim; the court is the witness; the court is the prosecutor and the court is the judge. It is perhaps a rare example in English law of an inquisitorial process.

It is usually appropriate for the judge who witnessed the contempt or whose proceedings are affected by it to deal with the matter himself. There is certainly no rule that it should be dealt with by another judge. This is apparent from the judgment of the Court of Appeal in *Wilkinson*.[8] The following passage from the judgment of Hale LJ is relevant:

> 23. Both the father and the Official Solicitor questioned whether the Judge should have dealt with the matter herself. The Phillimore Committee on Contempt of Court . . . saw three advantages in the matter being dealt with by the same Judge: she would be in the best position to deal with it because she had witnessed what had taken place: she might well be more inclined to take a lenient view after a period of reflection than another Judge who simply read the transcript and would be naturally anxious to protect a sister Judge: and the effect of immediate imprisonment is an effective deterrent. To these may be added the necessity for prompt action in cases where the trial is still going on and the impracticability of arranging for another Judge to deal with it if there is still a risk that the contempt hearing will itself be disrupted.

Precisely because of the need to avoid precipitate action and the need to ensure fairness, there is a power to remand the alleged contemnor in custody, at the very least overnight. In *Huggins* (see at 20.3 above) Moses LJ said:

> 23. The matter could and should have been dealt with by adjourning the case overnight with the appellant in custody whilst the Judge considered the appropriate course to take.

---

[7] (1985) 81 Crim App R 51, 53.
[8] [2003] EWCA Civ 95.

He went on to say:

> We emphasise that the court has the power . . . to detain a contemnor whilst he considers the proper approach to adopt.

In *Wilkinson* (above), Hale LJ said:

> 23. The question is, how long she can or should wait before bringing the case back. In many cases it need take no longer than the remainder of the court day . . . or overnight. But, where the delay is no longer than necessary in order to make arrangements for a summary trial in which the rights of the alleged contemnor can be properly protected, it cannot be unlawful. It would be illogical to hold that a Judge can impose up to two years' imprisonment virtually on the spot but not wait a short time in order to achieve a fairer procedure. As a matter of good practice, however, if the case cannot be heard the next day, the Judge should ensure that the alleged contemnor is brought back to court in any event, or if this is not possible, that enquiries are made and the case is mentioned in open court so that the reason for any further delay is both known and recorded and the question of bail can be considered.

20.5    Not only should a judge take time for reflection, he must ensure that the contempt proceedings themselves are fair. In *Griffin* (see at 20.3 above) Mustill LJ said:

> We are here concerned with the exercise of a jurisdiction which is *sui generis* so far as English law is concerned. In proceedings for criminal contempt there is no prosecutor or even a requirement that a representative of the Crown or of the injured party should institute the proceedings. The Judge is entitled to proceed of his own motion. There is no summons or indictment, nor is it mandatory for any written account of the accusation made against him to be furnished to the contemnor . . . nor is the system adversarial in character. The Judge himself enquires into the circumstances so far as they are not within his personal knowledge. He identifies the grounds of complaint, selects the witnesses and investigates what they have to say . . . decides on guilt and pronounces sentence. This summary procedure, which by its nature is to be used quickly if it is to be used at all, omits many of the safeguards to which an accused is ordinarily entitled and . . . the Judge should choose to adopt it only in cases of real need.

In *Hill*,[9] it was held that the power of the court to punish contempt was part of its inherent jurisdiction. It was for the judge to take steps to safeguard the court's authority. In appropriate cases, those steps will include:

   (1)  the immediate arrest and detention of the offender;
   (2)  telling the offender distinctly what the contempt is stated to have been;
   (3)  giving a chance to apologise;
   (4)  affording the opportunity of being advised and represented by counsel and making any order for legal aid necessary for that purpose;
   (5)  granting any adjournment that may be required;
   (6)  listening to counsel's submission;
   (7)  if satisfied that punishment is merited, imposing it within the appropriate limits.

[9] [1986] Crim LR 457.

The current position is well summarised in the decision of the Court of Appeal in *Grant*,[10] where Openshaw J said:

> 10. We turn then to examine the relevant principles which the Judge should have applied. There are currently no procedural rules dealing with summary contempt, but over the years the courts particularly in *Moran* have established certain principles which should ordinarily be observed when dealing with contempt cases. These include that (a) a Judge has the power to order the immediate arrest and detention of the suspected offender; (b) the decision to try a suspected offender summarily should be taken only when it is necessary to do so to preserve the integrity of the trial or the dignity of the court; (c) such a decision should never be taken too quickly and that time should always be allowed for reflection, if necessary overnight; (d) the suspected offender must be distinctly and clearly told what acts or conduct are alleged against him; (e) he should be allowed the opportunity of legal representation; (f) he should be allowed a reasonable opportunity properly to investigate the circumstances; and (g) the contemnor should be given an opportunity to apologise, which in an appropriate case might obviate the need for further action. We add that no one should be convicted of contempt unless they distinctly admit it, or if they do not, unless it be proved against them beyond reasonable doubt.

20.6    In *AS*,[11] the Court of Appeal examined the process whereby a judge tries a person for contempt of court. Referring to the power to adjourn, whether overnight or for a longer period, they drew a distinction between the 'truly summary' and 'a formal procedure'. *Griffin* (see at 20.5 above) was described as an illustration of the 'truly summary' where the judge deals with the contempt 'then and there'. *Santiago*,[12] where the question of trying the contempt was put off until after the end of the trial, was an illustration of the 'formal procedure'. In respect of this procedure, Thomas LJ said:

> 17(vi). The formal procedure will involve the calling of witnesses by a prosecutor, the opportunity of examining them, the opportunity for the defendant to give evidence and call his own evidence, and the provision of a reasoned judgment of the court against which an appeal to this court lies as of right. Such a procedure is these days very little different from a hearing in a Magistrates' Court, save that in a Magistrates' Court the charge will be set out in a formal document.

Given the steps which should be taken even when dealing with a contemnor immediately, it is not obvious that the difference between 'the truly summary' and the 'formal procedure' is very meaningful.

20.7    Certain miscellaneous points remain to be discussed.

(1)  In cases of criminal contempt, there is no power for the contemnor to purge his contempt. In *Phelps*,[13] Keith J said:

---

[10]  [2010] EWCA Crim 215.

[11]  [2008] EWCA Crim 138.

[12]  [2005] EWCA Crim 556.

[13]  [2010] EWCA Crim 2308; it should be noted that this case is a good illustration of a contempt dealt with as a 'summary contempt', ie then and there by the Judge – it involved an appalling outbreak of violence in the dock of the court.

10. In our view, the resident Judge was right to conclude that an application to purge the appellant's contempt could not be entertained. This was because the appellant had been sentenced to a determinate term of imprisonment for the criminal offence of contempt . . . at common law, a person committed to prison for contempt of court for a fixed term could not be discharged.

However, he did go on to say that:

11. . . . The Crown Court has the power under section 155(1) of the Powers of Criminal Courts (Sentencing) Act 2000 to vary or rescind a sentence imposed on an offender. Indeed with effect from 14 July 2008, the period during which it can do so was increased from 28 days to 56 days from when the sentence was imposed. Since the Judge had sentenced the appellant before he had had a chance to calm down and decide whether he wanted to apologise for his conduct, it may have been appropriate for the resident Judge to have treated the appellant's solicitor's request for a hearing to purge his contempt as an application for a variation of his sentence under section 155(1).

(2) It is up to the judge to decide whether to deal with the contempt himself or refer the matter to the prosecuting authorities to consider the formal laying of charges for specific criminal offences. In *Santiago* (see at 20.6 above), Hooper LJ said:

27. On the facts of this case it would have been quite disproportionate to have left the matter to the Crown Prosecution Service to bring a (possible) prosecution in the Magistrates' Court. That is certainly true when, as here, there was no dispute about the facts. It seems to us that the threat of summary contempt proceedings made at the time of the incident may well be effective in restoring or maintaining order whereas the risk of prosecution in the Magistrates' Court would not be so effective (if effective at all). It would be strange if having properly made the threat, the Judge was precluded in a case like this from hearing the proceedings.

In *AS* (see at 20.6 above), Thomas LJ said:

17(iv). In very many cases of contempt, a criminal offence is also committed . . . Whether the Judge should refer the matter to the Crown Prosecution Service for consideration of a prosecution for a specific criminal offence or whether the Judge should proceed to determine matters under the contempt jurisdiction is a matter of the Judge's discretion.

(3) By section 20 of the Juries Act 1974, a juror who fails to comply with a summons to attend for jury service is liable to be punished as if he were guilty of 'a criminal contempt of court committed in the face of the court'. In *Dodds*,[14] Hedley J said:

17. In our judgement the following are the minimum requirements for a fair hearing in a case of this kind:

(1) the juror must understand what he is said to have done wrong;
(2) the court must be satisfied that the juror when (by act or omission) he did wrong, had the means of knowing that it was wrong;

[14] [2002] EWCA Crim 1328; see also *Andrews* [2008] EWCA Crim 2394.

(3) the juror must understand what defences (if any) may be available to him;

(4) the juror must have a reasonable opportunity to make any relevant representations he wishes;

(5) if necessary, the juror must have an opportunity to consider what representations he wishes to make once he has understood the issues involved.

20.8    The uncertainties surrounding certain aspects of the approach to dealing with contempt cases should be considerably lessened from April 2011 when the new Part 62 of the Criminal Procedure Rules 2011 (SI 2011/1709) comes into force. So far as is relevant, it is set out hereunder:

62.1(1)  This part applies where the court can deal with a person for conduct:

  (a)   in contempt of court;

  . . .

62.2(1)  The court must determine at a hearing:

  (a)   an enquiry under Rule 62.8;

  . . .

(2)  The court must not proceed in the respondent's absence unless:

  (a)   the respondent's behaviour makes it impracticable to proceed otherwise; or

  (b)   the respondent has had at least 14 days' notice of the hearing or was present when it was arranged.

  . . .

62.5(1)  This rule applies where the court observes or someone reports to the court:

  (a)   in the Court of Appeal or the Crown Court, obstructive, disruptive, insulting or intimidating conduct, in the courtroom or in its vicinity, or otherwise immediately affecting the proceedings;

  (b)   in the Crown Court, a contravention of:

    (i)   section 3 of the Criminal Procedure (Attendance of Witnesses) Act 1965 (disobeying a witness summons);

    (ii)   section 20 of the Juries Act 1974 (disobeying a jury summons);

  . . .

(2)  Unless the respondent's behaviour makes it impracticable to do so, the court must:

  (a)   explain in terms the respondent can understand (with help if necessary):

    (i)   the conduct that is in question;

    (ii)   that the court can impose imprisonment or a fine or both for such conduct;

    (iii)   (where relevant) that the court has power to order the respondent's immediate temporary detention if in the court's opinion that is required;

    (iv)   that the respondent may explain the conduct;

    (v)   that the respondent may apologise if he or she so wishes, and that this may persuade the court to take no further action; and

    (vi)   that the respondent may take legal advice; and

(b) allow the respondent a reasonable opportunity to reflect, take advice, explain and, if he or she so wishes, apologise.

(3) The court may then:

(a) take no further action in respect of that conduct;
(b) enquire into the conduct there and then; or
(c) postpone that enquiry.

62.6(1) This rule applies in a case in which the court has ordered the respondent's immediate temporary detention for conduct to which Rule 62.5 applies.

(2) The court must review the case.

. . .

(b) in the Court of Appeal or the Crown Court, no later than the next business day.

(3) On the review, the court must:

(a) unless the respondent is absent, repeat the explanations required by Rule 62.5(1)(a); and
(b) allow the respondent a reasonable opportunity to reflect, take advice, explain and, if he or she so wishes, apologise.

(4) The court may then:

(a) enquire into the conduct there and then;
(b) in the Court of Appeal or the Crown Court:

  (i) postpone the enquiry; and
  (ii) order the respondent's release from such detention in the meantime; or

(c) take no further action in respect of the conduct.

62.7(1) This rule applies where the Court of Appeal or the Crown postpones the enquiry.

(2) The court must arrange for the preparation of a written statement containing such particulars of the conduct in question as to make clear what the respondent appears to have done.

(3) The Court Officer must serve on the respondent:

(a) that written statement;
(b) notice of where and when the postponed enquiry will take place; and
(c) a notice that:

  (i) reminds the respondent that the court can impose imprisonment or a fine or both for contempt of court; and
  (ii) warns the respondent that the court may pursue the postponed enquiry in the respondent's absence if the respondent does not attend.

62.8(1) At an enquiry, the court must:

(a) ensure that the respondent understands (with help if necessary) what is alleged, if the enquiry has been postponed from a previous occasion;
(b) explain what the procedure at the enquiry will be; and
(c) ask whether the respondent admits the conduct in question.

(2) If the respondent admits the conduct, the court need not receive evidence.

(3) If the respondent does not admit the conduct, the court will receive:

    (a) any statements served under Rule 62.7;

    (b) any other evidence of the conduct;

    (c) any evidence introduced by the respondent; and

    (d) any representations by the respondent about the conduct.

(4) If the respondent admits the conduct or if the court finds it proved, the court must:

    (a) before imposing any punishment for contempt of court, give the respondent an opportunity to make representations relevant to punishment;

    (b) explain in terms the respondent can understand (with help if necessary):

        (i) the reasons for its decision, including its findings of fact; and

        (ii) the punishment it imposes and its effect; and

    (c) in a Magistrates' Court, arrange for the preparation of a written record of those findings.

(5) The court that conducts an enquiry:

    (a) need not include the same member or members as the court that observed the conduct; but

    (b) may do so unless that would be unfair to the respondent.

# 21

## The Jury

## Composition of the Jury

21.1    Part 1 of Schedule 1 to the Juries Act 1974 set out a list of those involved in the administration of justice who were ineligible to sit on a jury. It included judges, practising lawyers, prison officers and members of the police force. This ineligibility is removed by Criminal Justice Act (CJA) 2003, section 321 and Schedule 33. Accordingly, and subject to exceptions which do not matter, every person aged between 18 years and 70 years and whose name is on the electoral register is eligible to serve and liable to serve on a jury.[1]

21.2    The responsibility for summoning a jury panel rests with the Ministry of Justice and the Minister/Lord Chancellor.[2] The fact that the eligibility and summonsing procedure does not make provision for a multiracial jury does not mean that section 1 of the Juries Act 1974 involves any contravention of Article 6 of the European Convention.[3] It is improper for a judge to try and manipulate the selection process for the membership of a jury in a particular case to seek to achieve some sort of racial or cultural balance. In *Ford*,[4] Lord Lane said:

> Responsibility for the summoning of juries to attend for service in the Crown Court is by statute clearly laid upon the Lord Chancellor ... It is not the function of the Judge to alter the composition of the panel or to give any direction about the district from which it is to be drawn ... The Judge has no power to influence the composition of the jury and it is wrong for him to attempt to do so.

Section 11 of the Juries Act provides that:

> 11. – (1) The jury to try an issue before a court shall be selected by ballot in open court from the panel, or part of the panel, of jurors summoned to attend at the time and place in question.

Normally, individual jurors are called into the jury box by name. However, where 'jury nobbling' is expected or anticipated, it may be permissible to refer to

---

[1] Juries Act 1974, s 1.
[2] Juries Act 1974, s 2.
[3] *Smith* [2003] EWCA Crim 283, where Pill LJ said (at para 42): 'We are not persuaded by the submission ... that section 1 of the 1974 Act is incompatible with Article 6 of the Convention'.
[4] (1989) 89 Crim App R 278, 282.

individual jurors by number.[5] It is not now necessary to devote any considerable space to a defendant's right to challenge a juror. His right to challenge 'for cause' remains[6] – he has to have a reason. Likewise, the prosecution retain the right to ask a juror to 'stand by'.[7] When the case is going to be a long one, which is likely to last well beyond the two week period for which a juror is normally summoned, Part IV.42.2 of the Consolidated Criminal Practice Direction provides that:

> it is good practice for the trial Judge to enquire whether the potential jurors on the jury panel will see any difficulties with the length and, if the Judge is satisfied that the jurors' concerns are justified, he may say that they are not required for that particular jury.

Where there is doubt about whether a person summoned has a sufficient understanding of the English language to function effectively as a juror, the judge should decide the matter and may discharge the juror from further service.[8] Likewise, where a person summoned as a juror has a physical disability giving rise to doubts as to his capacity to act effectively as a juror, the question of his capacity should be decided by the judge and, if not capable, that juror should be discharged.[9]

In any event, as Lord Lane said in *Ford* (above) (at 218):

> At common law, a Judge has a residual discretion to discharge a particular juror who ought not to be serving on the jury. This is part of the Judge's duty to ensure that there is a fair trial . . . A Judge must achieve that, for example, by preventing a juryman from serving who is completely deaf or blind or otherwise incompetent to give a verdict.

# Power to Discharge a Juror Before or During a Trial

21.3    A judge has power to discharge an individual juror from sitting or continuing to sit on a jury. As appears from the preceding paragraph, the power may be exercised prior to the jury being sworn or whilst the jury is being sworn. It may also be exercised during the course of the trial. This is implicit in section 16 of the Juries Act 1974 which provides as follows:

> 16. – (1) Where in the course of a trial . . . any member of the jury dies or is discharged by the court whether as being through illness incapable of continuing to act, or for any other reason, but the number of its members is not reduced below 9, the jury shall nevertheless . . . be considered as remaining for all the purposes of that trial properly constituted, and the trial shall proceed and a verdict may be given accordingly.

---

[5] *Comerford* [1998] 1 Crim App R 235, 246, where Lord Bingham said: 'It is highly desirable that in normal circumstances the usual procedure for empanelling a jury should be followed. But if, to thwart the nefarious designs of those suspected of seeking to nobble a jury, it is reasonably thought to be desirable to withhold a juror's name, we can see no objection to that course provided the defendant's right to challenge is preserved'.

[6] Juries Act 1974, s 12.

[7] As to the approach that the Crown should adopt in the exercise of its rights, see the Attorney General's Guidelines at 88 Crim App R 123.

[8] Juries Act 1974, s 10.

[9] Juries Act 1974, s 9B.

. . .

(3) Notwithstanding sub-section (1) above, on the death or discharge of a member of the jury in the course of a trial . . . the court may discharge the jury in any case where the court sees fit to do so.

The power of discharge was made explicit in *Hanbery*,[10] where Lawton LJ said:

Whatever doubts about the discharge of jurors existed before 1866, they were dissipated in that year by the decision in the Exchequer Chamber in *Winsor v Harris* . . . those summoned to serve as jurors are entitled to such consideration as it is within the power of the court to give them. If the administration of justice can be carried on without inconveniencing jurors unduly, it should be. Discharging a juror whose holiday arrangements would be interfered with by having to stay on the jury after being sworn no longer hinders the administration of justice: trials can go on as long as there are 9 jurors. Anyway, an aggrieved and inconvenienced juror is not likely to be a good one.

To similar effect is *Richardson*.[11] In that case, the husband of a juror died during the course of an overnight adjournment and the juror herself did not turn up for court the following morning. When the Judge was told of this, he immediately discharged her though he did not say anything about it to counsel when the case continued. In the Court of Appeal, the Lord Chief Justice said:

We have no doubt that she was properly discharged. It is not in our judgement right to say that the operation of the discharge of a juror can only take place in open court. All sorts of situations might arise. Jurors who are in considerable difficulties and who seek a discharge, should not have to come personally to court and make their application there. The fact that it [the discharge] was not done in open court is neither here nor there.

In *Hornsey*,[12] the Court of Appeal approved the decision of the trial Judge who discharged a juror who had become ill after the jury had retired to consider its verdict. Indeed, a judge has power to discharge a juror even after some but not all verdicts have been returned. The subsequent verdicts were not vitiated by the discharge of that juror.[13]

# Some Particular Problems

## The Sleeping Juror

21.4    In *Tomar*,[14] a juror appeared to fall asleep during the summing up. This was brought to the attention of the Judge. The Judge asked the juror whether he

---

[10]   (1977) 65 Crim App R 233, 236 *et seq.*
[11]   (1979) 69 Crim App R 235, 238.
[12]   [1990] Crim LR 731.
[13]   *Wood and Furey* [1997] Crim LR 229.
[14]   [1997] Crim LR 682.

had missed much and the juror said that he had missed very little! No application to discharge that juror was made. The Judge carried on and the defendant was convicted. His appeal was dismissed. The court held that:

> If it appears to Counsel . . . that the jury are unable to keep awake, then he or she must bring that to the attention of the trial Judge then and there. When the Judge deals with it, if he is asked to discharge the jury he can consider whether or not that is an appropriate course to take. If he is asked to discharge a particular juror he can decide whether or not that is an appropriate course to take . . . What is quite impossible is for us to take a decision which the trial Judge was not even asked to consider at the time.

## The Absent Co-defendant and the Defendant Who Pleads Guilty

Every case is fact-specific and inevitably the authorities do not necessarily point in the same direction. The overriding approach has to be fairness. In *Frederick*,[15] two defendants were facing allegations of fraud. There was no count of conspiracy but the case had been opened on the basis that both defendants were 'in cahoots'. One defendant pleaded guilty halfway through the trial. The Judge refused to discharge the jury in respect of the remaining defendant, who was subsequently convicted. The Court of Appeal held that the jury should have been discharged because they could not properly consider the remaining defendant's case in isolation from that of the defendant who had pleaded guilty.

In *Jenese*,[16] one of the defendants in a multi-handed case absconded. Application was made to discharge the jury but the application was refused. The trial went on against the remaining defendants, including the one who had absconded, and they were all convicted. The Court of Appeal said that there was nothing wrong with the approach of the Judge. The proper approach to the problem of the absconding co-defendant was fully considered by the Court of Appeal in *Panayis*.[17] In that case Potter LJ said:

> The situation arising as a result of a defendant voluntarily absconding during the course of a trial, together with the question whether or not it is proper to discharge the jury and allow the trial to continue, is entirely within the discretion of the trial Judge. The question must be decided having regard to the due administration of justice rather than to the convenience or contract of anyone. . . To introduce a rule, or even a presumption, that the absconding of one defendant should ordinarily lead to a retrial being ordered in relation to one or more co-accused would be to open an avenue to abuse by defendants on bail during the course of a conspiracy trial.

---

[15] [1990] Crim LR 403.
[16] [1998] Crim LR 679.
[17] [1999] Crim LR 84.

## Jury Hearing Things that They Should not Hear or Otherwise Learning of Matters not in Evidence

Again it has to be remembered that cases are fact-specific and that fairness is the key. A number of older authorities suggest that sometimes fairness will not require the discharge of the jury. In *Wright*,[18] a prosecution witness said in evidence that he had seen a photograph of the defendant in the 'rogues gallery' at Scotland Yard. Avery J said:

> We have come to the conclusion that in a case of this kind, where by accident an observation of this nature has been made, it may very well be that the best course for all parties . . . to pursue is to abstain from making any reference to it at all. The making of any reference to the matter may only lead to impress it more strongly on the minds of the jury.

In *Sutton*,[19] one defendant during the course of his cross-examination referred to the bad character of both of his co-accused. In spite of having told counsel that he would deal with the matter during the course of his summing-up, the trial Judge failed to do so. The Court of Appeal held that the judge was justified 'in letting sleeping dogs lie'. They said:

> We would certainly be slow to lay down as a general rule that when one co-defendant says something of this nature about his co-accused, a Judge must automatically allow a fresh trial, because it would simply make it too easy if a trial is not going well for one co-accused to say something which would secure his co-accused the advantage . . . of a new trial.

The modern approach is best exemplified in *Lawson*.[20] In that case, the Judge himself disclosed a piece of highly prejudicial information to the jury during the course of his summing up, having earlier ruled that the evidence should not be given. On appeal, Auld LJ said:

> 64. The ultimate question for the court in determining whether the Judge correctly ruled against the appellant's application to discharge the jury is whether, given the error he made and the steps he took to mitigate it, it is satisfied that the conviction is safe: *Docherty*. And in determining that question in a case such as this of wrongly admitted prejudicial material, the appropriate test for the trial Judge is that identified in *Docherty*, namely as to 'the most prejudicial interpretation' and its possible effect on the jury. Perhaps more useful is the simpler and more broadly expressed formulation in *Medicaments*, namely whether a fair-minded and informed observer would conclude that there was a real possibility or real danger that the jury would be prejudiced against a defendant by wrongly admitted prejudicial information.

---

[18] 25 Crim App R 35.
[19] 53 Crim App R 504.
[20] [2007] 1 Crim App R 20.

He went on to say:

> 65. Whether or not to discharge the jury is a matter for evaluation by the trial Judge on the particular facts and circumstances of the case and the court will not lightly interfere with his decision. It follows that every case depends upon its own facts and circumstances including (i) the important issue or issues in the case; (ii) the nature and impact of improperly admitted material on that issue or issues, having regard inter alia to the respective strengths of the prosecution and defence cases; (iii) the manner and circumstances of its admission and whether and to what extent it is potentially unfairly prejudicial to a defendant; (iv) the extent to and the manner in which it is remediable by judicial direction or otherwise so as to permit the trial to proceed.

During the course of the foregoing judgment, Auld LJ referred to *Docherty*.[21] In that case the jury heard evidence it should not have heard. Roche LJ said:

> In weighing up the danger of bias on the part of the jury arising from these answers, the Judge should have approached the issue on the basis of the most prejudicial meaning that could reasonably be placed on those answers rather than some lesser prejudicial interpretation.

In other words, the judge should assume the worst.

In *Thakrar*,[22] some six weeks into the trial and after the appellant had given evidence-in-chief, a note was received from the jury to the effect that one of their number had researched the Internet and discovered a previous conviction of the appellant. The Judge then gave a strong warning to the effect that that information must be disregarded but he declined to discharge the jury. In spite of that strong warning, the Court of Appeal were driven to the conclusion that there had to be a real possibility that at least some of the jury might not have followed that direction, particularly as all members of the jury knew about the previous conviction at an early stage in the trial but did not tell the Judge about it until much later. The conviction was quashed. It should be noted that judges are now strictly enjoined to tell the jury in terms that they must not make their own searches on the Internet.[23]

In *Wilson*,[24] jurors trying the appellant spotted his name on a court list in respect of another matter to be dealt with later in the week. As a matter of fact, evidence of his bad character was already before the jury. The Judge refused to discharge the jury. In the Court of Appeal, Hughes LJ said:

> 11. Whether to discharge a jury is a question for the judgement and discretion of the trial Judge. This court will not substitute its own view though necessarily, if the Judge's decision was one which was not properly open to him, it may well follow, though it will not necessarily do so, that the conviction will as a result be unsafe.
>
> 12. It is common ground that the test to be applied in some circumstances is that of the reasonable apprehension of bias . . . The question on that test is whether a fair-minded

---

[21] [1999] 1 Crim App R 274.
[22] [2008] EWCA Crim 2359.
[23] *Thompson* [2010] EWCA Crim 1623.
[24] [2008] EWCA Crim 134.

and informed observer would conclude that there is a real possibility, or a real danger, these two things being the same, that the jury would be biased.

13. Next, where inadmissible material is inadvertently disclosed to the jury and it is capable of more than one reasonable interpretation by jurors, the test ought to be applied on the basis of the most damaging reasonable interpretation.

## Miscellaneous

The following cases provide illustrations where the Court of Appeal has indicated that the judge should have ordered a retrial.

In *Boyes*,[25] at the end of the judge's summing up in a rape trial, the mother of the complainant shouted from the public gallery words to the effect that 'the defendant had attacked five other girls'. The judge did not hear exactly what had been said but was later told by counsel. He had the jury back and told them to ignore the outburst. It was held that he should have enquired of the jury if they had heard what had been said because if they had it was clearly highly damaging to the defendant and the judge should have considered the possibility of discharging them.

In *Blackford*,[26] on a charge of possession of drugs with intent to supply, a police officer in answering a question in cross-examination let the jury know that the defendant had previous convictions for supply. The Court of Appeal felt that this was a deliberate attempt by the officer 'to queer the defendant's pitch' and that the jury should have been discharged. (In my view, somewhat charitably so far as counsel was concerned, the court said that the Judge was wrong to conclude that counsel had asked for it by the way he put the question!)

In *Hutton*,[27] a notice under the Contempt of Court Act 1981 had been framed in such a way that it was obvious that further trials of the defendant were pending. The notice had been pinned to the door of the court and a juror was observed reading it. The Judge was not told of this until after the jury had retired. He refused to discharge them and nor did he have them back and give them a direction about ignoring what had been read. The Court of Appeal said that in so acting, the Judge did not clearly exercise his discretion and that the knowledge derived from the notice might have tipped the balance against the defendant.

*Barraclough*[28] indicates a practical problem which can arise when a jury is discharged after the defendant's previous convictions became known. In that case, a retrial was ordered for the following day. The Court of Appeal held that at a large court centre there is usually no problem with a retrial being held the following day: the court will assume that the jurors in the aborted trial will obey any instructions not to talk about it. However, at a smaller court centre where there is a

---

25  [1991] Crim LR 717.
26  (1989) 89 Crim App R 239.
27  [1990] Crim LR 875.
28  [2000] Crim LR 324.

greater likelihood of jurors meeting other jurors, the trial court may have to consider either discharging the first jury from further attendance or putting the retrial off for at least two weeks.

In *Azam*,[29] the Court of Appeal grappled with the problem of what to do with the uncontrollable witness. The witness had been the victim of a savage attack designed to kill him. Throughout his cross-examination he was prone to making outbursts, allegations against the defendants that were outwith the ambit of the trial, and referring to them as 'gangsters'. On instructions, defence counsel decided that they would not ask that the jury be discharged. The prosecuting counsel was concerned as to whether the trial could be fair. The Judge considered the matter and decided that the trial should continue. The defendants were convicted. One of the issues dealt with in the Court of Appeal was whether the Judge was right to have allowed the trial to continue. During the course of his judgment, the President made a number of observations relevant to all matters dealt with in this paragraph. He said:

> 48. The starting point for the submission arising out of [the behaviour of the witness] is that as an integral part of his duty to ensure that a jury trial is fair, the Judge retains, and where necessary should exercise, his right to discharge the jury.

He went on to say:

> 50. We immediately acknowledge that the Judge's decision on these matters is not simply a case management decision . . . If the Judge were to conclude that there were real grounds for doubting the ability of the jury to bring an objective judgment to bear on the issue, the jury should be discharged. The decision requires a balanced judgement of the things said to create the risk of bias in the jury, while simultaneously taking account of the directions available to be given by the trial Judge to address and extinguish the risk. In short, in the context of trial by jury, the question whether the jury may be biased or apparently biased, cannot be decided exclusively by reference to the material which is said to constitute the risk of bias, examined in isolation from the normal processes of the trial.

# The Jury Note

21.5   This topic obviously has to be considered bearing in mind the matters set out in the paragraphs which follow in relation to things which have taken place in the jury room and about which complaint is subsequently made. The general rule was set out by Lord Lane in *Gorman*.[30] He said:

> Certain propositions can now be set out as to what should be done by a Judge who receives a communication from a jury which has retired to consider its verdict. First of

---

[29] [2006] EWCA Crim 161.
[30] (1987) 85 Crim App R 121, 126.

all, if the communications raise something unconnected with the trial . . . it can simply be dealt with without any reference to Counsel and without bringing the jury back to court. Secondly, in almost every other case, the Judge should state in open court the nature and content of the communication which he has received from the jury and, if he considers it helpful so to do, seek the assistance of Counsel. This assistance will normally be sought before the jury is asked to return to court and then, when the jury returns, the Judge will deal with the communication. Exceptionally, if, as in this case, the communication from the jury contains information which the jury need not and indeed should not have imparted, such as details of voting figures, then, so far as possible, the communication should be dealt with in the normal way, save that the Judge should not disclose the detailed information which the jury ought not to have revealed.

In *Andriamanpandry*,[31] the jury sent 17 notes during the course of the trial, but none after retirement. The Court of Appeal stressed that *Gorman* should be followed and that unless the note related to something unconnected with the trial, the Judge should either read it out or hand it to counsel for them to have a look at. The President reiterated the importance of what had been said in *Gorman*, namely that:

> The object of these procedures which should never be lost sight of is this: first of all to ensure that there is no suspicion of any private or secret communication between the court and the jury and second, to enable the Judge to give proper and accurate assistance to the jury on any matter of law or fact which is troubling them. If those principles are borne in mind, the Judge will, one imagines, be able to avoid the danger of committing any material irregularity.

## Bias

21.6    Inevitably, matters in this paragraph overlap with matters already dealt with. In *Gough*,[32] Lord Goff said:

> The Judge in deciding whether to exercise his discretion to discharge one or more members of the jury should apply the same test which falls to be decided on appeal by the Court of Appeal – whether there is a real danger of bias affecting the mind of the relevant juror or jurors. Even if the Judge decides that it is unnecessary to do more than issue a warning to the jury or to a particular juror and thereby isolate and neutralise any bias that might otherwise occur, the effect of his warning is not merely to ensure that the jurors do not allow any possible bias to affect their minds, but also to prevent any lack of public confidence in the integrity of the jury . . . Finally, for the avoidance of doubt, I prefer to state the test in terms of real danger rather than real likelihood, to ensure that the court is thinking in terms of possibility rather than probability of bias . . . Accordingly, having ascertained the relevant circumstances, the court should ask itself whether, having regard to those circumstances, there was a real danger of bias on the part of the relevant tribunal in question, in the sense that he might unfairly regard (or have unfairly regarded) with favour or disfavour, the case of a party to the issue under consideration by him.

---

[31] [2003] EWCA Crim 1974.
[32] (1993) 97 Crim App R 188, 199.

This approach has now to be slightly modified in line with *Re Medicaments*.[33] In that case Lord Philip said:

> 85. When the Strasbourg jurisprudence is taken into account, we believe that a modest adjustment of the test in *Gough* is called for . . . The court must first ascertain all the circumstances which have a bearing on the suggestion that the Judge was biased. It must then ask whether those circumstances would lead a fair-minded and informed observer to conclude that there was a real possibility, or a real danger, the two being the same, that the tribunal was biased.

> 86. The material circumstances will include any explanation given by the Judge under review as to his knowledge or appreciation of those circumstances . . . The court does not have to rule whether the explanation should be accepted or rejected. Rather it has to decide whether or not the fair-minded observer would consider that there was a real danger of bias notwithstanding the explanation advanced.

In *Panayis*,[34] there was evidence of some out of court conversation between a solicitor's clerk acting for the defendant and a member of the jury. The juror told the Judge that what was said had not prejudiced her and she had not mentioned the matter to other jurors. Further evidence of contact emerged. The Judge sent a note to the jury through their foreman. They replied that nothing had influenced them. The Judge, having applied the *Gough* test, concluded that the case should go on. In the Court of Appeal Potter LJ said:

> Whether or not a jury may be taken at its word when it declares itself uninfluenced by some irregularity which has occurred, it is very much a matter for the Judge on the spot to decide . . . When a Judge has, in consultation with Counsel, followed an open procedure by which to ascertain the extent of any contact with a juror and whether any real danger of bias has resulted and when he decides that, subject to appropriate directions, no real danger exists, the court will be slow to form a different view.

In *Brown*,[35] the appellant was charged with indecent assault. His brother and brother's wife and daughter attended the trial. The appellant had bail during the trial. The jury had to pass through part of the public area to get to their room. Two jurors alleged that at lunchtime the brother and his daughter had made a remark directed to them as they passed. The appellant may or may not have been present at the time. One of the jurors also said that on her return after lunch another offensive remark was made. Another juror heard that remark. Two jurors complained to the Judge. He caused an investigation to be made by a police officer of all the jurors. The two complaining jurors gave statements. The Judge had the jury back and asked them two questions which required them to respond individually. In the Court of Appeal, Mann LJ said:

---

[33] [2001] 1 WLR 700; see also *Porter v McGill* [2001] UKHL 67, where Lord Hope said: 'The question is whether a fair-minded and informed observer having considered the facts would consider that there was a real possibility that the tribunal was biased'.

[34] [1999] Crim LR 84.

[35] [2001] EWCA Crim 2828.

24. Questions to a jury en bloc in open court and without opportunity to consider or respond to them individually and privately, may not have been the best way of dealing with the problem. We add for completeness that the Judge did not seek at any point in his summing up to address the problem that had arisen . . . Counsel for the defendant thus . . . accepted before us that it cannot be open to a defendant to obtain the discharge of a jury by deliberately creating some ground of aggravation or discord between himself and the jury, whether inside or outside court. But, in order for a Judge to rely on the appellant's responsibility for events occurring as a ground for not discharging a jury, the circumstances giving rise to such responsibility must, it seems to us, either be agreed or ascertained by the Judge to exist. They cannot be assumed simply because there is a prima facie case which the defendant disputes.

He went on to say:

31. We are not satisfied in the circumstances that he ever properly addressed his mind to the true test indicated by the European authorities, particularly the objective aspect of the test which has now . . . been authoritatively introduced into English law by the decision in *Re Medicaments*.

Finally, he said:

32. That the court can and that a fair-minded and informed observer would have in mind, as a background factor, the undesirability of discharging juries too freely and the hardship that any discharge can involve for complainants, not to mention the waste of time and costs seems to us correct . . . but they are part of the background to any consideration whether there is sufficient real risk of a lack of impartiality to justify discharge.

This last observation should be treated with caution. It is respectfully suggested that the proper position is set out in the speech of Lord Hailsham in *Spencer*,[36] where he said:

In considering such an application, the interests of justice should be paramount and neither the inconvenience of a second trial nor the necessity which would have been involved in calling again as witnesses the victims of the alleged assault, possibly to their detriment, should have outweighed the necessity of the accused receiving and being seen to receive a fair trial.

21.7   In the context of possible bias, a particular problem which has recently arisen is that posed by the presence of police officers on the jury.

In *Pintori*,[37] a juror worked in the communications department of the Metropolitan Police. She sat on a trial where a number of police officers gave contestive evidence. The defendant was convicted. Subsequently, she told an officer with whom she currently worked that she had previously worked with three of the officers who had given evidence. She had not mentioned this fact at the time. After referring to *Porter* (above), the Court of Appeal had no difficulty in finding that the fair-minded observer would conclude that there was a real possibility of bias on her

[36]   (1986) 83 Crim App R 377.
[37]   [2007] EWCA Crim 1700.

part. The more difficult question was whether the fair-minded observer would conclude that there was a real possibility that the bias of that juror affected the other members of the jury: the court said that the fair-minded observer could not exclude the possibility of contamination and the appeal was allowed.

In *Abdroikov*,[38] the House of Lords had to consider three cases, two of which involved police officers on the jury and the third, an employee of the CPS. It was a majority decision and it is not entirely easy to extract clear principles from the various speeches. Cases are fact-specific, but it is tentatively suggested that the following points emerged from the decision:

(1)   There can be no blanket ban on police officers sitting on juries: to hold otherwise would be to frustrate the clear will of Parliament. Accordingly, the mere fact that a police officer sits on a jury does not give rise to a risk of bias in the fair-minded observer. This is particularly so when the police evidence is not in dispute.

(2)   Where there is a dispute between the defendant and a police officer, especially where the police juror works in the same operational division as the witness, the fair-minded observer might perceive the risk of bias though, as we shall see, even this is not entirely clear from the subsequent cases.

The law has been clarified somewhat by the decision in *Khan*.[39] The following passages from the judgment of Lord Philips are important:

9.   It is important to distinguish between partiality towards the case of one of the parties and partiality towards a witness. Each can be described as 'bias' but they are different in kind and can have different consequences. Association with or partiality towards a witness will not necessarily result in the appearance of bias . . . Just because a juror feels partial to a particular witness does not mean that the juror will be partial to the case in support of which that witness is called. It may do so if the witness is so closely associated with the prosecution that partiality to the witness is equated with partiality towards a party calling a witness.

10.   Where an impartial juror is shown to have had reason to favour a particular witness, this will not necessarily result in the quashing of a conviction. It will only do so if this has rendered the trial unfair or given it the appearance of unfairness. To decide this, it is necessary to consider two questions:

(i)   Would the fair-minded observer consider that partiality of the juror to the witness may have caused the juror to accept the evidence of that witness? If so,

(ii)   Would the fair-minded observer consider that this may have affected the outcome of the trial?

(iii)   If the answer to both questions is in the affirmative, then the trial will not have the appearance of fairness. If the answer to the first or the second question is in the negative, then the partiality of the juror to the witness will not have affected the safety of the verdict and there will be no reason to consider the trial unfair. . . .

---

[38]   [2007] UKHL 37.
[39]   [2008] EWCA Crim 531.

29. [Having considered *Abdroikov*] our conclusion is . . . that the fact that a police juror may seem likely to favour the evidence of a fellow police officer will not automatically lead to the appearance that he favoured the prosecution. If the police evidence is not challenged or does not form an important part of the prosecution case, we do not consider that it will normally do so.

*Ingleton*[40] was post-*Abdroikov* but pre-*Khan*. As the jury were being sworn in, a potential juror disclosed that he was a police officer who knew all the officers who were going to give evidence in the case. At that stage it did not seem that there was likely to be any significant challenge to the police evidence and the Judge declined to discharge the juror. During the trial, one of the officers gave some evidence not included in her witness statement and which was contentious. The Judge did not discharge the jury. Quashing the conviction and stressing that unless it could be established with certainty that the evidence of the known witness really was uncontentious, Nelson J, giving the judgment of the court, said:

24. Where a potential juror informs the court that he personally knows anyone involved in the case, the Judge must establish the facts relating to that knowledge and then decide whether the fair-minded and informed observer, having considered the facts, would conclude that there was a real possibility that the tribunal was biased. . . .

28. It will be noted that both of the judgments referred to deal with whether there was an issue on the evidence between the police and the defence which the known witnesses would be testifying to. This will be a relevant and, in some cases, decisive point, although in many cases . . . knowledge of a witness alone will raise a real possibility of bias. . . .

36. Unless it can be said with certainty that the known witnesses to be called will play no contested as opposed to an agreed part in the determination of the issues, a person who personally knows a witness or witnesses should normally be asked to stand down.

The clear thrust of the above judgment is that personal knowledge of a participant by a juror should normally disqualify that juror, regardless of whether he is a police officer or not. Even if the evidence of a witness might appear to be uncontroversial, caution suggests that this must be right.

*Yemoh*[41] is a post-*Khan* case. It was a murder trial involving a number of defendants and raising difficult problems in relation to joint enterprise. After the trial started, the Judge learnt that there was a policeman on the jury but he did not tell the parties until the jury had retired, though he had made enquiries of the juror prior to this time. The officer concerned (who was the jury foreman) served on a different division of the Metropolitan Police from that of the officers who had given evidence and there was no suggestion that he knew them. The Court of Appeal were clearly of the view that the Judge should have told counsel immediately he became aware that the juror was a police officer but they declined to quash the conviction. Hooper LJ said:

---

[40] [2007] EWCA Crim 2999.
[41] [2009] EWCA Crim 930.

111. Although it might have been preferable for the Judge to have asked more questions of the juror, it seems to us that we should accept the answer as conveyed to the Judge that the juror knew nothing about the case . . . If he had inside information about the case or the background to the case as a result of his position as a police officer, we take the view that he would have told the court official. Likewise, the Judge made clear in his summing up that the jury had to decide the case on the evidence. If the juror was aware of information which did not form part of the evidence in the case then it seems likely to us that he would have made that clear. Unlike in the United States, jurors are only rarely questioned in this country. Jurors are often told the names of witnesses in case they know them . . . The system here proceeds on the assumption that a juror will reveal any difficulties that he or she may have in impartially approaching the case being tried and that other jurors will play a role in ensuring impartiality. No appeal should succeed on the speculative basis that a juror may have been partial towards a witness.

In *Ali*,[42] 'the issue for the jury was whether the appellant had been correctly identified by arresting police officers as the perpetrator of the assault and whether he was in possession of an offensive weapon'. There was a conflict of evidence between the appellant and the police officer. A member of the jury identified himself at the outset as a police officer and no objection was made. Later, there was an application to discharge him, which was refused. Having considered both *Abdroikov* and *Khan*, May LJ said:

16. Three things are evident from this – first, the question is obviously one of fact and degree and there is a measure of judicial discretion at the margin. Second and obviously, each case will depend on its own facts. Third, again at the margin, it is difficult to deduce clear-cut principles which are to be applied.

17. We remind ourselves that Parliament has decided that generally speaking police officers should not be disqualified from serving on juries. We take note of the fact that the Metropolitan Police is a huge organisation and we consider that it would be contrary to the Parliamentary intention if no Metropolitan Police officer could serve on a London jury in any case where significant evidence of a Metropolitan Police officer was challenged. The expression used in *Abdroikov* 'the same local service background' cannot extend to service in any part of the whole of the Metropolitan Police area.

The foregoing decision was clearly heavily influenced by the fact that no objection was taken at the outset. It is respectfully submitted that a judge at first instance should still be very circumspect where there is to be a police juror and the judge knows that there is a significant challenge to the police evidence.

In *T*,[43] very properly, the police officer summoned for jury service told the summoning officer of his occupation. That information was not passed on to the Judge or the parties. It was only discovered after verdict, the police officer having been the foreman of the jury! Although the case had involved allegations of police impropriety, they related to events many years earlier and involved officers who could no longer be identified and who did not give evidence. Although those

---

[42] [2009] EWCA Crim 1763.
[43] [2009] EWCA Crim 1638.

**DELIVERY ADDRESS**

**Cristina Alcov**
**49 Thackeray Drive**
**Nortfleet,**
**Gravesend**
**Kent,**
**DA11 8FS,**
**UNITED KINGDOM**

## Bookbarn International Ltd

Unit 1 Hallatrow Business Park, Wells
Road, Hallatrow,
Bristol
Somerset, BS39 6EX,
UNITED KINGDOM

## Packing Slip / Invoice
Price: £22.79

## Standard

| Order Date: | 03/12/2020 |
| --- | --- |
| **BBI Order Number:** | 1262672 |
| **Website Order ID:** | 202-2072692-8072334 |

**Customer Contact:** Cristina Alcov

NOS1

NOS2

| SKU InvID | Locators | Item Information |
| --- | --- | --- |
| 3168093 10572986 | C46-00-02 338777 Pink PAP ExLib - N U:G | **Case Management in Criminal Trials (Criminal Law Library)** Denyer, Roderick |

If you wish to contact us regarding this order, please email us via Amazon quoting your order number. **amzuk**

### Thanks for shopping with us

### www.bookbarninternational.com

**BOOKBARN**
INTERNATIONAL

Greetings from Bookbarn International,

Thank you so much for placing an order with us, in doing so you've helped us grow as an independent bookseller.

We hope you're happy with your purchase, however if you have any issues or queries please do not hesitate to contact us.
Log into the website you bought from, locate your order in your order or purchase history and **Contact Seller.**
Our small and committed team provides a fast response to ensure you are fully satisfied.

Kind regards & happy reading!
The BBI Team

---

Bookbarn Internationalからのご挨拶、

この度はご注文していただきありがとうございます。
おかげさまで私たちはインディペンデント系書店として成長することができております。

ご注文いただいた商品に問題がある場合や質問がある場合は、どうかお気軽にお問い合わせください。

連絡方法は、お客様がご注文されたウェブサイトにログインしていただき、注文履歴のリストから出品者に連絡するボタンより直接ご連絡ください。

当社の小規模で献身的なチームは、お客様が完全に満足していただけることを確実にするために迅速な対応をいたします。

どうぞよろしくお願いいたします。

読書をお楽しみいただけますよう願っております！
BBI チーム

---

Salutations de Bookbarn International,

Merci beaucoup d'avoir passé une commande chez nous. Vous nous avez aidé à grandir en tant que libraire indépendant.

Nous espérons que vous êtes satisfait de votre achat. Si vous avez des questions ou des questions, n'hésitez pas à nous contacter.

Connectez-vous au site Web où vous avez commandé votre livre, trouvez votre commande dans votre historique d'achat et contactez le vendeur.

Notre équipe petite et engagée fournit une réponse rapide pour s'assurer que vous êtes pleinement satisfait.

Bonne lecture!

Cordialement,
L'équipe BBI

---

Saludos desde Bookbarn International,

Muchas gracias por hacer un pedido con nosotros. Nos ha ayudado a crecer como librería independiente.

Esperamos que esté satisfecho con su compra. Si tiene algún problema o consulta, no dude en contactarnos: Inicie sesión en el sitio web que utilizó para efectuar su compra, busque su pedido en su historial de compras y comuníquese con el vendedor.

Somos un equipo pequeño, comprometido con brindar una respuesta rápida para garantizar su completa satisfacción.

Saludos cordiales y feliz lectura!

El equipo de BBI

---

Grüße von Bookbarn International,

Vielen Dank für Ihre Bestellung. Sie haben uns dabei geholfen, ein unabhängiger Buchhändler zu werden.

Wir hoffen, dass Sie mit Ihrem Kauf zufrieden sind. Wenn Sie jedoch Probleme oder Fragen haben, zögern Sie bitte nicht, uns zu kontaktieren.

Gehen Sie auf Meine Bestellungen, suchen Sie Ihre Bestellung in der Liste und klicken Sie auf Verkäufer kontaktieren.

Unser kleines und engagiertes Team bietet eine schnelle Antwort, um sicherzustellen, dass Sie voll zufrieden sind.

Mit freundlichen Grüßen und viel Spaß beim Lesen!
Das BBI-Team

---

officers belonged to the same force as the person on the jury, the events about which complaint was made happened long before she joined the police. In dismissing the appeal, and having pointed out that by statute police officers were entitled to sit on a jury so that the mere fact of being a police officer could not operate as a disqualification, Toulson LJ said:

> 74. Taking all those matters into account, we have reached the conclusion that the case of apparent bias is not made out . . . A fair-minded and informed observer would not consider there to be a real possibility of bias arising out of the occupation of the juror.

But, the concluding part of the paragraph should be noted:

> It is unfortunate that the juror's occupation was not communicated to the trial Judge before the trial proceeded. It is likely that out of an abundance of caution, the Judge would have asked her to stand down.

## Conclusion

(1) The mere fact of being a police officer is not a disqualification from serving on a jury.
(2) If the officer knows another officer who is going to give evidence, then:
    (a) if the evidence is entirely non-controversial, eg is going to be read, that may not necessarily give rise to the appearance of bias; but
    (b) as with any juror, common prudence would suggest that it is better that he not serve.
(3) If the prospective evidence of a police officer is likely to be contentious, then common sense and authority suggest that he not serve, particularly if he is from the same force.
(4) However, if no objection is taken at the outset (where the occupation is known) the appeal court may conclude that an allegation of apparent bias is not made out. Even where the occupation is not known, if a close scrutiny of the facts reveals no basis for the allegation of possible bias, then, on the fair-minded and informed observer test, the conviction will not necessarily be quashed.

# Investigations which Can be Made of the Jury

21.8 We must now consider what powers a judge has to investigate problems with the jury. It is necessary first to consider the provisions of section 8(1) of the Contempt of Court Act 1981, which provides as follows:

> It is a contempt of court to obtain, disclose or solicit any particulars of statements made, opinions expressed, arguments advanced or votes cast by members of a jury in the course of their deliberations in any legal proceedings.

In *Mirza*,[44] after the defendant had been convicted, a letter was received from a juror alleging that the other jurors were racially prejudiced. The Court of Appeal refused to admit evidence about the letter by reference to both section 8 and the common law prohibition on admission of evidence relating to jury deliberations. Insofar as they relied upon section 8, the House of Lords said that they were wrong so to do. Lord Slynn said:

> 57. It seems clear to me that in enacting section 8 . . . Parliament did not intend to fetter the power of a court to make investigations into the conduct of a trial. Properly construed, section 8(1) does not apply to the court of trial or to the court of appeal hearing an appeal in that case. It cannot properly be read as categorising what the court does in the course of its investigation as a contempt of the court itself.

In the same case, Lord Hope said:

> 90. The better view is that a court cannot be in contempt of itself. In my opinion section 8(1) is addressed to third parties who can be punished for contempt and not to the court which has the responsibility of ensuring that the defendant receives a fair trial.

In *Attorney General v Scotcher*,[45] Lord Rodger said:

> 16. Prior to the decision of the House in *Mirza*, the general assumption in the English courts was that the terms of section 8(1) was so broad as to apply to any court . . . which might have wished to enquire into a matter relating to the jury's deliberations . . . The House held, however, that if a trial Judge were informed about any misconduct during the jury's deliberations but before they had returned their verdict, then section 8(1) did not prevent him from looking into the matter.

To some extent, these decisions have liberated the Court of Appeal in dealing with matters which emerge after trial. However, it is less than clear that the new interpretation of section 8 assists the trial judge very much. This is because of the common law. In *Mirza* (above), referring to the common law, Lord Slynn said:

> 41. Thus the prohibition on receipt of evidence takes effect from the moment the jury is empanelled and covers not only what took place in the jury box or the jury room but covers any statement as to what the juror believed the attitude of other jurors to be as deduced from their behaviour . . . Once the verdict is given in the presence of all the other jurors, then that is the end of the matter.

In the same case, having gone on to assert that the present common law rule should be maintained but that section 8 did not preclude all enquiry, he said:

> 57. The court is restricted in its enquiry into what happened in the jury's deliberation, not by section 8 of the Act but by the long-standing rule of the common law.

Lord Hope said:

> 92. When allegations are made which suggest that a defendant is not receiving, or did not receive, the fair trial to which he was entitled . . . they must be considered and inves-

[44] [2004] 2 Crim App R 8.
[45] [2005] 2 Crim App R 35.

tigated. Any investigation must of course be within the limits that are set by the common law. Evidence which is struck out by the common law rule will be inadmissible and the court should not ask for or receive such evidence . . . the court must look to the common law for guidance as to the extent to which any such investigation is permissible.

He went on to define the common law rule as follows:

95. The general rule is that the court will not investigate, or receive evidence about, anything said in the course of the jury's deliberations whilst they are considering their verdict in their retiring room.

Accordingly, it followed that:

156. Allegations of misconduct by jurors may surface at any stage of a trial before the jury has retired for verdict. In such cases there is no reason why the allegation should not be investigated. The Judge must accordingly take appropriate steps to investigate and deal with any such matters that arise.

Such sentiments are of little use to a trial judge since no help is given as to what permissible steps may be taken to investigate problems that arise, given the common law prohibition. This dilemma was recognised (though not fully answered) by Lord Carswell in *Smith*.[46] He first set out the general position. He said:

16.(1) The general rule is that the court will not investigate, or receive evidence about, anything said in the course of the jury's deliberations while they are considering their verdict in their retiring room . . .

(2) An exception to the above rule may exist if an allegation is made which tends to show that the jury as a whole declined to deliberate at all, but decided the case by other means such as drawing lots or tossing a coin . . .

(3) There is a firm rule that after the verdict has been delivered, evidence directed to matters intrinsic to the deliberations of the jury is inadmissible . . .

(4) The common law has recognised exceptions to the rule, confined to situations where the jury is alleged to have been affected by what are termed extraneous influences, for example contact with other persons who may have passed on information which should not have been before the jury . . .

(5) When complaints have been made during the course of trials of improper behaviour or bias on the part of jurors, judges have on occasions given further instructions to the jury and/or asked them if they feel able to continue with the case and give verdicts in the proper manner. This course should only be taken with the whole jury present and it is an irregularity to question individual jurors in the absence of the others about their ability to bring in a true verdict according to the evidence . . .

(6) Section 8(1) of the Contempt of Court Act 1981 is not a bar to the court itself carrying out necessary investigations of such matters as bias or irregularity in the jury's consideration of the case. The members of the House who were in a majority in *Mirza* all expressed the view that if matters of that nature were raised by credible evidence, the Judge can investigate them and deal with the allegations as the situation may arise.

[46] [2005] 2 Crim App R 10.

He went on to say:

> 17. None of their Lordships specified the steps which it is open to the trial Judge to take in the last mentioned type of case, and the issue now before the House is the nature of the enquiry which can properly be made and the extent to which, if at all, it is permissible to question jurors about matters which took place during their deliberations.

His conclusions were as follows:

> 20. I am unable, however, to accept that it would have been appropriate for him to question the jurors about the contents of the letter, let alone that he was obliged in law to do so. If he had gone into the allegations, he would inevitably have had to question them about the subject of their deliberations . . . In my opinion the common law prohibition against enquiry into the events in the jury room certainly extends to matters connected with the subject-matter of the jury's deliberations. I do not think it necessary or desirable to attempt to draw up a precise definition of the situations in which it would be legitimate for the Judge to question jurors. There may be some matters into which the Judge can and should enquire in this way, for example that a jury has used a mobile phone to make a call from the jury room, but I would prefer to leave for future discussion the limits of any such enquiry.

> 21. I accordingly consider that questioning of jurors, even if it were within legitimate bounds, would have been likely to make the situation worse rather than better.

> 22. The Judge was accordingly left with the choice of two courses of action, to discharge the jury or to give them further instruction, along the lines of the familiar direction set out in *Watson*, re-emphasising their duty to carry out their discussions with proper give and take. The Judge took the latter course and I consider it was justified in the circumstances.

What follows hereafter is an examination of some of the cases which suggest what is and is not permissible by way of enquiry when dealing with jury problems, including bias. It has to be said that the authorities do not speak with one voice.

In *Orgles*,[47] there was friction amongst members of the jury and two jurors complained. The Judge asked those two jurors if they still felt able to give a true verdict and they said they could. The whole jury was then reassembled and the Judge asked them if they could continue to act as a body and the foreman said that they could. This was held to be the wrong approach. Holland J said that if the problem arose from something external to the jury and affecting only an individual juror:

> It is appropriate to commence and continue the enquiry with the juror concerned separated from the body of the jury, but 'such separation of a juror for the purposes of an enquiry cannot be justified if the circumstances are internal to the jury'. The problem is not the capacity of one or more individuals to fulfil the oath or affirmation, but the capacity of the jury as a whole. When this type of problem arises, then the whole jury should be questioned in open court through their foreman to ascertain whether as a body it anticipates bringing in a true verdict according to the evidence. It will be a

---

[47] (1994) 98 Crim App R 185, 190.

matter for the Judge's discretion as to how he reacts to the response, that is whether he makes no order, whether he discharges the whole jury or whether he discharges individual jurors up to three in number.

He went on to say:

What we regard as irregular was the initial separation and questioning of the individual members which, given the nature of their respective complaints, should not have happened.

*Bryan*[48] is broadly consistent with this approach. In that case and after the jury had returned some verdicts, they were sent home for the night. A woman on the bus overheard two jurors talking about the case, including a suggestion that one elderly member of the jury always thought the defendant was guilty. The woman reported the matter to the police, who in turn informed the Judge. The Court of Appeal said that the woman should have been brought to court to give evidence about what she had heard. Waller LJ said:

47. Some suggestion was made by the court during argument of the possibility that having established the position with the witness, the Judge ought to have gone on to identify the two jurors and possibly even thereafter to have identified the elderly juror. On reflection, we think that there would have been risks in taking that course and no benefits.

He went on to say:

48. Having established the position so far as the witness was concerned, we think that the Judge would have had to make up his mind whether a firm direction which warned the jury to approach the matter without any preconceived ideas and by reference to the evidence alone, would expunge any danger of an unfair trial. If he had concluded that such a direction could not suffice then the discharge of the jury in relation to the remaining counts would have been the only course open to him.

On the other hand, in *Blackwell*,[49] a female juror was seen talking to a man who had been present in court throughout the trial. Counsel asked the Judge to investigate. He refused. Later, having heard that the juror and the man were going to get married, he agreed to discharge the juror. He refused to make any enquiries of her before discharge and refused to make any enquiries of the remaining jurors. In the Court of Appeal, Morland J said:

If there is any realistic suspicion that the jury, or one or more members of it, have been approached or tampered with or pressurised, it is the duty of the Judge to investigate the matter and probably, depending on the circumstances, the investigation will involve questioning of individual jurors or even the jury as a whole. Any such questioning must be directed to the possibility of the jury's independence having been compromised and not the jury's deliberations or the issues in the case . . . When a Judge has completed his investigation . . . he is in a position to make an informed exercise of judicial discretion

---

[48] [2001] EWCA Crim 2550.
[49] [1995] 2 Crim App R 625, 633.

as to whether or not the trial should continue with all twelve jurors, or continue after the discharge of an individual juror, or the whole jury may have to be discharged.

In both *Zulhayir*[50] and *Brown*,[51] the Court of Appeal did seem to countenance the possibility of the concerned juror being questioned by the judge in the absence of the other members of the jury. In the former case, Hooper LJ said:

> 22. We say in passing that we have concerns about the juror's note being disclosed to the whole jury without any opportunity to consider the matter with the individual juror. If, as was done in this case, jurors are told to bring matters to the attention of the Judge if they have concerns, then it seems, to say the least, concerning to read this kind of note to the whole jury without prior discussion with the writer of the note.

He went on to say:

> 27. We have looked at some of the authorities and we note in particular paragraph 24 of the decision of another division of this court in *Brown*. In that case, in paragraph 24, Mance LJ expressed concerns about asking all jurors in open court in the manner that this Judge did about having first given the juror an opportunity to have the matter ventilated privately.

In *Oke*,[52] a member of the public was seen having a drink with a juror and that person had been in court during legal argument in the absence of the jury. The juror told the Judge that the man was her husband and the Judge declined to question her further. The Court of Appeal said it would have been better had the Judge asked a few more questions as to what had passed between her and her husband. It may be that this approach can be explained by reference to the distinction between something external to the jury and affecting only the individual juror, rather than circumstances internal to the jury as a whole.

In *Appiah*,[53] a juror noted that on three days she was being watched. This unnerved her. She told a fellow juror about what had happened and it subsequently became clear that she had told other jurors as well. The following day, having heard about the matter, the Judge discharged the juror. In respect of the remaining jurors, the Judge told them what had happened. He asked them individually whether they felt that they could properly carry on or whether they might feel uneasy about giving a verdict. No member of the jury indicated any unease. On appeal, it was argued that the jurors should not have been questioned individually but should have been addressed through their foreman. The Court of Appeal held that the Judge had adopted an entirely correct approach. There was no reason why he should not have asked each juror individually whether he or she felt intimidated by what had happened.

Perhaps the best approach is illustrated by what happened in *Momodou*.[54] After a four-month trial, the jury were on their second day of retirement when a juror

---

[50] [2010] EWCA Crim 2272.
[51] [2001] EWCA Crim 2828.
[52] [1997] Crim LR 898.
[53] [1998] Crim LR 134.
[54] [2005] 2 Crim App R 6.

wrote a letter to the Judge saying that two of her fellow jury members were being discriminatory and prejudicial against the defendants and not judging the case on the evidence. The Judge did not discharge the jury straightaway. What he did was as follows:

(1) He had them back into court and expressed his concern about the contents of the letter.
(2) Each juror was then provided with an edited copy of the letter.
(3) The jury were then told to retire and consider the letter and decide whether they felt able to continue deliberating together impartially and to consider whether their collective ability to give an impartial verdict had been compromised.
(4) He indicated that he would only accept a response in general terms and would not consider individual responses.
(5) Through their foreman, the collective response was that they took their obligations seriously and would try the case fairly.
(6) He rejected counsel's request that more detailed enquiries of individual jurors should be made.

The Court of Appeal upheld this approach.

Once the judge has decided that a fair trial with the jury in question is no longer feasible, there is a clear duty to discharge that jury regardless of considerations of convenience, cost, and such like. This is apparent from *Spencer* and the passage from the speech of Lord Hailsham already quoted. In *Bryan*,[55] Waller LJ said:

> 48. If the Judge had concluded that such a direction could not suffice, then a discharge of the jury in relation to the remaining counts would have been the only course open to him. The fact that the trial had got so far; the fact that there were verdicts already returned on some counts; the fact that a discharge might lead to no trial at all on the remaining counts were simply irrelevant and should not have been taken into account in making the necessary ruling.

# Jury Tampering

Section 13 of the Criminal Justice Act 1967 came into force on 1 October that year. For the first time, it allowed a majority verdict to be returned by a jury in a criminal case. The relevant provisions are now set out in section 17 of the Juries Act 1974. The change was prompted, at least in part, by fear that trials were being derailed because one or more jurors had been 'got at'.

As dealt with at 21.3 above, a judge has always had power to discharge an individual juror during the course of the case. In theory, therefore, if it became apparent that an individual juror had been 'got at', it would be open to the judge

---

[55] [2001] EWCA Crim 2550.

to discharge him and continue with the remaining members. In reality, though, it may be very difficult for a judge to be satisfied that the other jurors had not in some way been affected and the likelihood is that the whole jury would have to be discharged. CJA 2003, section 46 is designed to deal with this problem, ie 'nobbling' or tampering once the trial has started. The section reads as follows:

46. – (1)  This section applies where:

    (a)  a Judge is minded during a trial on indictment to discharge the jury; and
    (b)  he is so minded because jury tampering appears to have taken place.

(2)  Before taking any steps to discharge the jury, the Judge must:

    (a)  inform the parties that he is minded to discharge the jury; and
    (b)  inform the parties of the grounds on which he is so minded; and
    (c)  allow the parties an opportunity to make representations.

(3)  Where the Judge, after considering any such representations, discharges the jury, he may make an order that the trial is to continue without a jury if, but only if, he is satisfied:

    (a)  that jury tampering has taken place; and
    (b)  that to continue the trial without a jury would be fair to the defendant or defendants.

But this is subject to sub-section (4):

46. . . . (4)  If the Judge considers that it is necessary in the interests of justice for the trial to be terminated, he must terminate the trial.

(5)  Where the Judge terminates the trial under sub-section (4), he may make an order that any new trial which is to take place must be conducted without a jury if he is satisfied in respect of the new trial that both of the conditions set out in section 44 are likely to be fulfilled.

(6)  Sub-section (5) is without prejudice to any other power that the Judge may have on terminating the trial.

(7)  Subject to sub-section (5), nothing in this section affects the application of section 44 in relation to any new trial which takes place following the termination of the trial.

One of the difficulties that arises in connection with this section (and indeed with section 44 dealt with later) is that the decision of the trial judge to conclude that tampering has taken place may be based, in whole or in part, on material shown to him by the prosecution which is subject to public interest immunity (PII) and which therefore cannot be disclosed to the defence. In *KS (No 1)*,[56] the trial judge ordered discharge of the jury, in part based on materials subject to PII. This was held not to be a ground for overturning the decision. In the Court of Appeal, Lord Judge said:

20. It is an inevitable concomitant of the extended powers of the court to control jury tampering but there will be occasions when public interest immunity principles will apply to the material brought to its attention.

[56]  [2009] EWCA Crim 2377.

In *Tinnion*,[57] Lord Judge said:

> 20. The fact that the Judge has been invited to consider material covered by PII principles, whether during the trial or in the course of considering the application, should not normally lead to self-disqualification.

In summary, therefore, the consideration of PII material by the judge in arriving at the decision to discharge the jury on tampering grounds and his subsequent decision to deal with the case himself:

(a)   does not vitiate his decision to discharge the jury;
(b)   is not a bar on 'bias' grounds if continuing with the trial and giving a verdict.

So far as (b) above is concerned, the Court of Appeal has made it very plain that normally the trial judge should continue with the hearing. In *KS (No 1)* (above), Lord Judge said:

> 23. . . . if a Judge decides that the trial should continue, he must take it over at the point it has reached, however late that may be. There is no particular moment when it must be deemed inappropriate for him to do so.

In *JSM*,[58] Lord Judge said:

> If during the course of this, or indeed any trial, attempts are made to tamper with the jury, to the extent that the Judge feels it necessary to discharge the entire jury, it should be clearly understood that the Judge may continue with the trial and deliver a judgment and verdict on his own. The principle of trial by jury is precious, but in the end any defendant who is responsible for abusing the principle by attempting to subvert the process, has no justified complaint that he has been deprived of a right which, by his own actions, he himself has spurned.

However, there may be situations when the judge has learnt so much about a particular defendant that it is simply not appropriate for him to continue the trial on his own. In *KS (No 1)* (above), apart from PII material, the judge had presided over a series of related trials during the course of which much information about the defendant, which would not normally come to the attention of a jury, had been made available to him or had been heard by him whilst dealing with other defendants. In those circumstances, the Court of Appeal concluded that there was a real danger of the perception of bias. Lord Judge said:

> 41. In this jurisdiction we cannot countenance, let alone permit, the verdicts in a criminal case to be returned by a jury which is actually or apparently biased. An identical principle must apply whenever a verdict is to be returned by a Judge sitting on his own . . . It is clear that the absence of judicial bias does not answer the separate question whether an informed objective bystander might legitimately conclude that such bias is a realistic possibility.

---

[57]   [2009] EWCA Crim 1035.
[58]   [2010] EWCA Crim 1755.

We must now deal with the scenario which arises when the prosecution apply pursuant to CJA 2003, sections 44 and 45 for the trial to be conducted without a jury. The relevant parts of the sections provide as follows:

> 44. . . . (3) If an application under subsection (2) is made and the judge is satisfied that both of the following two conditions are fulfilled, he must make an order that the trial is to be conducted without a jury, but if he is not so satisfied he must refuse the application.
> (4) The first condition is that there is evidence of a real and present danger that jury tampering would take place.
> (5) The second condition is that, notwithstanding any steps (including the provision of police protection) which might reasonably be taken to prevent jury tampering, the likelihood that it would take place would be so substantial as to make it necessary in the interests of justice for the trial to be conducted without a jury.
> (6) The following are examples of cases where there may be evidence of a real and present danger that jury tampering would take place:
>> (a) a case where the trial is a retrial and the jury in the previous trial was discharged because jury tampering had taken place;
>> (b) a case where jury tampering has taken place in previous criminal proceedings involving the defendant or any of the defendants;
>> (c) a case where there has been intimidation, or attempted intimidation, of any person who is likely to be a witness in the trial.
>
> 45. – (1) This section applies:
>> . . .
>> (b) to an application under section 44.
> (2) An application to which this section applies must be determined at a preparatory hearing.
> (3) The parties to a preparatory hearing at which an application . . . is to be determined must be given an opportunity to make representations.

The Court of Appeal has set its face firmly against the notion that such trials should become commonplace. In *JSM* (above) Lord Judge said:

> 8. We must emphasise as unequivocally as we can that, notwithstanding the statutory arrangements introduced in the 2003 Act . . . this remains and must remain the decision of last resort, only to be ordered when the court is sure (not that it entertains doubts, suspicions or reservations) that the statutory conditions are fulfilled. Save in extreme cases, where the necessary protective measures constitute an unreasonable intrusion into the lives of jurors . . . the confident expectation must be that the jury will perform its duties with its customary determination to do justice.

In *KS (No 2)*,[59] Lord Judge said:

> 7. We emphasise the link between the nature of the threat of jury contamination and the steps reasonably available to be taken to reduce the risk to manageable proportions and caution against any unduly alarmist proposals, alarmist both in the sense of the

[59] [2010] EWCA Crim 1756.

likely adverse impact on the members of the jury themselves, and on the drain on precious police resources of providing them. The new statutory arrangements do not undermine, but rather confirm, the need for the issue of jury protection to be handled in a realistic and proportionate way.

As already described, CJA 2003, section 45 deals with the making of the application. Section 49 envisages the making of criminal procedure rules to flesh out the same, but as yet no such rules have been made. Accordingly, the guidance given in *Tinnion* (above) governs matters:

> 32. Confining ourselves to what we anticipate will be the rare case which arises with decisions under section 44 . . . and to ensure consistency of approach . . . for the time being arrangements should be made for the case to be referred to one of the presiding judges of the circuit for a listing decision. The application will normally be heard and decided by the presiding Judge.

# Index

# Index